A Struggle To Be Heard

To Brian

Best wishes

John Laird
December 2010

A Struggle To Be Heard

By a true Ulster liberal

JOHN LAIRD

Published by Global & Western Publishing Ltd
PO Box 151
Exeter
EX4 4WG

First published 2010

ISBN: 978-0-9566507-1-9

Designed and Typeset in Bembo 10.5/13.5pt
by Jeremy Mills Publishing Ltd
www.jeremymillspublishing.co.uk

Edited and produced by Fiona O'Cleirigh

Printed and bound in the United Kingdom by
Riley Dunn & Wilson Ltd., Huddersfield

A CIP catalogue record for this book is available on request from the British Library.

Dedicated to my dear wife Carol, daughter Alison and son David,
with whose support everything is possible.

Contents

Preface 1

Acknowledgements 5

Executive Summary 7

CHAPTER ONE
The Inst Boy 9

CHAPTER TWO
The Honourable Member 41

CHAPTER THREE
The Rebel 69

CHAPTER FOUR
The Public Relations Consultant 111

CHAPTER FIVE
The Inst Governor 137

CHAPTER SIX
The Noble Lord 159

CHAPTER SEVEN
The Chairman 205

CHAPTER EIGHT
The Ulster Scot 239

APPENDIX
The Presidents' Trail 263

Index 277

Preface

'BIG LAD, YOU'RE getting above yourself – Laird writing a book!'

I can just hear my friends' and others' reaction at the idea of me writing about myself. And I agree with their viewpoint. I have not undertaken the usual worthwhile tasks that are generally considered to make an autobiography interesting beyond one's close family. But this book is not an autobiography. At least that is how I see it.

This is the story of an ordinary Ulster Scot, Ulster Unionist or Ulster Protestant making his journey through life in his native trouble-racked province, in the latter part of the twentieth century and on into the twenty-first. What it is not, is a day-by-day or a month-by-month or even a year-by-year account of an average enough life.

I have been interested in current affairs, which in Northern Ireland includes history, from as early as I can remember and long before achieving a number of recognisable positions. As a result, I am constantly asked to explain the Unionist case or to outline my Ulster Scots background.

There seems to be little analysis of those two topics for the ordinary punter. Why did, and why do I, spend so much time upholding Unionism and why am I so pleased to be of an Ulster Scots background? These questions and more I try to answer in these pages.

I believe that we are all made up of our reactions to that which has happened to us, directly and indirectly. So, using selected sections of my life, I map the journey from the small boy steeped in Unionism, or 'the Cause', to the rational grown-up of pension age. I still have most of the basic values and beliefs intact. But as a result of that journey, I am no longer a 'paper Unionist' or 'paper Ulster Scot', but one who has, almost day-by-day, thought out his position and now regards himself as a practical exponent of those two major beliefs.

The journey from the atmosphere in which I was born to this day was strewn with doubt, mixed messages, confusion and occasional revision of my views. And it was none the worse for any of that.

As well as our backgrounds, we are created by the circumstances we meet in life. I try to explore the circumstances, both positive and negative, that I encountered in my life, and consider how they affirmed or changed my views. I examine my Ulster Scots background, or Scotch/Scots Irish as they call it in America, and come to terms with how it affected my community, my family and me.

The Ulster Scots people are often regarded as that section of the Scottish race that was hardened on the anvil of Ulster. Their story is one of hardship, independence of spirit and a search for equality and justice. The Ulster Scots community produced some most remarkable people including seventeen American presidents, two men who would stand on the moon, some major figures of business, the church, science and of war. Their story is one that changed the course of history at many points. They had the vision and drive to help create what is now the United States of America. For a small group moved mostly from the border of Scotland and England to the northern part of the island of Ireland, their contribution to the modern world is out of all proportion to their size. Yet by our nature, we of that ethnic group either play down or do not know who we are. I sincerely hope that this publication will inform at least some.

My brother Jimmy and I were reared in a home that was dominated, although not in a negative way, by our father. He laid down little law, he almost never raised his voice, and indeed he spoke as sparsely as possible. It was his presence, even when not there, which hung over everything.

At a low point in my life, in the year after our father died, Jimmy offered me advice when approaching any difficult decision: 'Think what our dad would have done.'

That worked as a short-term solution. But both of us, as time went on, began to see that Dr Norman Laird was not the man we thought he was. His inability to change an opinion once expressed was, for me, most unsettling. If we are the sum of our reactions to life's experiences, why was he an unmovable rock? When you are young, a rock is of great importance and value. But seeking the truth, whatever that was, or is, requires a totally open mind.

There is no man whom I loved more than my father; I still do. I followed his every word and he, in turn, provided a set of rules and values that were unchanging. Importantly, when under pressure, I could refer back to him for an acceptable reason or view, one that was clear and never, but never, changing. That was a great comfort. Analysis of any position was not required.

On 28th April 1970, the most important event in my life happened. My father suddenly died. I was cut adrift. No more certainty, no more firm hand on the tiller. Worse, everything, every institution by which we, the Laird family, ran our lives was under attack. The Troubles had started. Worse still, I was pushed, although I created much of my own momentum myself, into taking over one of his positions. I became a Northern Ireland Member of Parliament for a working class area of Belfast, one that felt day-by-day under attack from Republicans and by the media. Cut adrift, my community was to face its greatest challenge for several generations.

In these pages, I have tried to document and so explain that journey and how it created the John Laird of today. I am not my father and not, anymore, a pale imitation of him. But I worked out and tested opinions by a different path and I have arrived at the same conclusions as my father did, on the importance of Unionism and the need for equality and freedom. The key difference is that I was forced to put these beliefs to the test almost daily. On other major issues, my ideas today might surprise him.

To put it another way, I feel that my father was right in some of his values. It's just that his thinking, to me now, was mixed-up and his presentation skill only just saw him through his life. It is a strange thing to say, but the best thing my father, who I loved in unbearable measure, did for me was to die when he did. This started a journey of failure, change, modest success; one that he could not have understood.

This is not John Laird's autobiography. I have only been a bit-part player in the events of the last forty years. And it is not a history book. I am not a historian. The book does relate some history, as I understand it, which helped to mould my life. It is not unique upon the shelves, but it is my contribution to a bit of Ulster's social history.

If you do not think of yourself as being of the Ulster Scots tradition, then I am delighted. What is about to unfold may help you to understand people like me. But please do not be offended. Contained are my genuine opinions concerning Irish Republicanism, as well as many other topics. I am a plain-speaking Ulsterman. I state my case clearly but I do not intend to offend anyone. Why should I? These are just my opinions. I have as much right to be correct or to be wrong as anyone else.

I have had massive pleasure in putting this tome together. It is that journey shaped by my dread of bullying, and in particular that of so-called Irish Republicanism, and by my identification with the Ulster Scots which is before you, if you care to read on.

John Laird
Belfast, November 2010

Acknowledgements

I OWE A deep debt of gratitude to very many people who helped in the preparation of this publication. Most I have included in the pages, as a part of my life experience. I hope that they will take their inclusion as recognition of their importance to me.

I also wish to thank Kevin Cahill and Fiona O'Cleirigh, who formed the editorial and publishing team. Without their commitment and expertise, this work could never have been published. To them all praise is due.

I would like to mention two good friends whose help and encouragement were important. Dr James Dingley is an academic of some standing and is well known for his enlightened thinking. I regard Peter Houston, of Houston Green Photographers in Belfast, as being the most creative photographer that I have ever met.

I could acknowledge many from the world of politics who have helped me over the years with ideas and new thinking. However, I think it is only right to highlight Desmond Boal, a former MP for the Shankill. Desmond's mind is sharp and insightful on any topic. I am always delighted to spend time with him and receive the benefit of his experience and clarity of thought.

Executive Summary

1. Modern liberal thinking holds that nationalism, in all its forms, is backward looking and out of tune with the modern world.

2. Ulster Scots cultural thinking is broad based and forward thinking, with an important role to play in the development of the modern world, in keeping with its contribution over the last four hundred years.

3. The Irish, when not politically motivated, are amongst the finest people in the world.

4. 'Equality deferred is equality denied.' A small group of politically motivated Irish people control sections of the Northern Ireland civil service and the BBC, in such a way as to hold up the manifestation of Ulster Scots culture and thinking. This, I feel is due to a lack of self-confidence, and fear.

5. Those who are dyslexic will continue to increase their influence in society.

6. We must all be convinced, by peaceful means, that the world's future lies in larger political units. The only idea of borders is to keep money in and unwanted cultures out.

7. Artigarvan is a wonderful place in which to spend a childhood.

8. Irish nationalism has been a negative influence on the British Isles.

If we do not understand our history, we will remain forever children.

CHAPTER ONE

The Inst Boy

THE GERMANS ARE IN FULL RETREAT
THE BBC HOME SERVICE

IN NOVEMBER 1942, a BBC Home Service news bulletin proclaimed to the citizens of the United Kingdom that, for the first time in the dark days of the Second World War, the allies were pressing home an advantage, and the Germans were in full retreat. I believe that these are the most important words of my entire existence and they were uttered over a year before I was born.

Belfast was, and to an extent still is, one of the great industrial cities of the United Kingdom. In the early 1940s, it was hard at work hammering out both ships and planes, making a major contribution to the war effort. Every weekday morning, twenty-five thousand men reported in to Harland and Wolff, once the world's largest independent shipyard. There they built ships to replace those that were lost on the Atlantic crossings. As a result, Belfast had been heavily bombed by the Germans. The city had the questionable distinction of having sustained the largest single night's air raid of any city outside London and Coventry.

In days without proper radar, the Germans used the Cave Hill in north Belfast as a reference point in order to navigate their way into the city. Passing over the streets of blacked out houses, which the locals hoped they could not see, they spotted the Belfast

Waterworks near to where my parents and other relations lived. Mistaking this area for the shipyard, they bombed north Belfast, as if it was the industrial heart of the city. My father, being a general practitioner, and my mother, a nurse, were in charge of the local Cave Hill Road first aid post, which provided succour and support for the good people of that area for the nights of the air raids. It was extremely busy, tending to those who were injured and frightened and, in some cases, tending to the dying. This clearly made a tremendous impression on my parents.

At the start of the war, they had evacuated their only son, my elder brother James, to family in Artigarvan, County Tyrone. My mother and father suffered like every other United Kingdom citizen with the ups and down of the war. There were good days and, more particularly, there were bad days. But finally came the day of the BBC announcement, crackling across in the correct, clipped Oxford tones of the war period, with the news that the Germans were in full retreat, after the second battle of El Alamein. To the day my mother died in 1983, she could make the hair stand on the back of my neck, by talking about the night they heard the news. She would quote what the newsreader said, with particular emphasis on the word 'full'. Looking back now, it was not that the Germans were in retreat; it was the fact that the Germans were in full retreat. The mood, certainly, in the Laird household, in Ballysillan Road where it crossed the Cave Hill Road, improved dramatically. There was going to be a future. There was going to be victory. The Germans were not invincible. The war could be won and society could get back to something like normality.

In April 1944 I was born, two months prematurely. I was very small and many expected me not to survive. I was never told that this event was a consequence of El Alamein, but it was quite clear, from my non-demonstrative parents (this was, after all, the 1940s), that I probably was conceived as a result of the new and renewed faith in the future. I was born into a middle class, professional household. Houses around ours had been flattened, including that of my aunt and uncle. A bomb had fallen on our own house but it was of the incendiary type and had been put out very quickly by the Home Guard. I remember nothing of that house. All my information from that period comes from the continual chatter of my parents and our friends about what was clearly the biggest event ever to happen in their lives; the war. From then on and until their deaths, everything was calculated against the time frame of 'before the war', 'during the war' or 'after the war'.

They say that one's reaction to events moulds one's personality, and I believe that. I received my upbringing from two totally honest, decent parents who were born in the Edwardian era. They had lived through two world wars and the creation of Northern Ireland. These events certainly began to shape who I was, from a very early age.

In 1946, my mother had come into an inheritance. Although pitiful in size by today's figures, it was sufficient for the family to buy, without mortgage, a large semi-detached house on the Somerton Road in North Belfast. This had been an extremely fashionable area, and we lived right beside Dunlambert House, the traditional and ancestral home of the Clark family. They had been involved in shipbuilding in Belfast in a similar way to Harland and Wolff. We also had as neighbours a large section of the Jewish community. North Belfast was the home to some two and a half thousand members of this community, who were mostly, and possibly even exclusively, middle class. In years to come, they were to build the new Belfast synagogue next door to us, and thankfully it is still in operation today. A Hebrew school formed part of the synagogue complex and, consequently, a lot of my friends in the area were Jewish. Meeting them, understanding them and knowing them became a significant part of my growing up. They were different to me in that they attended, as I did, one of the local grammar schools, but, in the afternoon, in gleaming school uniforms, they came to the Hebrew school to learn about Jewish culture. By contrast, I and a few of my local Presbyterian compatriots only attended a church-based school on Sunday, albeit that it was an hour's intensive grilling into what it was felt that we should debate as Presbyterians. It seemed odd to me that they should be attending their school every day and I only attended the school organised by my religion once a week.

Many things in those days seemed odd, and it is only with hindsight that one is able to put the pieces together. Even to this day, I still have flashes of inspiration when I find myself revisiting some event or scene from my childhood. At such moments, it is possible to see, with the insight of maturity and common sense, that what had seemed so strange, as a child, was absolutely normal and totally explainable. I learned a lot from the Jewish community. In common with many young people of that age, I met up with friends in the Somerton Road and Fortwilliam area, after school. But our Jewish compatriots were at school and so we could not play with them; as a result, we saw a difference with them. Also, they were better dressed than us. To my shame, but totally naturally, we considered them to be different to us and therefore, in the way that small boys do, we 'made a difference'. In those days (as he does to this day), my brother seemed to be the font of all knowledge. He had a tremendous understanding of life that was disproportionate to his age; he was almost six years older than me. Jimmy told me about the persecution of the Jews during the war. I was shattered. I felt totally ashamed, realising that I had accidentally fallen into the error of making a difference of people who only a few years before had been made a difference of by the leadership of an entire country. And that was only the recent past. I discovered that Jewish people had not had life easy for at least two thousand years. From that day forward, I did not treat the Jews as equals, as I should have done. It could be argued that from that day forward, I treated them in a favourable light. It is for others to decide whether I was exercising undue discrimination.

The Jewish community in Belfast have played a most honourable role in public affairs. Many were, and still are, active members of pro-Union opinion. Several were members of the Belfast Corporation and at least one was a very popular Lord Mayor in the early part of the last century. There is a farm near Millisle in County Down that is still referred today as the Jewish Farm. There, for several decades from the early 1930s, children of that religion were reared away from their unsafe homelands in Eastern Europe. When recently I discussed what the Jewish community had done for Northern Ireland with a senior member of that community, he pointed out that I was looking in the wrong direction. He then revealed a story which I had never heard before and which I was pleased to hear. The Stormont Unionist government during the war had unofficially helped Jewish people escaping Europe; mostly from Germany. John M. Andrews, the Inst-educated local Prime Minister for part of the War, Harry Midgley, a cabinet minister, and other senior party members had organised housing, accommodation and employment, mostly at their own expense. To this day, senior members of the dwindling Jewish community express gratitude for the help of Ulster men of other religions. I am deeply proud of this.

For a few years from 1948, I attended a small local school, run by a headmistress called Miss Shaw. Brookvale was a private school in a converted terraced house. I remember my first day there, when, without complaint and without tears, I left my mother and was taken away by what then seemed to be an extremely elderly woman. It is easy to see, now, that Miss Shaw was probably only then in her fifties, but to me she looked positively ancient. I was, after all, just four-years old.

There I met a lot of boys and girls whom I had not come across before. There was a new category of person that I was not used to and it came under the heading of 'female'. I remember from a very early age being totally intrigued by a fellow pupil with long pigtails. Her name was Freda. I do not know if it is possible to be infatuated at four or five, because if it is not I must have had some other disease. Besides, I later realised that I was too young to 'wash behind my ears', as they say in my native city.

My father was born in 1906 at 162 Agnes Street, a semi-main thoroughfare that crossed the Shankill Road, which, to this day, is regarded as one of the Protestant heartlands of Belfast. Even considering that Agnes Street might have looked down on other streets, it was still a Belfast back street.

My grandfather and his widowed mother ran a shop there. I knew of my Agnes Street connections only after my father's death in 1970. He was of an age and time when you did not reveal the fact that you were from a working class background. He never spoke of it; he never referred to it. For myself, I am desperately proud that he was from a working class area, an iconic area; the Shankill. It is better to have climbed a mountain than to be born at its top.

The Lairds seem to have come originally from around Berwick-upon-Tweed, which they probably regarded as part of Scotland. They were sent over in the plantation of four hundred years ago, initially to Donegal. They then moved about quite a bit through the province of Ulster, as middle and low ranking planters tended to do. My particular connection ended up just outside Ballymena, at Kells, in a townland called Lisnawhiggle. My relatives were members of Kells's first Presbyterian Church. Kells is a small town predominantly, if not almost totally, Presbyterian, with two massive Presbyterian churches. Stuck in a little side entry was a small, and it still is small, Church of Ireland place of worship.

The great Protestant Revival of 1859 started, as far as I understand it, near Kells and possibly even in Kells's first Presbyterian Church. The cottage of my great great grandfather, William Laird, is still in existence. His son was called Jesse. Jesse and his wife, Agnes, had a significant number of young Lairds, the eldest of whom was my grandfather. Unfortunately, Jesse, who was a labourer in the local Francis Dinsmore linen mill, died at the age of thirty-seven, causing his widow to bring her family to Belfast. By all accounts, she was a sturdy and totally determined, independent, hard-working caricature of a Presbyterian woman. In an age without social security or welfare benefits, she took them onto the Shankill Road, and there reared the family.

My grandfather was well-known for a number of things, not the least of which was that he, James Davidson Laird, had only one leg. At the age of sixteen, he had stood on a rusted nail. This caused such a bad infection in his foot that, in those pre-antibiotic days, it had to be removed. He was an entrepreneurial type, regarded as a hail fellow well met sort, and, according to all reports, the life and soul of any gathering which he attended. He died at the age of fifty-nine, on 8th April, 1939.

James Davidson Laird was known as a rent-collector, although he did have an interest in his mother's shop. He started an estate agency business, named after himself, on the Grosvenor Road, somewhere in the region of the current Police Service of Northern Ireland station. He bought property, and lots of it. After his death, it became clear that he did not own houses; he owned streets, particularly in his native Shankill Road area. He was heavily interested in Masonic activity and in the Boy Scout movement, being one of the founding members of the 6th North Belfast troop.

My father, Norman Davidson Laird, was his eldest son. All my aunts and uncles on my father's side, and my grandfather, had the middle name Davidson. This came through a relation of my great-grandmother. The Reverend Samuel Davidson was a Presbyterian theologian who came from Kellswater. He taught in the school to which I went and spent a long time in Germany as a theologian. And, typically of Presbyterians, he managed to fall out with every other Presbyterian he met and possibly did not, as a consequence, achieve the recognition he should. He was always regarded as the greatest theologian that the small hamlet of Kellswater ever produced. Which is, in my opinion, not difficult, as I am convinced that he is the only theologian that the small hamlet of Kellswater ever produced.

It is clear that my grandfather was the most dominant person in my father's life. Norman Laird had a totally different personality to that of James Laird. My father was shy, introverted and deep. Looking back, he was quite clearly a man who, despite the image that he portrayed, was unsure of himself. As was fashionable in the earlier part of the twentieth century, he took his guidance and his lead totally from his father, who informed the young Norman that he would be a doctor. From reading records regarding the young Norman Davidson Laird, it is quite clear that he did not like being a doctor. Nevertheless, he was a good and successful doctor in a working class area in Belfast, which covered the lower Falls Road,

Sandy Row and Donegall Road. Before he ever went into general practice, at a surgery on the Grosvenor Road, he declared on paper no interest, and no liking, for medicine. But he had been told to be a doctor, and he had been told so by his father.

James Laird had worked hard to take his son out of the Shankill Road every day and send him to the Royal Belfast Academical Institution, or 'Inst'. This was, and is, one of Northern Ireland's premier schools. Samuel Davidson, the pride of Kellswater theologians, had been a master at this school. It was a school that espoused Presbyterian ideals. The Royal Belfast Academical Institution, which my brother, myself and, subsequently, my son were to attend, was one of the greatest influences on my life. Being a Presbyterian school, by nature, it was not a school for Presbyterians. Because to be a Presbyterian school, it is necessary that the school should take no cognisance of anybody's religion, but treat everybody on a totally equal basis. Unlike other religious establishments, perhaps, which are intended for children of that particular religion, a Presbyterian school is a school for everyone, run on strict lines of equality.

In Northern Irish Presbyterian terms, Inst would be regarded as following reason-based 'New Light' principles, in contrast to the Belfast Royal Academy. That establishment was started over twenty years earlier, in 1789, also by Presbyterians. It became a beacon of Bible-based 'Old Light'; the other face of Presbyterianism. However, the Academy was not considered by the liberal-minded Presbyterian commercial class to be satisfactory. The New Light school of thought, to which I would subscribe, felt the need to start again in the centre of Belfast. Consequently, Inst came into existence in 1810. The original intention was for the establishment to become Belfast's university, with a specific mission to further New Light learning and science. The two sections of Presbyterianism will be further explained later.

Sending my father to Inst was important for the family, because it pulled him out of the working class background on the Shankill and led him to Queen's University to study medicine. Back in 1935, an aspiring general practitioner was required to buy himself a practice, or have one bought for him. My grandfather duly made the purchase, and set his son up as a GP.

In my possession is a document that my father wrote on 1st January 1934, at the age of twenty-seven. In it he said, startlingly, that he had no interest in medicine: his life's ambition was to be a member of the Stormont Parliament, which in 1934 was only thirteen years in existence. The other stated ambitions in this document were to marry his girlfriend Margaret, my mother, and, with his close friend, J.N. Dick, to write a history of Ulster. It is so typical of my father, this meticulous, careful planner of events, that he listed his life at the age of twenty-seven, and almost stuck to it. My father was not known for spontaneity. He was not known as a personality that you would invite round for tea, and he was not known as a man who had the slightest understanding of small talk. If you discussed the weather with my father, it always seemed to strike him with astonishment, for he would not have noticed that there was any weather that day.

Norman Laird was introverted and seemed to speak only on very rare occasions, which meant that when he did speak it was with great authority and his words were significant. It was this attribute that made him a considerable success in the working class areas. He himself would tell me that he believed that eighty per cent of his patients had illnesses that were imaginary. Therefore, when he sat and talked to them and listened to their complaints, and uttered one or two well-chosen words, it could seem like the answer to their problems. He had the ability, which I witnessed on many occasions, to ease the worries of a patient, who in many cases could hardly move, or who was going into hospital for a difficult operation. 'Look, Mrs Smith,' he would say, taking her by the shoulder. 'What you're going in for is a minor operation. You will be all right and, in the very near future, you will walk again and your health will be restored.' I could see the physical status of the patient improve, the chest would swell, the patient would become erect, catch a hold of my father's arm and say 'Doctor, thank you doctor, I believe you, doctor. I thank you'. If that was what my father did for patients, he did a lot. Of course, he did much more.

I learned a lot from his silent power, which was possibly accidentally created and accidentally exercised. He had the gift of being able to relate to people with great authority, in such a way that his words almost had a godly resonance. He was never a man who said one thing one day and said something else another day. This affected my mother during his lifetime and she took on many of his attributes. My father, if he said something, if he gave his opinion on a topic, then that was it; it was carved in stone. That opinion was never changed. What he said was what he believed and that was what he carried to the grave. At the time, I considered that to be a tremendous strength. Looking back, I see that it was a weakness. Looking at this fault now, I see it to be Old Light thinking to never question received wisdom. My father never mentioned any type of light. I just think he did not have the self-confidence to allow his mind to flow. As a consequence, he was unable to change his opinion or be open to new ideas.

However, he was ultimately a man of his time. He did represent the period from which he came. He was of that generation that went through the climax of the Home Rule debate during the early part of the twentieth century. He witnessed the effect of the rising tide of concern that rose to a fever pitch between 1908 and 1910, concerning the possibility of a Roman Catholic-controlled Ireland, one in which the people of Ulster felt they may be required to live.

Events of that period were significant, not the least of which was a real life court room drama; the McCann Case. A Protestant woman married a Catholic man, and proceeded to produce a series of children. The couple then sought to separate. The papal decree of Ne Temere insisted that the children of a mixed marriage were brought up as Roman Catholics. However, she wanted to take the children with her and bring them up as Protestants. There was a lengthy custody battle. To the extreme alarm and amazement of Ulster Protestants, the court of the land upheld the Roman Catholic decree as having priority over any counter wishes. If the courts were holding up papal decrees, then what was it going to be like if we ended up with Home Rule? The popular cry became 'Home Rule is Rome Rule'. My father lived through the signing of the Ulster Covenant on a sunny Saturday, 28th September 1912. I have in my possession the original covenant that James Davidson Laird signed at the City Hall, in a great blaze of enthusiasm and the massing of crowds. That very historic day was never to be forgotten by anyone who was there.

My father lived through the First World War, albeit as a developing young boy, and he lived through the Troubles in the early 1920s. The island of Ireland, which for many of its residents, including me, was never a nation but was at least two nations, possibly more, was divided and two parliaments were set up. There was trouble in Belfast, and there was a civil war in the Irish Republic, known at that stage as the Free State. My father remembered stories about relations of his mother, who worked in public transport. They had become vulnerable to suitcase bombs, which were a common Republican murder weapon of the period. My father made his way, on more than one occasion, back to his home in Agnes Street, both from Inst and later from medical school, only by lying on the floor of a tram, while bullets whistled through the windows. Any human being would have been affected by those events.

Ambition is one thing, but having the drive to fulfil that ambition is another. Unfortunately, my father's lack of drive and, possibly, of self-confidence, meant that his aspiration to become a Member of Parliament in Northern Ireland, outlined in the document of 1st January 1934, did not come about for thirty-five years and three weeks. At an age that probably meant it was his last opportunity, he became a Member of Parliament for his beloved St Anne's constituency, in January 1969, succeeding one of the Unionist old guard, Edmond Warnock QC.

As a family, we canvassed through the St Anne's area, which I knew because my mother, at that stage, was a councillor for part of it. All my political experience had been there; Sandy Row, Donegall Road and Roden Street were all main parts of the seat. In 1955 my mother had allowed her name to go forward for a local government position. Although a little hesitant at first, she was encouraged by her husband. Possibly this was a part of my father's grand plan to prepare the voters for himself. Regardless, Councillor Mrs Margaret Laird took to her task with great gusto. My mother was more sociable than my father. She would talk to anyone and nearly always did. She had a great interest in the people of her electoral ward. Not long into her career, she was to become the chairman of important committees such as Welfare, Education and Libraries.

My father was extremely well-known. He was the local doctor. Even during the turbulence surrounding Unionism in 1969, he seemed assured to be elected. However, with hindsight, I realise that he did not have the qualities or the charisma of a candidate. This, I think, requires a bit of showmanship; the ability to stand on a doorstep, talk to a potential voter and leave a memory that he or she might never forget, and will certainly hold until election day. My father could really only perform on a doorstep as a canvassing unit when accompanied by one of his relations, such as myself or some senior Unionist lieutenant from the area. But in the early hours of a Tuesday morning, at the end of January 1969, he was declared elected by the returning officer, as the member for Belfast St Anne's division, to serve in Her Majesty's Northern Ireland House of Commons; an unlikely Member of Parliament.

He took to it like the proverbial duck to water. He left his solitary existence as a general practitioner, which, between 1935 and 1969, was single-handed; no receptionist, no appointment system, no backup, no support. Although he interfaced with patients on a daily basis, his working life must have been soul-destroying. Suddenly my father was catapulted into a place of deference, into his life's ambition and into a place where he met, and possibly palled up with, new colleagues; the other Unionist MPs. It was the first time I have ever seen my father acting as the classic male might act in a male herd, talking about 'the boys', and gaining great amusement from schoolyard jokes and boyish activities. Even then, at the age of sixty-two, he was learning and I was seeing him in a way I had never seen him before. He reported back to his wife and sons, with tales of little incidents and misunderstandings and, to my great surprise, sexual innuendo, at which the boys had laughed uproariously. My father had been a rugby player in his student days and therefore must have been involved in all that rugby entails, including the aftermath of a match and the downing of the beer. However, the spirit of those student days seems to have deserted him during his thirty-five years as a solo operator in a GP practice. It was amazing to see him so intrigued by the behaviour of the collective male herd, even at that advanced age.

My father did the classic thing, I think, when he got away from his father, and first worked in hospitals in the early 1930s. I did not know until well after his death that my father drank, let alone had a drink problem. I did not know until well after his death that my father had also been in his youth a compulsive gambler. No drink was allowed in our household in my day. My mother, particularly, poured a disproportionate amount of scorn and anger on anyone who, in any way, drank or gambled. My father supported her in this. He had the enthusiasm and the fervour of the convert. My father owed his rehabilitation from those two weaknesses to my mother.

Margaret Dunn, as she was, was born as the eldest daughter of Robert John Dunn and Rebecca Dunn, in a farmhouse called Ballyskeagh, on the outskirts of a small hamlet called Artigarvan. The Dunns were also border reiver people, who had been planted in Ulster in 1610 from their homeland a few miles from Berwick-upon-Tweed. This move was part of King James's ethnic cleansing of the borders. The transportation of the border people to Ulster subsequently became known as the main plantation of Ulster. The Dunns were moved to Donegal. It is notable that the Laird family and the Dunn family lived not far from each other in Donegal, before the Lairds went to County Antrim and the Dunns went to County Tyrone. My father and my mother were, over three hundred years later, to come together and unite the two families. Incidentally, Dunn is the Scottish word and, subsequently, the Ulster Scots word, for brown complexion. That is why you will get, to this day, pubs in the north of England and in the border area called the Dun Cow; a dun cow simply being a red cow. And to this day, relations of mine who are Dunns do have a red complexion, copper or red hair, and a ruddy face.

Otterburn, in what is now Northumberland, was their home. Up until 1610, as border reivers, we regarded that as either Scotland or England, depending upon our audience. From not long after the period of Edward the Hammer of Scotland, the activities at Stirling Bridge, and the input of William Wallace, the people who had grown up on the borders of Scotland and northern England were known as reivers, which was the Scottish word for a raider. On the borders there existed a whole culture and a whole different lifestyle. This was the engine house that produced the Ulster Scots, that particular race of people that has dominated my life and defines who I am.

For three hundred and fifty years we ran the borders. We ransomed everything, working our way up and down the land. An army never passed through the borders unless we got a ransom. We did not regard ourselves as owing allegiance to any king or sovereign. When we of the borders rode out with our lances, we did not put any overlord's flag on them; this is the origin of the expression 'freelance'. Because of our status as a small group of people spread the whole way across the borders, we became totally independent, working on the concept that you have nothing else to depend on but your own right arm. This was to become, in subsequent years, a very important Presbyterian philosophy.

The border reivers were not nice. The border reivers were the troublemakers of the day. We had our own, perhaps Mafia-style, code of ethics. If you offended us, we killed you. It was nothing personal; it was just what we did. We raided, particularly in England. Our wives would tell us the family was hungry and the larder was empty by putting our riding spurs on the centre of the plate and serving that to us for dinner. That meant that we had to get on our horses and go and get the dinner.

We raided heavily to the south, and, as many of the traditional

Scottish border songs still record to this day, we burned and plundered, raped and pillaged our way as far south as Durham. The English were not enamoured with this behaviour and they built a settlement to try and keep us out. Being new in the land, it was known as Newcastle and it is there today. We were not on the same line as Hadrian's Wall but there was a rough sort of a connection. The whole area along the border became known as 'the debatable land', particularly on the eastern side, because, being freelancers, we worked the border to our best advantage. If somebody came from London to administer us, we said: 'That's a bit of a pity: you'd a long way to ride up here, because we live in Scotland. You see, the border is down there.' Then, if someone came from Edinburgh to administer to us, we would say: 'My goodness, this is a wee bit embarrassing; we actually live in England! You see, the border is up there.'

We were accountable to no one. We were independent. We lived in families and we were loyal only to our family. When we had to fight battles, we fought in family units. This is interesting because, particularly on the western side of the debatable land, battle order was always an echelon (V shaped). This meant that every second family was bred to fight left-handed. So, depending on who you were, you were either left- or right-handed. To this day, coincidence or not, almost fifty per cent of people called Kerr, who live in Northern Ireland, are left-handed–they fought on the left-hand side of the echelon. I think the Elliotts are much the same, although their statistics are not quite as impressive as those of the Kerrs.

All these families along the borders, and there are many of them, were tough guys who subscribed to a code. Maybe it was a blood code, but you did have a code of honour, bound together with your next-door neighbour family. You came together to fight a common enemy. The reivers were never particularly known for being religious, although they did believe in insurance, and they did like to pray the night before a battle. But they would fight each other and they had a process of once a month settling all their disputes. They also had a process whereby you could legitimately raid your next-door neighbour's or someone else's premises. You had a right known as 'hot trot'. You could actually go down as far as you liked into the opposition's ground, taking as much as you wanted, for a period, if they had caused you wrong; but only for a period.

The reivers were the origins of being bereaved. It was believed locally that if you dealt with the reivers you would be be-reived; you would lose somebody. The origins of the expression 'blackmail' also lie with the reivers. We would head down from the borders and steal a neighbour's daughter or a neighbour's wife or, best of all, an Englishman's daughter or an English wife, and then send, by hand, a letter to the opposing family. The letter envelope would have a black line around it, as a helpful indication of the contents. We also did a nice line in green mail. This involved taking somebody else's herd of cows or flock of sheep and sending a ransom letter with a green line around it.

Much is written about our exploits. Border reivers, according to legend, did not have any fear. They just fought and fought and fought. As a modern Ulsterman, I am heavily dictated by individual days out of history. Possibly one of the most important days that defines who I am is 24th March 1603, when Queen Elizabeth I died. Horsemen rushed to Edinburgh, arriving there around 28th March, to inform King James VI of Scotland that he was now also the King of England. We regard him as King James VI; Sassenachs regard him as King James I.

He was a rather unprepossessing gentleman, with some peculiar habits. But he was a very successful king of Scotland, and was known around the courts of Europe as the 'cleverest fool in Christendom'. When he became King of England, he found himself confronted with a number of problems, which he duly sought to iron out. From his position, he dealt with them well; not always successfully, but well. And his decision on how he would handle the making of Scotland and England into one kingdom is crucial to my background. James decided that in order to forge one kingdom, he needed to remove those people who made their living out of the border between the two parts of the kingdom.

James also had a problem in Ireland. Nearly ever ruler of England claims to have had a problem in Ireland. But like a modern day Nobel peace prize-winner, he thought he could solve the problem in Ireland, which was really centred on Ulster. The crisis reached a climax with the Flight of the Earls from Ulster to Europe, in 1607. They were never to return. James thought he would ethnically cleanse the border reivers by forcibly moving them into Ulster. Thus, he would solve two problems at once. He would clear the troublemakers from the border between Scotland and England and he would put reliable mainland Protestant tough guys in to Ulster, to plant it, to calm it down and to fill a major vacuum left by the Flight of the Earls.

It was some day in 1610 when the knock came to the door, in what is known still to this day as the Dunn land, near Otterburn. We were bundled out, along with all the other families, and sent to Ulster. That significant year, four hundred years ago, changed the course of history. Through the Plantation of Ulster in 1610, King James changed the course of British history, he changed the course of Irish history, and he changed the course of world history. Events were started which led on to the creation of the United States, as well as to the development of new systems of banking and agriculture, the advancement of academia and the creation of a race of warriors, who are still about today.

There had been plantations in Ulster before, during the time of Elizabeth I, involving mostly English settlers. The 1610 Plantation relocated a population of 400,000 from the border area to parts of Ulster. This plantation differed from earlier ones both in scope and the groups of people involved.

Until then, Ulster was virtually an empty area depopulated as a result of the Elizabethan wars. There had been a collapse in authority, a collapse in population, and a collapse of morale on the Irish side, with the Flight of the Earls. Our move to Ulster might have been difficult for us. But it was good for the world, and good for Ulster. The Plantation brought to the land a totally different way of thinking. It brought over a Protestant way and a Protestant ethos. It led to a different type of agriculture, to a development of a different style of early town planning. It introduced more modern, commercial approaches, market-orientated and more capital-intensive. This is a reflection of the Protestant ethic of individualism and personal salvation. They built the first real towns, roads and trading links and opened Ulster up to economic developments. This was a challenge to the semi-nomadic economy based on Brehon law, which had an emphasis on communal rights and ownership.

Plantation towns do not have market squares; they have diamonds. This feature of town planning later went to America with the Ulster emigrants. It resulted in the development of the classic American grid system in large cites, with streets going in one direction, at right angles to avenues. Our activities on the borders of England and Scotland notwithstanding, the plantation brought people who genuinely seemed to want a new way of life. It is true that Ireland's wetter climate was not what we would have chosen. And it is also true that some of the natives, albeit small in number, could be irritating. They kept trying to kill us and throw us out, which is good cause for irritation. However, there were also instances where relationships were often quite good, at least at first.

Not all plantation people from Scotland were Protestants or Presbyterians. Possibly as much as fifteen per cent of the planters was Roman Catholic. One of the areas from which my ancestors came, Strabane, was noted as being a Roman Catholic planters' area. But from 1610 onwards, the Plantation had started and nothing, but nothing, would ever be the same again.

It was from this stock that my father and mother came. Both had a Presbyterian background, each with shades of both wings of Presbyterianism. Strict Presbyterianism was the order of the day for both the Lairds and the Dunns, a feature that worked to mould my personality.

The only culture I ever knew in my home was Scottish. My father referred to his church as his kirk. One of his life's ambitions was to wear a kilt. Unfortunately, his lack of self-confidence let him down and he never donned such a garment, to my knowledge. All the songs that my mother would sing to us were Scottish. The term 'Ulster Scot' was bandied about in our home, as that was who we were. It was not desirable to call ourselves Irish. In fact, in the heartland of Artigarvan, if you wanted to insult somebody you referred to them as Irish. It was in the complex area of northwest Tyrone that I first heard, in full measure, the language of Ulster Scots. It is a language that has made a considerable difference to Ulster and it is still spoken in some degree by every native, regardless of religion or politics, in the form of its grammar and its words. Sometimes they call it slang, incorrectly, and sometimes it is called a dialect. Who cares? It is recognised by both the British and Irish governments, and by the European Union, as a language.

At home in the sleepy days of the 1950s and 1960s, Scotland was regarded as the homeland. Hogmanay was the big festival; Scottish culture was second nature. Irish was nowhere to be seen. Ulster Scots was all that you knew and all that you wanted to be. It is into that mix that I closed, in the early 1960s, an unsuccessful career at school. Lacking ambition, because of my own circumstances, I plunged into Ulster politics.

'Dyslexia is a funny business,' someone once said to me. He was right in the sense that it is strange. Of course, I did not know that I had such a difficulty until I was in my forties. I just thought that at school, Sunday school, the scout troop, at home, away from home, with relations and without relations, I was stupid. So did everyone else, or that was how I felt. From Brookvale School at the age of seven, I went to Inchmarlo, which was the junior school of Inst. It was a preparatory school and a very pleasant one for young gentlemen.

They seemed to spend a disproportionate amount of time out gardening and doing things of a non-academic nature. I did not at all enjoy my time at Inchmarlo. It is not Inchmarlo's fault. They taught me the best they could in the 1950s but it was not a pleasant process, as far as I was concerned. I took it into my head that I was the stupidest person in the school. In fact, I felt, I was setting new standards in stupidity. First of all, I was small, coming as I did into the world after seven months, and I seemed to be sickly. My father regularly took me off school. I do not know if he was just being kind or whether I actually was sickly, but I was absent from school a great deal, on health grounds. When you are small, scruffy, the last in the class, you become the butt of all jokes. I heavily resented that. I simply resented everything. I regarded myself as a disaster, with no future and with very little present.

I was bullied; a number of us were bullied. It was nasty at Inchmarlo, as it is probably nasty at any junior school, to the extent that I had to enlist my father's help to appeal to the headmaster about the major school bully. I realise now, of course, that the school bully needed to be treated as we all did, with compassion. He was to be pitied; it was his problem, not ours. It is interesting to note that subsequently that school bully went on to become a Church of Ireland clergyman. The headmaster was a friendly and kind gentleman called Edgar Lockett. He had an enthusiasm for teaching that was infectious. Looking back now I see him as a man of the 1950s.

I was totally unable at school to read or spell phonetically. To an extent, this is still the case. I could not and cannot convert sounds into letters and so place them into a word. Reading came very late to me and is still slow and painful. 'Relax and read a book' is an oxymoron. Under any pressure, I misread or I read words that were not there. One of the greatest challenges at school was to avoid reading 'out loud' to the class. The stress was massive and the teacher's reaction explosive, not to mention the mirth generated by the rest of the boys in the class. I invented any excuse to avoid that painful task.

Writing, too, was difficult, and still is. Apart from the unusual spelling I use, my brain seems to work much, much faster than the pen or keyboard. It is selecting the next word while I am still trying to write the previous one. Total disaster and embarrassment all around. To add to my difficulties, until fourteen, I was one of the smallest in any class. Small, stupid, unable to tie my shoelaces, I was marked out as an object of ridicule. Hand and eye co-ordination were difficult as a dyslexic, which meant there was little point in trying any sport. I knew that my father had been good at athletics and rugby and I felt that I was a total failure in his eyes. He did, on a very few occasions, lambast me for not trying but on the whole he kept his counsel and I festered in silence. But all that said, I cannot complain about my upbringing. I would not have changed it – if I could. It was of its time and, in my view, began to make me the person that I am today. It causes me to think and examine everything in detail. It filled me with resentment, which gave me the drive the show 'them' wrong by being a success.

Dyslexics find their input of information in either a verbal or visual way – but not through reading. If someone says anything to me I have a better than average chance of remembering all or part of the information. I have always been amused by those who ask what I am currently reading. I answer: 'The House on Pooh Corner by A.A. Milne – it's very good you know!' However, even from my time at Inchmarlo preparatory school, I realised that I could, and very often did, beat anyone of any academic level at chess. But I could not spell the word 'chess'.

During the period I was at junior school, I felt myself to be inadequate, lacking in confidence, the butt of humour and quite the worst pupil ever to have attended Inchmarlo. My first teacher there, at the age of seven, was a strict, difficult spinster. She presided over what was, perhaps, one of the very worst years of my life. I do not hold anything against the lady today. She was a well-respected teacher of her time and she did her best. In the long run, she helped me. I developed a strong-burning desire to prove that she was wrong about me.

Throughout the academic year I can recall only once being praised by the lady. 'Good,' she said, pointing a long bony finger at me, one day at a sports day race when, for reasons I cannot explain, I had tried to take part and compete and arrived at the finishing line early in a band of boys who made up my class. I can still see her saying that four-letter word. Surprised? I was delighted! Most of the time in her class, there was a slap to the leg or, on a few occasions, the head. I became distant.

It seemed that few of my classmates would want anything to do with me. I played on my own. I retreated into one of the make-believe worlds that provided me with sanity and comfort. In this all-enhancing existence I was the hero. I could do anything, and generally did, much to the acclaim of my imaginary onlookers, classmates or devoted public. The rest of the years at Inchmarlo were better, if not perfect.

One day in later life, in the mid-1980s, I attended a function in Newry. There I met a fellow pupil from those Inchmarlo days. He had inherited a farm nearby in Armagh and so achieved a comfortable living. To my surprise and upset, he began to make fun of me to some other guests, with the most hurtful remark being about my inability to tie shoelaces. Memories came flooding back and I felt sick. Later, on the road out of Newry and on the way home, I was driving my large Mercedes (for show purposes), paid for out of the business that I had started with £200 and which was then paying for the education of my kids. I sailed past my former Inchmarlo colleague, who was driving a very battered Ford, or Lada, or something else of that status. I blew my horn to say goodbye and I wondered exactly what point he had tried to make at the function and, more importantly, why?

The early 1950s were still the aftermath of the War. Rationing was still going on. Bomb damage was visible in Belfast and the general rule of 'make do and mend' was the order of the day. My father, for professional reasons as a doctor, was allowed a car during the war. By the fifties, he was driving a Hillman, a large car for that time. It was black, with leather seating and a beautiful red 'cherry' on a silver pole on the passenger mudguard, to keep my father aware of his nearside.

He was the only one in the house who could drive. The Belfast roads were not crowded and public transport, trains, trolleybuses and buses were regular and quick. On either side of where I lived on the Somerton Road there were tram depots; one on Salisbury Avenue, off the Antrim Road, and the other on the Shore Road. I loved anything on rails or indeed, failing that, any form of transport.

With my mother's relations living in Artigarvan, County Tyrone, I was outstandingly lucky to be introduced to railway journeys from well before I can remember. Artigarvan is five miles outside Strabane. Five or six times a year the excitement mounted in our home. Out came brown leather suitcases; on went our best clothes with a heavy coat. It seems that weather was more extreme in those days. A taxi took my mother, my brother Jimmy and I to Great Victoria Street Station, a place that entranced me. The smell, the crowds, the trains: the steam trains going to, or coming from, exciting places whose names were called out from the ticket barrier. Newcastle, Armagh, Cookstown, Enniskillen, Clones and Londonderry; Londonderry – that was ours. We settled down in first class accommodation, an apartment to ourselves, and enjoyed, or at least I did, the three hour journey to Strabane. The Lairds, according to my father, only travelled first class! This was fine by me.

If we were lucky it was a steam train; if not so blessed, one of the new diesel railcar sets. I loved these journeys to Strabane and later back home again. Heaven must surely be Strabane Railway Station. There the Great Northern Railway, which ran the line from Belfast to Londonderry, met the County Donegal Railway. I could not contain myself. The beautiful red and yellow carriages, the magic rail buses and the red, yes the red, steam engines. Somewhere inside of me something stirred, a thrill which still exists to this day.

Summer holidays were different. Then we went by car to Portrush, that most beautiful seaside town on the north coast. Seaside was on both sides. Portrush sticks out into the Atlantic and has an east and west strand. It seemed to me the pinnacle of existence was a visit to the White Rocks, set amongst the sand hills. The beautiful, massive strand was just perfect. My father shared my love of railways. He cunningly marked out, with a stick, two lines in the sand, two feet apart. This 'railway track' ran around our part of the beach. I was safe. Pretending that I was a train, with a service to be provided, I could be found at any time between the two lines. Sometimes, I carried a stick over my shoulder and thus became a tram with a trolley. Several years later and at home, I was to be modernised. I obtained a second stick and became a trolleybus.

But at school I struggled through, not playing any games to a scientific level, not having passed any exams and not doing anything worthwhile. At Inchmarlo, I had been mistreated both physically and mentally, which scarred me at the time. I do not hold any resentment, although I hated it then. I hated everything to do with it. I hated the teachers; I hated the pupils. I can think of nothing that I liked about the school, except going home. But I do not hold it against them and, in subsequent years, I was to be on the board of governors of that Belfast school, along with its senior school, Inst. Today, Inchmarlo is a top rate school that looks after the interests of those who are educationally disadvantaged. More of Inst later.

I went on to Inst, the senior section of the school, although I failed twice to pass the Eleven Plus exam. Surely this is a record. I have never met anybody else who twice failed to pass the Eleven Plus. Inst was a revelation. First of all, I was now meeting people with broad Belfast accents. This was a shock. I was interested in classroom subjects beyond the mere reading and writing. I was gaining ground in maths, learning algebra and geometry, which I found that I could understand. I learned history and to my surprise, and that of some of my contemporaries, not to mention the history teacher, I blossomed at history, and at geography, despite the dyslexia. I even became semi-good at Latin, and obtained a little bit of French. I could always do the science topics, but generally I began to learn the skills of the dyslexic, and how to bluff your way through life. Dyslexic pupils learn to develop strategies to hide their dyslexia, and I was no exception.

Humour – some people just laugh at it but I take it seriously. If you are the butt of jokes, if you are small, if you are stupid, if you are open to bullying, then what is your reply? What is your response? Mine was humour. If people were going to laugh at me anyway, then I could lessen the mood, menacing or not. I could be of value to a group. I began actively to seek to be funny. Not successfully; humour did not run in my life. It almost seemed that Presbyterians did not do humour. Perhaps it was seen as a waste of time and resources and there can be no waste!

I have always felt that it was important to be of a Presbyterian background. As I have gone through life to date, there are more positive sides to negatives. But one negative, which was compounded by the atmosphere of the 1950s in Ulster, was 'offer no praise'. To praise someone might give them 'ideas above their station' or 'make them complacent'. Looking back, no doubt, I was searching for praise or at least recognition, or any encouragement at all. Again, I do not hold the lack of warmth or support as anyone's fault. Nothing was deliberate. Those were just the times we lived in.

I was not perfect. I was bad mannered and badly behaved. When I could be, I was loud. From the age of seven, I clearly preferred to play by myself, which I did day after day. Except, of course, when Jimmy brought some of his friends around. Then I was cheeky. However, Jimmy had a particular friend with what seemed to be an unlikely name; Popplestone. Robin Popplestone, known to all as Pop. Pop was the son of a teacher of French at Inst called Jack, who had settled in Ulster during the war and brought up a fine bunch of sons. The eldest, and perhaps the cleverest, was Pop.

How Pop and my brother came to team up is a mystery to this day. Pop was extremely left wing; a supporter of Russia of all things! He was, like me, a railway enthusiast. Many long hours I spent with Pop on my model railway while he rearranged its electrics, its timetable, its layout and anything that was lying about to match his expertise and act as an outlet for his brain. Jimmy looked on with boredom and disinterest, or even concern, because I had stolen his friend.

For Pop, nothing was simple. We played Monopoly but his version included stocks and shares, advanced banking with forms of interest of which I had never heard. Any plaything that we or I had, Pop enhanced to meet his standards. He argued politics with my brother. Rather unusual, I thought at the time. The arguments were not about the border or about the freedom which Ulster offered, vis-à-vis the Republic of Ireland; a grim, church-dominated hellhole with imperialist aspirations over Ulster. Pop and Jimmy debated the importance of something called Communism, as opposed to Capitalism. A new type of political thinking, I felt, and one that would never catch on. Clearly, the freedom of Ulster was the only world issue of any concern.

In 1960, I took to railways in a big way. That summer I received a remarkable letter from the appropriate education authority telling me that I had passed the Junior Certificate. Goodness, I had passed an exam, and with some high marks as well! Perhaps the world was not such a bad place. Since the previous year, I had taken a practical interest in the local railway system. I began to spend some time at the end of platforms at the two major railway terminals in Belfast, which still had steam. I met fellows of my own age who treated me as an equal. I could learn their railway language, full of bogies, paths, goods, and so on and so on. Passing the Junior, that state exam, moved me up the confidence league.

My father was not an ungenerous man but he had amongst his faults a total misunderstanding of money, how it worked and its role in every day life. To mark my exam success, he funded me to obtain several runabout tickets for a week's travel on the railway system. At £3.50, I could not be expected to purchase one myself, let alone the food and other requirements for travelling the countryside.

My world gained a totally new dimension on Sunday, 9th July 1960. While using my runabout ticket, I was on the 6.20pm Belfast to Dublin reading an internal railway timetable, known as the 'working book', while the time ticked away as we waited to leave Great Victoria Street. In 1960, such a train was full, or almost full. I was sitting facing away from the front on a seat one removed from the window, in other words on the inside. As the train was not steam, there were no requirements to sit at a window on the milepost side, in order to 'log' the outing.

I was aware of a dark cloud as it passed down the aisle. It seemed to be taking an interest in me. The cloud returned and this time it faced me and enquired if it could be permitted to examine my timetable. And so I came face to belly-button with Cecil Thomas Bell. Cecil, I am very pleased to say, is perhaps my very best friend, as opposed to a relation, to this day. As we pass through life, we meet people who help to mould and shape us. Without doubt,

Cecil Thomas Bell was such a person for me.

Although it was mid-July, Cecil was wearing a Methodist College tie as he sat down opposite me to share information with a fellow railwayman. During the course of the hour and a quarter run to Goraghwood, our place on a Sunday to catch the steam-hauled return from Dublin, I enquired as to why he was wearing a school tie during holidays. Cecil explained that he was twenty-three years old and had been away from school for eight years. The tie was his regular mode of dress. Cecil Bell could be hard work and difficult to know, but he is a true, loyal, lifelong friend. His understanding of life, his politics and importantly his sense of humour were to make a positive impression on me, and one for which I am most grateful.

Inst was indeed a revelation. It set me free. I owe a lot to Inst. I have tried to pay that which I owe over the years as should become clear. But I did leave the school in a fit of lethargy. In 1963, I was ill equipped for university, certainly; that idea was laughable. I was equipped only to join a bank. And that was a revelation of monumental proportions, because I discovered a job that I could do, which was relatively easy and that I could be good at. Most significantly of all, it was the first place I had ever been, in which I had praise and recognition.

Burnt into my mind is the night I was working late in the bank's head office in Arthur Street in Belfast, towards the end of 1963. The caretaker, who was also a commissionaire, Sergeant Fred Turner, was waiting for me to finish work. And he said to me: 'Laird, this office doesn't work so well without you. This office is actually different when you're not here. This office springs to life and works faster, and better, on the days when you're here.' No one had ever said anything like that to me before. No one had ever encouraged me in anything that I can think of before. It was always the back of your hand before, not physically, but mentally. I can remember exactly where I was in the bank when he said that to me. I could not believe it. That started a short, slightly remarkable banking career, which, again, began to fit me for my future existence.

As I have indicated, Inchmarlo, the preparatory school for Inst, had been a very difficult time for me and I hated the place with a passion. That first teacher, the particularly tough spinster, and her literal hands-on approach would be against the law in today's society, thank goodness. But the most damaging thing of all was the continual rubbing away of one's self-confidence. If all you are ever told is that you are absolute rubbish, and a disgrace, and the worst they have ever seen, there is a point at which you become all those things. The particular lady was liked by some at the school, but disliked by most. I remember a friend telling me that he was walking down a corridor, past her class door, and had his hands in his pockets. And he happened to be whistling a tune. She came out of her room and circled round him like a beast of prey about to pounce. She roared at him and she shouted at him, giving him all sorts of abuse for his behaviour. And he was not a pupil; he was a member of staff.

Years later, in the early 1980s, when my son David went to that school, I met my first teacher again. The elderly spinster was a guest at the sports day, in her capacity as a retired teacher. I spied her there, wrapped up in rugs and felt obliged to go over and introduce myself and perhaps indulge myself by explaining how I had got on in life since leaving school. She looked surprised to see me. The lady did not know who I was until I introduced myself. I thought she might have known me because I had been a very high-profile Member of Parliament at that stage. I proceeded to try and tell her what I had done since leaving school but before I could get in to the point, she asked me about my brother, whom I did not know that she knew. How was Jimmy, she asked. 'Jimmy? He's fine. Now I want to tell you about me.' And before I could get the point made, she said 'What's he doing now?' I said: 'Jimmy, he's a medical consultant; he's a senior consultant at the Royal Victoria Hospital. Now, I just want to say that I've been a member of …' She said: 'Is he keeping well?' I said: 'Jimmy? He's keeping very well. He's got two daughters, and they both go to Victoria College. And I … ' She said: 'That's very interesting. Tell Jimmy I was asking for him.'

I'm really not very sure what that conversation was about, but, once again, it backed up the point, at that stage, that she seemed to have an inability to remember her part in my life, or she thought of it and was trying to hide it. But I think it was the former and not the latter.

Unfortunately, it was a time that fitted in a little bit with the rough side of the Presbyterian ethos. That is, you don't actually praise or seek praise, for that's bad for the soul. Because I was small at that junior school, and it was an all-male school, I was usually selected for female roles in any of the Christmas shows. I thought I was quite good there. I would come off after the show expecting praise, because the audience seemed to like it, and all I got pointed out to me was that I had not combed my hair. I played a lot of female roles while at Inchmarlo. One of my proud boasts is that, by the time I left junior school, I had handled many female parts!

Inst was different. The bank was different. I got on well at the bank. I liked the bank, its atmosphere, its routine. I got a lot of pleasure out of strange things at the bank. I loved the concept, even as a junior in the office, of opening the door at a certain time for business. I loved, in subsequent years, watching the television series, *Open All Hours*, because it had the same kind of ethos, of opening the door and trying to serve the public. Strange to say, I took the bank exams and was fairly successful, again, much to my amazement, and ended up on the bank inspection team. We would nowadays be called auditors. So, at a young age I found myself as a bank inspector, touring around the province, in what I thought was a fast James Bond-type car, with three other inspectors. We visited isolated branches throughout Northern Ireland, and carried out our inspections; this was an enjoyable period of my life.

The bank that I joined in 1963 had high stools, dip pens and high desks, and with the exception of a few machine-offices, everything was written with pen and ink on card. In 1968, the bank decided that they were going to be computerised, whatever that meant in those days. And to save money, and to be prestigious, they were going to be computerised by the bank's existing staff. So in 1968 we were all subjected to an intelligence test, an aptitude test. Now, it never actually seemed to dawn on me that I would not be successful at that. For an intelligence test I could gobble up any day of the week. An aptitude test, answering simple maths problems seemed to be no problem to me. Lo and behold, in this entire test of every member of staff for selection as programmers, I came second and ended up in October of that year in Manchester, beginning to train as a computer programmer. Computers in those days were the size of massive rooms. They were kept in larger halls, which were air-conditioned, and you were only allowed into them under certain conditions. It was almost like a sterile laboratory. The size of the computers we had, and how we programmed them, was like the Stone Age compared with what is available today. But the facts are that the bank was using its own staff and completed putting up an online banking system by February 1971, the first outside the United States. What we did was impossible according to computer experts, but as nobody had told us that at the time, we just went on and did it.

During my time in the bank, I began to be profoundly affected by my clear-sighted boss, Bryan Johnston. Bryan led the small team that carried out the impossible. Today it is interesting to note that the trailblazing location for the very first branch to be put online in real time was the Ardoyne branch and the date was 24th August 1970. A first indeed for Northern Ireland. We should all be proud of what happened at Ardoyne that summer.

Other members of that outstanding team were Don Campbell, a long suffering and most pleasant systems analyst, Mervyn Bishop, Maurice Carson, Anthony Swan, Allister Young and Gerard McAdams, all of whom started as programmers. They were soon to be followed by John Acheson and Andy Lovatt, who worked as operatives. I learnt a considerable amount from this period; in particular, the importance of focusing on a task, no matter what problems it entails. It is for this latter point that I am most grateful to Bryan Johnston. It was he who had the vision and drive to turn an old-fashioned savings bank into a modern full service organisation. He gave many years of public service in the 1990s and in the first decade of the current century. Rightly, he was awarded the OBE in 1991. Carol and I are delighted to consider Bryan and his wife Helen amongst our good friends.

To my delight, the Lord Mayor of Belfast, Councillor Pat Convery, hosted a reception in the City Hall on 24th August 2010. The event was designed to mark the part the city had played by being the pioneer of real time, or online, banking, forty years previously. I was delighted that all the computer staff from that time were able to attend, along with the staff of the Ardoyne branch, the first to 'go online'. Ardoyne is a name that should go down in history as the very first site of this type of modern banking outside the United States. Yet another first for Northern Ireland!

I was becoming more interested in politics. I came from a political background. My mother was in the Belfast City Corporation. My father had his ambitions to get into Stormont and was the chairman of the local Unionist Association and a big time, if not flamboyant, Unionist. It seemed natural to me that I should take a part in this type of activity. I joined the Young Unionists and began to work for the party. As a result of this, and in combination with my work in the bank, I did seem to go up in my own mind and up in the world. It was good to feel accepted, to never be questioned but to be praised. I gained the impetus to rise up through the Unionist movement fast and ruthlessly, politics being a ruthless profession. But the day that changed my life forever, and was to be quite the most significant event that ever happened to me was yet ahead of me.

After working late at the bank on Monday 27th April 1970, I went home at about 10 o'clock. My father was there; my mother was at a meeting in the Belfast City Hall. I sat and had a chat with my father. It was a detailed sort of a chat, which was not a common occurrence. We talked about things. He asked me to go into town, the next day at the bank, to buy some items for him. He was a keen stamp-collector, despite my jibe that philately would get him nowhere, and he asked me to buy some particular sheets. He took me down to his office in the house and showed me what he wanted. Then we went back to sitting in front of the fire and talking, in the way I loved to talk to my father. I did not do it often enough. We had a cosy, two-man chat; father and son. My mother came in, and had a cup of tea. Good nights were said, and we all went to bed. Twenty minutes later, my father was dead. It is an irony that I have to live with, but the best thing the man I loved most in the world ever did for me was to die when he did. I came in my own mind from being Donald Duck to Einstein in a matter of hours. Nothing was ever the same again.

In the early hours of 28th April, I went to bed as a carefree bachelor, with a good job at the bank, a frivolous sense of humour and a developing personality. And I set off the next morning, a shattered, broken individual, fighting back the tears, to visit the family solicitor, and other significant people, including senior members of the Unionist party, to tell them that my father was no more. From that day on, responsibility has seemed to me to have lain on my shoulders in full and strong measure, in a way I could never have envisaged. The pressure was such that I almost cracked: it is possible to argue that I did crack. The next twelve months were absolute hell. But, I suppose, it is that which defines the making of a human being.

CHAPTER TWO

The Honourable Member

FOR THE ST ANNE'S DIVISION OF BELFAST

HANSARD

'THE BIGGEST MISTAKE ever made by the British people of Ulster' is the way that I now think of the compromise they made in 1921, in accepting a devolved parliament. After four decades of grim determination not to accept Home Rule, we did just that in 1921. This error of judgment was to cost us dearly and was to leave us in a most difficult position. But then, of course, in developing my opinion today, I did not come through the Great War.

'The war to end all wars', as the Great War was to be called, must have been the most shattering experience for everyone involved. Clearly it was for the massed ranks of fighting men right through to the ordinary citizen – if such a person exists. Unlike the 1939-45 War, it could have been avoided. The world could have been spared the later destructive events.

Millions died between 1914 and 1918 or, in some parts, 1919. Borders in Europe were redrawn with the ease of a child writing on a wall. But from my viewpoint, the legacy consists of the change of attitude and the attendant political atmosphere. Many feel that a major war or civil unrest is a time for humanity to move on, develop and to be creative. In my view, this is correct. The First World War left its mark on Ulster.

Life in and around Belfast in 1912 to 1914 was exciting. Emotions seemed to have run in many directions. The Ulster Covenant, a document designed to underline the determination of Unionists not to have Home Rule, was signed in 1912 in a wave of emotion and loyal fervour. The Titanic set sail that year, to the pride of all in the city. The threat of Home Rule was always on everyone's mind – what was going to happen? The Unionist leadership of Sir Edward Carson and Sir James Craig held rallies all over the place to keep the faithful at boiling point and plans were being laid for resistance of a tougher type. The Ulster Scots people were doing what they were always good at; digging in with their backs against the wall.

Through my life there can be no doubt that the sections of the Scottish nation who had been forged on the anvil of Ireland – the Ulster Scots – liked nothing more than to exercise their inherited right of making a stand. Also, there can be no doubt that, were I there at the time, I would have been amongst their number.

In August 1914, the people who had armed themselves with German guns only a few months earlier in April, were ready to turn them on the Germans and to fight to remain British. The German guns had arrived under cover of dark at Larne and were distributed overnight all over the province in what is now called the 'gun-running'. Up to that date, Carson's Ulster Volunteer Force could have been seen as a paper-threat but, literally over one night in a well-organised exercise, the force became fully armed. That night entered the loyalist folklore and is revered to this day.

The development of the original UVF had taken the loyalist community by storm. 'Ulster will fight and Ulster will be right,' said the father of Winston Churchill, when addressing a meeting in the Ulster Hall in 1889. These words still rang in every ear.

My grandmother on the maternal side, Rebecca née White of Killynaght outside Artigarvan, was no exception to the spirit of militancy. It is interesting to note that if you draw a line north from the Dunn's farm at Ballyskeagh to Killynaght, a farm on the other side of several fields, and draw another almost due south, you will hit a farm at Artigarvan called Lowry's. My great-grandmother,

Isabel, was a Lowry and my grandmother was a White, both several fields' length away from the Dunn household at Ballyskeagh. In the 1800s, people did not move too far and communities were family-orientated.

Isabel Lowry had an important effect on the Dunns. She was a Victorian of the latter period, when women wore black with hair parted in the centre and tightly combed to each side. This look was not feminine, at least not as I understand it. A photograph of her and my great-grandfather was displayed in the sitting room at Ballyskeagh. For very many years I was convinced that it was of two men! For reasons I can only guess at, the Dunns called their sitting room the upper room.

Miss Lowry was the strong, so strong, Presbyterian female of her time. The new Mrs Dunn remoulded the Dunns' religious character to be purely Presbyterian. The Dunns might have considered themselves as perhaps, just perhaps, Church of Ireland at that stage. But a Dunn was not going to remain Church of Ireland for long, if he was to be lucky enough to marry a Lowry. Isabel's husband, my great-grandfather, in common with all Dunns who owned Ballyskeagh from 1826 to 1993, had a John as a Christian name. By all reports, he seems to have been a most friendly and pleasant gentleman. My uncle Jack (John), who was born in 1907, knew his grandfather well until the elder man's death in 1921.

John, my great-grandfather, was five years of age at the height of the famine in the mid 1840s. He often recalled the shortage of food in that part of Tyrone and how he and his family had to walk many miles due east to find provisions. This and many other stories he told my uncle, his grandson, and they were passed on to us all before his death in 1993. That sort of thing makes history seem short. The Irish famine of the 1840s is always remembered but it was only one of many in both Scotland and on the island of Ireland. Many were much worse than the one of the 1840s.

When the Home Rule crisis deepened, the Dunns, the Whites and the Lowrys, along with almost everyone else in Artigarvan, were involved. Rebecca White was one of five sisters, who, to the unbiased eyes of family members, were five stunners. The Whites were Presbyterians of a more liberal sort. For example, they were known to take a drink. Rebecca's father's usual routine was to head for the excitement of Strabane on a Saturday night. He would proceed to get so drunk that he could only get home because his pony and trap knew the way. Looking back on that story, I suspect that the pony was due more credit than the trap.

At the formation of the UVF, Rebecca joined the local attached nursing unit in Artigarvan. As I would expect, her history, when told by the family, indicates that she was a 'leading member'. The unit met and trained in Artigarvan Orange Hall, which is still there today. The hamlet of Artigarvan and its local area could also be referred to as Leckpatrick. At least, the creamery and the local school were, but the appropriate railway station on the narrow gauge from Strabane to Londonderry was called Ballyheather. Confused?

The local area, like very many others in the province, was to provide fertile recruitment for the army, come 1914. Many from the UVF became members of the 36th Ulster Division and saw outstanding service at the Somme. Hundreds of them marched on the nearby road to Londonderry on their way from Finner camp, in Donegal, to board ships to take them to war. The sight of the soldiers marching to their destiny was long remembered and recalled in the areas it passed through. A feature, that was to interest me, was that almost everyone who joined up was sixteen years old and therefore underage. Or so they said. Interestingly, when I worked in the bank with many who had fought in the Second World War, their tales always involved exciting derring-do that took place on well-known campaigns, and nearly always on the first day. Stories were never about the catering section or the like. Perhaps I was just lucky that I worked with the twenty or so men who were responsible for winning the war.

One of the farm workers in Ballyskeagh was an elderly, round man by the name of Andy Forbes. Andy, in common with many such workers at that time, wore a cap, a striped shirt which had seen better days and was without the detachable collar. His trousers were blue pinstriped and were held up by binder twine tied at the front. Forbes had signed up to join the 36th Ulster Division at, of course, the age of sixteen. When I knew Andy in the 1950s, he liked nothing more than to puff at his foul smelling pipe.

Private Forbes was to survive the great battles, including the Somme. To the pride of his family and many friends in Artigarvan, he was awarded the Military Medal for extreme bravery on the battlefield. The tale that was often repeated in that Tyrone village, by almost everyone except him, was simple. One night, with his comrades, he got smashed drunk. A German machine-gunpoint, which had been annoying the whole British line, started up again. Andy, in this drunken state, grabbed a gun, raced over the top and right up to the German point and shot directly into it killing the three gunners. The gunpoint was never a problem again but the British officers now had a new dilemma. What were they to do with Forbes? He had disobeyed orders by going over the top but he had destroyed an enemy gunpoint. Thankfully, the decision was not to court-marshal but to award him the Military Medal, a reward of great distinction in wartime. Andy lived out an unassuming life near his native village, like many of the lucky ones who were able to return home.

At the start of the Great War, Carson had asked all UVF members to show their loyalty and sign up for King and Country. Almost all the UVF did so and were joined by many more. Many from a nationalist background and from the south, too, also joined and they acquitted themselves well. On the fateful 1st July 1916 at the Somme, the 36th Ulster Division, along with countless others, entered the dreadful and wasteful battle. Seen in its entirety, it was a massive failure. The Germans had not been knocked out as expected, after considerable British bombardment. The only division to reach its targets for the day was the 36th. German points called the Stuff and Schwaben redoubts were captured but because the support failed, the territory had to be given up again.

That day 5,500 men of the Ulster Division were killed or wounded. Four soldiers – Private William McFadzean, Private

Robert Quigg, Lieutenant Geoffrey Cather and Captain Eric Bell – were awarded the Victoria Cross, three posthumously.

An English officer wrote in his official report: 'I am not an Ulsterman, but yesterday, the 1st July, as I followed their amazing attack I felt that I would rather be an Ulsterman than anything else in this world. My pen cannot describe adequately the hundreds of heroic acts witnessed... The Ulster Volunteer Force, from which the Division was made, has won a name which equals any in history. Their devotion deserves the gratitude of the British Empire.'

I suspect that, just after the war in 1919, the fight had been knocked out of even the Ulster Scots. The whole atmosphere had changed and perhaps the time had come for compromise. The narrative was that the blood of the 36th Ulster Division at the Somme had paid for the freedom of Ulster. There was not a town, village, hamlet or group of cottages in the province, which had not been affected by the Somme.

The Unionist Council accepted a local parliament, which was duly opened by King George V in June 1921 at Belfast City Hall. The arrangement set out in the Government of Ireland Act of 1920 was for a bicameral, or two-chamber, affair, run on Westminster lines. The Upper Chamber was composed of twenty-six Senators and the Lower House was the Commons with fifty-two members, known as MPs, of all things. The production was almost exactly the same as at the Mother of Parliaments. It could only administer and legislate for devolved subjects; foreign affairs, tax-raising and defence were restricted to London. That was during a time when we had to make do with what we had.

I am always pleased to point out that the Government of Ireland Act had two interesting inclusions that seem to have been overlooked in recent years. Section five ensured that any legislation that the new Parliament passed and which discriminated against any individual or group, on grounds of their religion, was null and void. Section eight outlined that any administration undertaken which discriminated in the same fashion was also illegal. In later years, I could never understand why protesting groups did not take up some of the allegations of discrimination against Stormont in the courts, instead of on the street. It would have saved much death and destruction.

By 2000, the Government of Ireland Act had been repealed to allow the Police Bill to pass and thus permit religious discrimination in the recruitment of officers to the Police Service of Northern Ireland. The United Kingdom government had decided that the local police needed more Roman Catholics officers, a point on which almost everyone agreed. However, their solution was to draw up a system of fifty-fifty recruitment which people like me, who hate discrimination, have opposed. Infringing human rights can never be an answer to anything.

In 1921, the Northern Ireland Parliament took over running the new country, but where did the country start and end? The issue of the exact extent of Northern Ireland would not finally be settled until 1925 and then in some households, during that period, all hell broke out – if it had not already done so.

In many areas throughout the island of Ireland, hell had been on hand since 1920. The Irish Civil War in the south set nationalists against nationalists and against Protestants. The argument amongst nationalists was about accepting the offer of self-government of twenty-six or so counties inside the Commonwealth or not accepting it. The issue against Protestants seems to have been that Protestants were seen as part of the ascendancy and therefore could not have a part in a 'Free Ireland'. Besides, nationalists wanted the Protestants' land, jobs and homes. So much for Republican ideals!

Figures vary, but somewhere in the region of 60,000 Protestants were removed from that new country, most coming to the new Northern Ireland and some going to Great Britain. Also mixed up with the violence was death most crude. Many Protestants were murdered, from Cork in the very south to the other end of the Free State. This informed and shaped opinion in Protestant circles in Northern Ireland for decades. It still lurks in the corporate memory.

For the sake of fairness, things were not pleasant in the northern state either. Protestants killed Roman Catholics and Roman Catholics killed Protestants. The whole island moved towards anarchy. Some bold actions were taken on all sides, by those in authority during those initial years, which managed to diffuse some issues and a sort of normality descended in the mid 1920s. Over the next couple of decades, Northern Ireland had to fight to continue to exist. On one hand, it required all the traditional Presbyterian determination but, on the other hand, its siege mentality helped to undermine some traditional Ulster Scots values. Again, it is easy for me to see that now, removed as I am from that atmosphere.

Only thirteen years after the creation of what became known as the Stormont Parliament, my father decided that his life's ambition was to become a member. Westminster I could have understood, but why Stormont? Perhaps it was the grandeur and deference of the place. It may have been a smaller version of Westminster but when, from 1933, it was set in the regal surroundings of the Stormont Estate, it did look and sound like a parliament. It was on 1st January 1934 when he listed his ambitions, only months after Stormont came on-stream. My father, that man of his time, that Ulsterman who came through the most difficult of periods of 'no Home Rule', had bought into the system. As I would learn, perception is more important than actuality.

In Stormont, as I found out, the staff treated members with full deference. Called Members of Parliament, we thought that we were important and we became confused with those who attended Westminster. The elections from 1921 were by proportional representation, similar to that used in the Free State. Also, similar to their elections we had all the big nationalist names standing for Ulster elections. For example, Eamon De Valera became a Stormont MP. He never attended!

By the end of the 1920s, Stormont had decreed that elections should be 'first past the post' to complete the copy of Westminster. There were thirteen members in the national Parliament from Northern Ireland so, with fifty-two members at Stormont, it was a rule of thumb that each Westminster constituency should divide into four Stormont constituencies. In Belfast, for example, there were four Westminster seats; East, West, North and South. These in turn were divided much as a cake is divided into four, slicing from the centre. So each Westminster constituency translated into four pieces of cake for Stormont and St Anne's Stormont constituency was thus a quarter of West Belfast. St Anne's covered most of the area in which Dr Norman Davidson Laird practiced medicine and was to become the local member. As expected, he held the seat for the Unionist Party in January 1969, more or less holding the outgoing gentleman's majority. It was to that area that I was elected in his place on Friday 13th November 1970 – a day unlucky for the other candidates.

In keeping with all significant events, the aftermath of my father's death can be looked at in several lights. The political dimension needed to be agreed and this kept me focused and driven. The added responsibility also had a major effect on me. Within minutes of our father's death I needed help. As a family, we made tea for ourselves and for the medical support that had turned up to work on our father's heart attack, his cause of death. It seemed unreal. Tea and gentle sympathy were served in the very room in which I had spent some time talking to him, only a very few hours before.

When left on our own, around 2.30am, my brother took control, organised the spare room for our mother and made a point of offering comfort to me. James, or Jimmy, as we in the family called him, was – and is – the most gentle of people, kind and thoughtful. Like everyone, he has many faults but being a bad brother is not one of them.

At the turn of the stairs in our large house that night, he added to the massive change that my life was to undertake. Offering comfort, he told the shattered me to think political, think about the upcoming by-election and did any member of the family want to stand? I asked him if he did. I held my breath. He had just been appointed as a consultant to a major hospital in Londonderry. I felt strongly that he would not want to be side-tracked but he was, and is, my eldest, if only, brother.

Jimmy said 'no' but that I should 'go for it'. I was careful never to ask that question again. Whatever I expected by 'going for it' I cannot remember, but whatever it was, it was not what I got! An Ulster Scot was about to be tested.

June 1970 was a month selected by Harold Wilson, the Prime Minister, to call a UK-wide general election. So with my father's death at the end of April, a by-election for Stormont could not be held until the autumn period. The first viable date selected was Thursday 12th November, with the count being made in the City Hall on Friday 13th.

All summer I prepared and worked, worked and prepared. When nomination day arrived, I was the duly selected Unionist candidate at twenty-five years of age. I was determined that I should obtain every possible vote as a tribute to my dad. I set about the streets of St Anne's that I knew so well – sometimes with others and sometimes on my own. I restricted myself to the Protestant areas. In Belfast West, there was neither cross-voting nor floating voting.

There were two other candidates, both very decent people. One was NI Labour and the other SDLP, on that party's first outing. The Social Democratic and Labour Party was only formed that year. It was mainly made up of former Nationalist Party members and independents. The leader was Gerry Fitt MP, of whom more later. I should win, but how? Although I say it myself, I worked hard and between that and the emotion of my father's death I never, but never, met anyone who said that they were not going to vote for me.

On Friday 13th the count took place. I had increased my father's vote and doubled his majority – most unusual for a by-election. The Returning Officer, after reading out the votes cast, said, 'I, the undersigned, do hereby declare that the above named John Dunn Laird is duly elected to serve as the Member of Parliament for the St Anne's Division.' It was like a dream. A crowd of supporters carried me shoulder-high, in the time-honoured fashion, out of the City Hall into the daylight of the street. My poor mother, overcome with the electoral success, kept saying that she wished Norman, her husband, was there, he would have enjoyed it. While I knew what she meant, I knew she was carried away. After all, it was his very death that caused the day's events to happen! That night's Belfast Telegraph had the large front-page headline: 'St Anne's gives Laird double majority win'.

The following Tuesday, my youthful form was introduced into the Northern Ireland House of Commons as its newest member, its youngest ever Unionist and, as it turned out, its last addition. Within days, the election and the related excitement subsided and the new life, new surroundings and new colleagues took over. This was November 1970. There were no facilities such as those recognised today. No office, no staff, no expenses of any kind, just a salary of £1,750 a year. More importantly, there were no arrangements for new members to be 'educated' in this demanding and frightening job. You just started and made mistakes and then more mistakes. Somehow I would learn. Candidates who win a seat anywhere will talk about the post-election period, when the excitement is over, as depressing. I did not know anything about that classic aftermath but I was soon to find out.

The first issue is disbelief. The target of one's recent life has been achieved after several months, or more, of hard work. You are in the 'forum' but as a burnt out shell! To that date, I had never been so tired and flat. I was in at the deep end, out of my depth, filling my father's shoes, missing him as well and determined not to 'mess up' his reputation. Any politician who dies in office is just about untouchable. His failings are forgotten and the emotion of losing a well-known figure remains. Constituents and others, when first meeting with me were likely to say: 'So, you are Dr Laird's son. He will be badly missed.' While I knew that they did not mean this as an insult, I took their point and my burden increased. Throughout my time associated with the St Anne's area, I was always referred to by everyone as John. But my father was only referred to as Dr Laird. While I liked to be called John and even

I saw my father as Dr Laird, the way we were addressed by the same people seemed to mark out the difference.

I soon started my weekly advice centres at, of all places, No.1 Primitive Street. This was a central location, off Blythe Street in Sandy Row. Monday night after Monday night I interviewed or was interviewed by anyone from St Anne's who had a problem of any size. It was necessary to keep a sense of balance and also a sense of humour. On one occasion, I was asked to christen a small child in its mother's arms. I explained that there are many things a Member of Parliament can do, but accepting children into a church is not among them. 'Try the Church of Ireland,' I advised. 'I think they are not as fussy.'

I met all shapes and sizes. People sometimes just wanted to chat, perhaps as my father had chatted to them. On one occasion, late into a November evening when I was about to go home, a large lady pushed open the office door, looked at me and shouted to her husband outside, I supposed: 'He's in here!'

In came the large Belfast woman and a small, frightened-looking Donegall Road male. 'Sit down,' she invited her husband. 'Now,' she said to him. 'Billy, that is Mr Lurd, he is going to help you. You tell him your story, hold nothing back.' She then turned to me. 'Mr Lurd, do you see that man there?' I was only two foot from his face. 'He is the bestest wee man on the Donegall Road.' I was silent; there was no gap in which to speak, anyway. 'Mr Lurd, my Billy,' – in Sandy Row all males seemed to be called Billy – 'he is going to tell you something which you will not believe. For he is the bestest wee worker in Belfast.' In this way we seemed stuck for about ten minutes while he was told to tell me all and I was told about how bestest he was at everything.

At last, the moment seemed to have arrived when she said: 'Now Billy, you explain.' Billy opened his mouth but to my amazement it was her voice again. 'I will tell him myself.' Once again, she started to ensure that I could see Billy and that I knew how good he was. Billy looked worried and most uncomfortable, like a hen not knowing if it should lay an egg.

After what seemed like a long period, I suspected we were getting nearer to the point – if one existed. 'My Billy is a painter in the City Hospital. Last March he was up a ladder painting an outside wall. Do you know what happened to him?' she enquired. How could I? 'He fell the whole way down, landed on his head and has suffered post-natal depression ever since!' A month later, I took the case to an industrial tribunal and won for Billy a meagre compensation, but not for a post-natal anything.

The Northern Ireland Administration, in keeping with all other such organisations, had some points that were good and some that were bad. The first ten or so years were very difficult. There was the issue of the exact border, the unrest as people came to terms with the new arrangements and the very problem of creating a local administration with its own statute book. The political and cultural atmosphere of the time could do nothing but create a siege mentality for all but the strongest. The Free State, once it got itself organised, ran a boycott of Northern Ireland, its people and its goods. This was in the well-worn tradition of uniting a people against an outside enemy; in this case, us. It required nationalists on either side of the border not to recognise the new Northern State. Some tried more direct action to destroy our institutions. The new administration was sorely tested.

Now problems began to kick in. Unfortunately for the future stability of our part of the United Kingdom, a defensive stance took hold. This represented a missed opportunity, in that it prevented problems from being addressed in an open way. The Unionist Council, and thus the Party, was not created to run a country, or even a part of the UK. It was a single-issue cause. Upholding the Union was the cause, as Unionists saw it as their only chance of fair play. Asking the Unionist Party to administer an area was like councillors elected only on a platform of wanting a swimming pool for Holywood being asked to run North Down Borough Council.

The Unionist compromise of 1921 produced not just a Home Rule Parliament, but one with its own difficulties inbuilt. A one-party state is possible for a period but it puts both the governing and the governed into a straightjacket out of which it is almost impossible to move.

Again, I must point to my not being there and so I am unable to compare my reaction then with now. But the lack of long-term vision was missing and the usual failures caused by the guise of power set in. I use the word 'guise' because that was also a problem. Stormont was a Parliament only in name. It was a county council with law-making powers. To give the guise of power without the actuality is the road to madness. In my short time in that local Parliament, it was clear to me that our voters – the public – thought that we had real power, but we had not. The MPs, me included, were caught in the seductive vice of looking like having real power. The grim reality was that we had little.

This communication is intended to outline those events that shaped my outlook, not to be an academically researched account of any period. That point being made, it is always important to remember that there is at least one other side to all stories.

Northern Ireland played its part in the Second World War, although not to the extent that many Unionists would have liked. But as a training area, a major manufacturing point, providing manpower and withstanding bombing raids, the province was important. The community acted as one with very few exceptions. The Republican maxim that 'England's problems are Ireland's opportunity' never seemed to take hold. The stakes were too high. The Irish Republic played its usual multisided role of trying to please the Allies and stay friends with the Germans. The country was neutral; a position that it thought would be helpful, were the Germans to win. The case of Norway proved the nonsense of that policy. Norway had been neutral but was invaded and subjugated by the Germans.

A Unionist maxim is: 'give Republicans enough rope and they will hang themselves.' And so it proved once again. De Valera, the Irish leader, when he heard of the suicide of Hitler in 1945, could not wait to get round to the German Embassy to sign a book of condolence. Bad timing and a good example of a rat joining a sinking ship! Winston Churchill, the British war leader, vented his and the nation's anger in no uncertain way. The Hitler death issue gave much comfort to the Unionist people for many decades. 'What can you expect from a cow but a kick?' my mother would proclaim on very many occasions when this topic was paraded. She was right. The Irish nation was out of step from the rest of the world. Inward looking, backward and poor, it was as if it had slumbered undisturbed since 1921. If the new Irish state looked unattractive to Northern Protestants in the early 1920s, then it was a hundred times worse in 1945.

At this point I become critical again of the Ulster Scots, or Unionist, people of my homeland. It is easy for me to look back over the decades. I can only guess at the victory atmosphere of the period and the feeling of invincibility we had against outside forces and, especially, with regard to the Republic. However I do feel that the Ulster Scots people should have taken a more global view and tried to make the people of Northern Ireland more like one community. The area was, for some, a cold house. Pointing to the Republic as not being welcoming for any one except those of an Irish or a Roman Catholic background may give short-term satisfaction as an excuse. But we were the people who made America; we were the people of the Scottish tradition of equality and fairness. Narrow-mindedness should not be in our nature.

There is no doubt that there was discrimination of an ethnic and religious type in Northern Ireland. So, also, was there in the Republic. Every part of the universe was the same. This was the 1940s and 1950s. That was how people conducted their business and other affairs. Without modern ideas of human resources management, the only proper way of employing a reliable person was to take that person from your own community. The offspring of a good employee or someone from the same school would fit the bill. None, but none, of this was promoted or even allowed by the local Parliament. How could it be? The Government of Ireland Act would simply have made it null and void.

It is interesting to note that the Province today has a complementary set of rules and regulations governing employment, which ensure complete fairness in all related areas. But the Irish

Republic does not. As recent examples have shown, employment there is biased towards Irish and Roman Catholics first and, where possible, only them. Also in Eire, another name for the Irish state, jobs in the state sector are regarded as rewards for political tasks and awarded regardless of merit to 'place men', cronies and party hacks.

The 1950s were good times for many in Northern Ireland. Engineering was still important, with the shipyard being by far the biggest employer. Tobacco, linen, ropes and aircraft were also amongst the thriving industries. The country, the creation of 1921, was bedding in, imperfections and all. The IRA, which 'never goes away, you know', tried to unsettle everything with a totally useless campaign from 1956 to 1962. Again, if you are trying to convince one million people to join your land of 'milk and honey', then blowing them up and shooting them does seem rather counterproductive. And so it proved.

The 1960s saw modernisation in work, home and in politics. It could be said that we became too comfortable. In common with other parts of the world, in the late 1960s, people were looking for enhanced rights. In a few cases, this was fully justified. At a meeting of the Young Unionist Council in 1968 in the Ortine Hotel at Lisnaskea, County Fermanagh, the governing body of the youth movement discussed our involvement with the rising Civil Rights Movement (CRM). This movement had been running street demonstrations, some of which had turned violent. Their demands were for civil rights, an issue that should have engaged us all. However, their claims were one-sided and their ranks were increasingly filled with well-known malcontents. We had the spectre of people from the Republic demanding 'rights' for citizens in the United Kingdom, forgetting what the position in their country was very much worse than it ever could have been in ours. Our members had been involved from the start but we were now getting information about a move to Republicanism in the CRM. Collectively, we were disgusted; our knee-jerk response was to be careful and to pick our friends with more care.

It is a minor point, but I often wonder that would have been the outcome if 'our people' had stayed and tried to exercise leadership. Perhaps things would have been no different. The ifs and buts of history are only a dead end, not a main road and not a place in which to waste too much time. From here the facts are well-known. Northern Ireland descended into its own worst nightmare. In 1969, the Troubles began. Much has and will be written about that period. The death toll itself had been the subject of many publications. From my viewpoint, coming around the period of my father's death, it all helped to underline the end of one era and the start of another. Everything changed. I sometimes think that my father was lucky to die when he did. He could not have understood what was happening to his beloved province. His timing was a major problem for me but saved him considerable distress.

The year turned into 1971 and on the streets of Northern Ireland things just got worse. The IRA developed a deliberate policy of attacking the Unionist community, so in the easily accessible areas leading from the Donegall Road and Sandy Row, bombs were heard. Not military targets, not commercial targets, just houses which belonged to the good, honest working people. Night after night, or so it seemed, some part of St Anne's was attacked. The night-time was dark and menacing. Out of the dark, at any corner, trouble could appear.

The temper of the ordinary people was sorely tested. In one case, a car bomb left in Hope Street, which is just off Sandy Row near the city centre, damaged over 250 dwellings. Many were beyond repair. Special services were made available to repair, in some form, such destruction, but nothing was repaired to satisfaction – how could it be? The real victims in this period were the ordinary people. Why should they put up with this? Day after day, I explained the feelings of St Anne's people to the Northern Ireland House of Commons. Each time I asked for special measures. Little came.

For me, this period was the depths. I was tired, in over my head, lacking in experience, trying to look after an area at war and unable to get new security measures that were mostly in the hands of Westminster. I hit rock bottom. Even in the middle of the problem I was aware that I had a balancing act to perform. On one hand, I had to show leadership to my area and, on the other, I was aware of the need to be reasonable and so to leave lines open to the 'other community'. Not an easy task. I think that I often failed. To add to my unrest, I took dreadful flak from friends who should have known better. The country was in turmoil and so was I. It is easy for others to attack me and dealing with that was part of my job. But I felt that they did not understand the pressure or the perceived pressure that I was under. In my mind everything seemed unfair and I was getting more and more stressed. I did not go home at night and relax. I sat and worried. Was I doing the right thing or not? In other countries, public representatives could make mistakes but in my case those mistakes could affect life or death. There was only one thing that had placed me in this position and that was ambition, so I had to live with it.

I was a democratically elected representative for a people under the cosh and when they turned to me I could do nothing. During history classes at Inst, ten years earlier, I had wondered why the German people were willing to elect, by popular vote, someone like Hitler. Now I was beginning to understand. People reach a point of desperation when all seems against them; no-one seems to care, so something had to be done. And it was. From that period, the seeds were sown which would grow into the Ulster Defence Association, or other so-called Protestant paramilitary groups. Most reasonable people thought that this step was wrong – but how could you argue against it? I was swept to one side. 'Laird, you're a decent man doing your best but get out of our way, this is no time for democratic politics,' the polite ones said.

As an individual, I was clinically depressed. I hated the situation that I was in. At times I would not even answer the phone. I was frightened stiff by the news on the radio or television. I began to dislike visiting St Anne's. People were collectively in a bad temper. I seemed to get the brunt of it. Unable to offer a defence of the government's case, or lack of it, I became useless, or so I felt. I learnt about depression. I seemed to assume that I was responsible for everything that went wrong. The feeling of isolation was frightening. The buck stopped with me in every field and I was not used to such responsibility.

After much discussion with some family members and friends, I took medical advice. I had treatment; medical, mental and physical. Slowly I began to come round and out of the bunker, but it took time and support. One most interesting side affect was the mental battle. I began to realise that the most important part of living was to control your mind. If, by whatever means, I could look at things in a positive light, then the issue could be won. But the mind battle was a very slow process which took a considerable amount of thought, over the years. Again, I feel that I was very lucky. My journey was taking me through new areas that I could turn to my advantage. Besides, I convinced myself, how could you know how good sugar tastes unless you had sucked a lemon? Slowly I came through that phase, a much better and more rounded person.

I began to understand and to practice positive thinking. The idea that a glass is half full rather than half empty, appealed to me. Always look on the bright side of life, as the song goes. It took considerable time to learn, as I developed ways of controlling my mind. However I got into the 'positive zone' and I hope that I never look back. Controlling one's mind is the most important thing in life.

The year 1971 had one major high spot. I married Caroline Ethel Ferguson on 24th April 1971 at Benmore Church, near Derrygonnelly in County Fermanagh. In a county known for rain, that was the wettest day I have ever known there. My relations, coming mostly from Belfast, could not find the church. Carol's people, whose church it was, had no bother. As the organist struck up the Wedding March, I looked round to see the Ferguson side of the church with what seemed to be standing room only and three, yes, only three people on my side. I said to my brother, who was my best man: 'If they take a vote here now, we are beat!'

Throughout the ceremonial side of affairs, repeatedly, I could hear behind me the sound of the big door opening and a Belfast voice say: 'This is it.' Then footsteps would guide the new arrivals to my side of the church. Carol Ferguson, as she was called from birth, is one of six children born to William and Mary Ferguson of Dromore, Derrygonnelly. The Fergusons are a big name in that area and, as I was to find out, rightly so.

When people talk about the salt of the earth Ulster people, for me they are the Fergusons. They were hard working and honest, farming from early in the morning to late at night to feed a family totalling eight. To me, from Belfast, their existence was a daily grind. There was little comfort or time-off to enjoy their beautiful surroundings. But the Fergusons and their like never complained or, as they say in Fermanagh, 'pass no remarks'. As a family, they were involved in the church, the local Orange and associated bodies, the Unionist Party and in the case of father-in-law Ferguson and his son, Fred, the Crown Forces. Not just being prepared to live and work in the isolated areas during the day, they turned out night after cold and wet night, to defend it – and never complained. Finer people could not be found.

Ferguson is a planter name coming from the Ayrshire area of Scotland. Also included in the family mixture of my wife were other planter names like Kerr, Scott, Elliott and Abercrombie. An Ulster Scots union was formed. I had met Carol about five years before at a Belfast social gathering. Carol was the classic country girl at that stage – or so I thought. Pushed into Belfast to become a nurse, at seventeen she first faced the challenges of city dwelling. Carol had much in common with my mother. Both were theatre nurses, both farmers' daughters and both from the West of the province. But, importantly, they had a sense of decency and common sense which could surprise me at very odd times. Carol, whom I was lucky enough to marry, is hard-working, dedicated to things being clean and, in common with her branch of Fergusons, has her own views and an ability to express them with great clarity. She has four sisters with much commonality of personality. My brothers-in-law were soon able to cope with the sisters.

Marriage in 1971 began to stabilise the home base for me once again. Lack of money caused us to live with my mother in the Somerton Road and, later, on the Belmont Road. Lack of funds was a problem at that stage and would be well into the 1980s.

Without doubt, 1972 was the worst year in the recent Troubles. The number of deaths, incidents, political upheavals and general bad feeling mark the twelve months out as one we would all like to forget. January saw an important and tragic event, when, on the last Sunday, thirteen men were shot dead in Londonderry while attending a street protest. Much has been written, and more will be, about what is now called 'Bloody Sunday'. But the facts are that over a dozen died and, with them, the idea of peace for years to come.

The Westminster government had had enough bad publicity around the world or so they thought. It wanted complete control of all aspects of security or else it would suspend the Stormont Parliament. We had had enough also. As Unionists we felt pushed around, unable to take action and were being blamed from all sides of our community. The Protestant paramilitaries were recruiting and organising and so people like me felt uncomfortable. Things could not be grimmer. Now we were being asked to have no say in sorting out the mess but, as MPs, we looked and sounded responsible. Feeling let down and sick at heart, we threw in the towel. In late March, Stormont was suspended, but we were still to be MPs for over another year. Suspended? Everyone knew that, once suspended, we would never return. The Home Rule Parliament created in 1921 faded without a battle into the pages of history.

On the last day of the Northern Ireland House of Commons's existence, the final debate was on the adjournment. This was a device to allow any topic to be raised. We all knew that, from midnight, the Parliament was to be suspended. On that day, late in March 1972, one of the last speakers was The Honourable John Brooke, who was to become Viscount Brookeborough. He was the

Unionist member for Lisnaskea and was the son of Basil Brooke (the first Viscount) who had been Prime Minister for twenty years. Fittingly, he chose a poem by Rudyard Kipling, entitled *Ulster 1912.* The words still ring true today.

The dark eleventh hour
Draws on and sees us sold
To every evil power
We fought against of old –
Rebellion, rapine, hate,
Oppression, wrong and greed
Are loosed to rule our fate
By England's art and deed.

The faith in which we stand,
The laws we made and guard,
Our honour, lives and land
Are given for reward
To murder done by night
To treason taught by day,
To folly, sloth, and spite,
And we are thrust away.

The blood our fathers spilt,
Our love, our toils, our pains
Are counted us for guilt
And only bind our chains –
Before an empire's eyes
The traitor claims his price.
What need of further lies?
We are the sacrifice.

At that moment, on the Unionist side, there was not a dry eye. Kipling had informed us of the oncoming realpolitik. Later, the vote was called for the adjournment. Three others and I, in an act of final defiance, voted against it. The others were Mrs Anne Dickson, Reverend Billy Beattie and James Stronge.

Over the previous nine months, I had taken an interest in our bad image in the British Isles and further afield. I sought information about public relations; where did it fit with press relations and what was the role of the Government Information Service? My dedication was such that I was noticed by whoever notices such things in both the party and in the Government Information Service. Perhaps to keep me quiet, I was sent to work for the Northern Ireland government in New York, in a public relations agency called Oliver Beckman.

On site in the Big Apple, I gave interview after interview to printed media, radio and television. Fed by the Irish Americans, who were everywhere in that city and stoked up by anti-British feeling, the media believed almost anything bad about Northern Ireland, its existence, the Protestant people and about the native Irish population who could not vote, own property or get employment. That year the theme of the Saint Patrick's Day parade was: 'Get England out of Ireland'. I spent some time in television studios explaining that to carry out that slogan, Patrick would have to be dug up and carried back to England. This argument did not go down well in the Bronx, New York's main Irish area. I visited Irish pubs there and, to my disgust, witnessed collections every time a soldier was killed back home. What a gruesome way to collect money.

Many years later, in 2000, while attending the Democratic Convention in Los Angeles and while being hosted by the Massachusetts delegation, I met a former head of police in Boston. He looked after me kindly for three days. All he seemed to understand was that I was from 'Ireland'. One day he said to me: 'When I was in charge in the 1970s, we all knew what the boys were doing. When they wanted to move guns, they let us know and we looked the other way. In fact, in the force we collected money for the IRA.' I did not have the heart to tell him I was a Unionist and so opposed to the IRA. I do not think that he would have known what I was saying anyway. Such was the power and grip of the Irish community in the north east of the USA.

In a way, the former chief of police was underlining the difference between Irish Americans and the Scots-Irish. (The term Scots-Irish is synonymous with what we in Ulster call Ulster Scots.) The Irish clearly believed that they live in a part of the 'old sod'. They were Irish, no matter how many generations removed into the New World. Everything had to be done to support the Irish collective. After all, as I often told them, they would do anything for the 'old sod' but live in it.

The Troubles took a new and dangerous twist at the end of July 1972. On a sunny, warm Friday, the last in July, the IRA launched a concerted daytime bombing attack on the centre of Belfast. The bank for which I had been working was completing a computerisation programme and it allowed me to retain a part-time position there for several years after my election to Stormont.

I was working in the Head Office, in Arthur Street in the city centre, on that fateful day which was to go down in the sad history of our Province. Around 2.30pm there was a loud bang, which seemed to be near, very near; too near. Before we had time to evaluate the implications, there was a second and then a third. The staff, and those members of the public who were attending to banking business at the time, became alarmed. Where next would there be a bomb? Just then, further away this time, came another bang. All this was accompanied by the shattering of glass, screaming and, after a few seconds, the sound of sirens.

In the way that these things develop, rumour began to rush from worried face to worried face. Each was more dramatic than the last. Then it filtered through that, in nearby streets, commercial premises had been blown up. In keeping with the conditions of the time, the decision was quickly taken to close the bank and send everyone homeward. Out on the street, we could see the destruction. This time, the Belfast medley of sirens was accompanied by shouting and crying. The scene was like anyone's worst nightmare.

There was fury in the eyes and in the voices of the workers on the street. 'How could this happen in daylight, in surroundings that we all found so familiar?' Strangely, there seemed little fear at that stage; we were past that. The emotion was raging anger. From the distance of a few streets away, there was another bang! The crowd, like a tide, swayed to the end of the road, to the corner of Chichester Street. This time, a further bang came from the direction in which I and the crowd were going, so we turned back and flowed in the other direction. There was nothing that we could do for any of the injured. The rescue forces were in charge. So the tidal crowd quickly began to flow back the way it had come. I passed an elderly middle class woman, on her own, waving her fist in the air and shouting: 'If there is going to be a civil war let it start now. I cannot stick more of this!' Although we passed her in silence, I suspect most of us knew what she meant and even, in the heat of the moment, agreed with her.

If a bomber, or a person who was even suspected of being one, had been sighted I would not have given any odds on him, or her, seeing another sunrise. I had never been in a crowd situation before when the collective had lost its temper and could have become a lynch mob. And I was, or would be, a willing part of it. I am not proud of that point but I must he honest. Democratically elected public representative I may have been at that time, yet my temper had gone. Like me, I am sure that day, many in the crowd were experiencing something totally new, scary and out of our depth. In fairness, under the circumstances, perhaps I was entitled to feel the way I did.

The day was to become known locally as 'Bloody Friday'. In dreadful carnage in the commercial and shopping heart of Belfast, nine died appalling deaths, some so badly blown up that there was only jelly left for a body. One hundred and thirty were injured. In all, twenty-six bombs went off in and around the centre of the city that afternoon. Businesses were torn apart, vehicles were left as mangled metal. The transport stopped; it was a target. Thousands of city-dwellers, office-workers, shoppers, schoolchildren and old age pensioners struggled to make their way through familiar streets covered in rubble, glass and dust. A smell was in the air like nothing that I had sampled before. I joined the swarm looking for, and slowly finding, a safe way home.

In common with many, I will never forget watching the evening news on another occasion on BBC television. A young reporter, Andrew Coleman, was trying to read live, on air, a report of what he had seen at a fatal explosion at a place called the Abercorn Restaurant. He just could not continue the report. He broke into tears, shook his head and put down his script. It was one of the most powerful pieces of television reporting that I had ever seen.

Bloody Friday and similar events had ensured that the middle classes of all creeds were now involved in the Troubles. To me and many like me, the IRA had scored another own goal. Did they think that any Unionist, anywhere, was going to change his or her views about a 'United Ireland' as a result of such cowardly attacks? But then that could be said about all the Troubles.

The civil unrest continued. The year of 1972 was the worst, by any standard. The problem was that the Westminster government, which was in charge of all activities in Northern Ireland, by then was following a policy of trying to find common ground with the Republican terrorists. In turn, the terrorists were trying to strengthen their bargaining position by killing as many of the pro-British population as they could. From our traditional Unionist position, we knew that the only thing that would satisfy the IRA was a United Ireland, whatever that was. There was evidence that there would be no room for us. The case was one of life or death for my community.

The concept of 'Brits out' and 'Ireland for the Irish' was not just an interesting policy to be debated in pleasant debating clubs, in centrally heated chambers. It was the ultimate realpolitik, involving not just our freedom but also our very lives. The question that occurs on a regular basis in Ulster circles was being put to us both verbally and by terror. That was: 'When are you going home?' Home to where – and why? It is easy to talk about a special Ulster spirit, which helped the population through this dreadful period. But logic demands that any people, anywhere, will resist the activities of the thug or the bully. Killing people in large number in random attacks may cause havoc but it did not, nor will it, change minds. 'Thank you, Mr Bomber, thank you, ruthless bloodthirsty killer. I now see your argument and I want to join you in your new 'land of milk and honey' in which you will allow me 'freedom'.' The idea is laughable.

The Secretary of State for Northern Ireland, the first ever, was William Whitelaw. He was a large caricature of a Borders landowner. His constituency was Penrith in the north west of England. His face was easy to cartoon and he had one major asset. His always-worried face did not look like that of a slick, not to be trusted politician. He looked like someone whom you would meet at the market in Ballymena and with whom you could do business. The Ulster Unionist Party was being ripped into two bits. Those who seemed prepared to swallow at least some of the London line and those who would not. I fell into the latter camp. The problem for me was two-fold. The continual appeasement of the Republican terrorists only had the effect of creating more violence against the Unionist people. Secondly, there was the suggested involvement of Dublin in any solution. The very idea of including the Irish in policy issues brought back, collectively for Unionists, all the inherited wisdom of: 'You cannot trust the Irish with our freedom and our future.' In the wind, there was a suggestion of the development of a Council of Ireland, similar to that proposed in 1921, but ignored by the Irish. From late 1972, the sound of alarm bells in all sections of the Unionist community was unmistakeable.

In June of 1973, an election was held, to appoint the very first Northern Ireland Assembly. Seventy-eight members were elected by proportional representation in the twelve Westminster constituencies. I was now fighting West Belfast, a traditionally nationalist seat, which included the area of the Falls, Andersonstown, Twinbrook, Ballymurphy and other nationalist areas. But it also took in the Unionist area of half the Shankill and my old stomping ground of Sandy Row and the Donegall Road. Battle-lines in Unionism were drawn. Apart from the split Unionist

Party, now led by Fermanagh farmer Harry West, there were the Democratic Unionist Party, under Dr Ian Paisley, and a new grouping led by former Home Affairs Minister, Bill Craig. It was called the Vanguard Unionist Party.

The Rev. Dr Paisley must be included in any consideration of Northern Ireland. Paisley is a large man with a personality to match. It is fair to say that he ranks alongside Bill Clinton as someone whose charisma can fill any size of room or hall. His firebrand style of preaching is compulsive listening. He has the ability to make everyone in his company want to please his every wish. In 1970 he started his own party, the Democratic Unionists, in opposition to the Ulster Unionists. Many of their concerns were similar to mine. Some say that there are many Paisleys. The one that I have dealt with since 1970 is always most correct, warm, friendly and supportive. My mother regarded his wife Eileen (now Baroness) as a close friend, while both were members of the Belfast City Corporation. Today, I may be out of step, but I have a high regard for their politically minded son, Ian Junior. On a point of principle, I never attack other Unionists in public. I find Ian Junior and the rest of his party to be true and honest colleagues at both Stormont and, now, in the House of Lords.

Much to my surprise, and in spite of the Unionist divisions, I topped the poll in my new area coming in with over two quotas which meant polling over twelve thousand votes. Thus, at that time, I added more records to my newly acquired list. I was now the first ever to be elected to a Northern Ireland Assembly, the first since 1929 to be elected by proportional representation to Stormont and, even after almost three years as a representative, I was still the youngest. These points could now be added to my earlier achievements of being the last ever elected to the Northern Ireland House of Commons, the youngest ever Unionist and the youngest in that Parliament at the time. While I enjoyed these honours, I was aware that none of them could be eaten for dinner.

CHAPTER THREE

The Rebel

UP THE REBEL

SLOGAN ON A BELFAST WALL

IN ALL OF us who come from a Scottish background, albeit that my family has lived in Ulster for four centuries, there is the potential to be a rebel. Not a rebel without a cause, but a person who is prepared to take on anyone, or any organisation, if he, or she, thinks that they are right. After fifty years of 'running' Northern Ireland and therefore being seen by many as the establishment, it can be hard to consider people like me as being rebels. Add to that the inability of my community to explain itself with a wilfully misleading use of words, unlike our Irish counterparts, and anyone would have problems. The best example of that is the United Irish rebellion of 1798, but I am getting ahead of myself. An asset on the journey of life was the ability to think differently and to examine new information. You cannot be a rebel if you only accept the established views. In this area I owe much to two gentlemen, one of whom has already been introduced. However, it was the other one that I encountered first.

'Always be a lark, never be a frog'. To some, this may seem to be a racist remark, depending, perhaps, on whether you are French. However, these words hold the essence of the most important lesson in the most important period of my school life. Inst, the

Royal Belfast Academical Institution, was, and still is, an influence on my life. This point has been established. The involvement of a lark and a frog, if it were to be the only thing that I learnt there, would have been worth it. The Reverend John McConnell Auld is a Presbyterian minister who, when he taught at the school, was only about ten years older than me. He is a Belfast man, educated at the Belfast Royal Academy, that other bastion of Presbyterian thinking already discussed. Following ordination, John Auld, who prefers to be called Con, joined the American Army with the status of an entertainer. Several years further on and following time with a church in Australia, he returned to his native province and, through a curious set of circumstances, was recruited as a fill-in teacher at Inst. The job grew and, before too long, the Rev. Mr Auld was a full time member of staff instructing the boys in a range of subjects.

Religious education was not a topic that sent the pulse of many of my school friends racing. For most, the class was an opportunity to relax; for others, to further relax. However, during the years in which Con instructed my class, things were different. He had an interesting way of using the periods. Rev. Auld would invite the class to discuss any one topic each time. At the start, we selected stupidly and suggested all the foolish ideas that passed through our minds. Geese and the role of sex in modern society were two that I remember. Our clerical teacher never blinked and spent the period dissecting the topic offered. We soon learnt to take the subject seriously and as a result we discovered a great deal that was to be useful in later life. Lesson one – or round one – to Rev. Auld!

The day that he introduced the concept of existentialist thinking is the one period that I remember almost word for word. The basic idea was that if you were a frog on ground which was surrounded by water, your decisions about your future would be limited. All that informed you was the ground and the water. However, if you were a lark soaring in the sky above the frog, and could see that the ground surrounded by water was in fact a pond and so had land all around, then your decisions were based on more and better information. By implication, the lark's future plans were more likely to be the correct ones. This is a very simple piece of philosophy based on the ideas of Danish philosopher Søren Kierkegaard. It was so simple, but to me, as a small youth at that time, it taught me a lot. Always consider the wider picture; take nothing without questioning the information. And, importantly, it gave me an interest in philosophy that was to take me to several years of night classes at Queens, a local university in Belfast, in the 1990s. To this day, I am grateful to the Rev. John McConnell Auld. Years later, he became a Unionist councillor on North Down Borough Council, and rose to the position of Mayor. No better man!

I was later to realise that Kierkegaard was also part of that Enlightenment tradition that influenced Ulstermen. This very idea of thinking widely and critically contrasts antipathetically with Romantic ideas of rural, peasant simplicity and bounded ethnic identities.

The other mentor, Cecil Bell, played an increasing part in the development of my thinking and personality in the 1960s and 70s. In the late 1950s, a number of railway enthusiasts teamed up. All were driven by a desire to learn every aspect of railway practice, particularly regarding stream traction. Railways in Ulster, at the time, were out of fashion. Much to my disgust, the local administration was heavily focused on road transport for all our needs. Many of us could see that this policy was throwing away the vast, if worn out, infrastructure that railways had provided. But the official view, in the oil-rich society of the time, was that our province was too small for rail and more suited to motorways.

The band of railway-men, as we saw ourselves, had a number of common features. We spent all our spare time 'on the railway', we were in the same age bracket – more or less – and we seemed like a bunch of misfits. Put another way, we thought that we were odd and the world seemed to agree. We could see nothing wrong with spending all day on the railway system, logging all activity with a brace of stopwatches while carrying two still cameras, a cine version and a large but portable tape recorder. Why did people stare at us? Why did they ask us what we were doing, in a tone of disbelief? Was it not clear? Had they never seen groups of young men at the line-side, with the same equipment, recording every move of a steam engine? Could they not understand that when a dozen such men jumped out of a train at Warrenpoint before it stopped, ran across the platform and boarded one which was already in progress from the other platform, it was normal Saturday afternoon activity? We marvelled at the narrow mindedness of our fellow citizens.

I met and developed a liking for unusual characters when 'on the railways'. People like Bob (Robert) Hunter, now a retired public servant, with the best memory for detail I have ever encountered; John Richardson, who worked for years in the Northern Bank and is dedicated to helping all and everyone in life; the late Irwin Pryce, with whom I attended school. Irwin went on to become a schoolteacher himself and was dedicated to steam engines; Drew Donaldson, another teacher who had a rather different way of conducting himself than that which society normally accepts. The list of unusual people is endless.

Cecil's relationship with me developed to more than just swapping railway information. We discussed life in general and politics in detail. Being eight years older than me, which was a big gap at that stage, he seemed full of interesting ideas. He is from a Protestant background, albeit Church of Ireland, but sees things differently to me. In the Laird household there was a general sense of insecurity. Everything that we valued in Ulster was always under attack. As a Unionist people, we had to be on guard: the enemy could strike at any time. There can be no doubt that this concept developed in us a siege mentality. But Cecil was different. His major area of political interest was the larger stage. To him the question of Northern Ireland as part of the United Kingdom was settled in 1921. We were British, in his view, so now let us get on with doing what Britons do in terms of politics. I was taken by his views. By exploring them, I could see difference perspectives. I was naturally afraid to venture too much on to new and untested ground and, anyway, I failed to see how it could fit into the comfortable politics of the Laird family. Even if that politics was paranoid there seemed comfort in that to which we were accustomed. Why change? On reflection, the correct position was somewhere in the middle, where we were on our guard but considered ourselves to be fully integrated into the United Kingdom.

Cecil Bell took the next step in advancing my schooling and offered opportunities to debate the eternal Presbyterian question: 'Why?' He became my Con Auld figure and many a day I went home, head buzzing with new ideas, wondering how could I fit them into my belief system. In the 1970s, Cecil went on to become the Secretary of the Ulster Liberal Party. Its leader was a New Light Presbyterian minister, Reverend Albert McElroy. I have problems with the label 'liberal' and I suspect that, if I pushed hard enough, so would Cecil. Most of us are liberal because we seek information upon which to base our beliefs. Liberalism emerged out of the Reformation values of individual salvation and the right to find one's own way; its sense of enquiry was also vital to the emergence of science. As a result, Ulster became the centre of science, Protestantism and liberalism on the island of Ireland.

In recent decades, it bore in on me that had I lived in the late nineteenth century, I would have been a Liberal Unionist. Without doubt, I would have supported Prime Minister Gladstone's disestablishment of the Church of Ireland, non-denominational education and the whole area of land reform. The older I get, the more liberal ideas, or the ideas of those referred to by that name, seem to match my own. Perhaps it is the Liberals who have matured! At the very start of the 1970s in Northern Ireland, an unusual and upsetting type of liberalism sprang up amongst the Protestant middle class, in response to the Troubles. Coming at an important time for me, it helped to develop my dislike of the middle class, a point of view I still tend to hold today.

The so-called Protestant middle liberals were smug, well off and out of the firing line of the IRA, or so they thought. They calculated their liberalism by reciting the number of Roman Catholics that they actually knew. Rather like reading off a score card in bridge, they wished to outsmart their neighbours by arithmetic. How crude, tasteless and plastic! Worse, they looked down their noses at those prods in the thick of it, as far as the Troubles were concerned. I was attacked at gentle Belmont dinner parties for associating with the working classes and for having the nerve to seek to represent them. My contempt for the middle class could not be measured. However, during the course of the summer of 1972 they had to change their collective mind when the Troubles came home.

I still live with my mistrust of the middle class's idea of liberalism. To many of us, that sort of sentimental confused thinking was a betrayal of the original idea of liberalism and its association with science and mental discipline. It was superficial and lacked the rigour and depth of truly scientific liberalism that goes beyond appearances. It amounted to romanticism and was ultimately a betrayal of liberal values. I am trying to get to a mental state where I can countenance the very word 'class'. Life is probably not long enough.

One of my liberal heroes was Thomas Sinclair and I used to wonder what he would have made of the middle class liberals of 1970. Sinclair was a major figure during the second half of the nineteenth century and the early part of the twentieth. Educated at Inst, he was believed to be the best student that Queens University had ever had at that time. Sinclair was an active member of the Liberal Party in Belfast, but in 1886 with Gladstone's drive to give Home Rule to 'Ireland', he passionately took up the Unionist cause. In April of that year he said: 'We shall show the world that come what may, Ulster will never consent to yield up her citizenship, or be expelled from the Imperial Parliament to be degraded to a junior partnership in a subordinate colony.' Sentiments of the time indeed!

Thomas Sinclair went on to organise the great Unionist Convention of June 1892 and was the author of the famous Ulster Solemn League and the Covenant of 1912. He was a strong Presbyterian and there is a church in the centre of Belfast named after his family – the Sinclair Seaman Memorial in Corporation Street. Sinclair never forgot his Ulster Scots roots and often referred to his Scottish heritage. My friend Cecil and a small band of like-minded people did represent a proud vein of liberalism in Ulster. Much damned for Gladstone's Home Rule Bills and misunderstood after 1921, nevertheless it was a good cause and one to be respected.

Cecil Bell's father had died when Cecil was less than a year old. He pulled himself through the education system and spent a number of years at Methodist College Belfast, before family circumstances forced him to leave early and start earning. One of Cecil's greatest strengths is the ability to see humour in almost all circumstances. In my view, he would have made an outstanding comedy scriptwriter. In the area of humour, I learnt much from CTB, as he called himself. In 1952, young Bell went for an interview for a job in the Belfast grain trade. The grandee of the company was so impressed with the applicant that he told Cecil that his firm had offices in South America. 'But,' he confidentially said, 'I will say no more'. The excited Bell raced home to tell his mother that he was bound for South America. However, as Cecil pointed out to me on his retirement in the mid 1990s, the grandee was as good as his word. He never mentioned it again.

Cecil's input into my thinking, over the years, has been invaluable. At times of dark clouds, when gloom was everywhere and when personal decisions were required, he could be expected to give of his time and wisdom freely. It pleases me to say that my family regarded him as one of its members. From the funeral of my mother, whose coffin he helped to carry, to our children's birthday parties, we have regarded Uncle Cecil as a vital participant. However, the most important task that Cecil ever undertook for me was to expose me to close examination of my views. For that, no reward could be too much.

After the various plantations in Ulster, the area did not settle down, as King James I desired. The space left by the Flight of the Earls, when they fled to mainland Europe, was partially filled by planters. Some of the native Irish resented the newcomers. But it is not as if we were willing new residents in that country of wet land and difficult people. Anyway, during times of stress some of the locals requested that we go home. At least, that was the view of the more polite. Strangely, this sentiment still comes through in times of similar tension today, four hundred years later. It would be a mistake to think that the plantations were the cause of the modern difficulties on the island. They may have played a part, but the Troubles are more to do with the creation of Irish heritage stories about self-perceived past wrongs. In large areas of Ulster, the various peoples, Irish, Scottish and English, settled down to work the land and feed their families. Also, it should be noted, they converted many native Irish to Protestantism.

In 1641, things did come to a head. Nothing in history is simple and when one considers the island of Ireland, things get even more complicated. Charles I was on the throne. His policies on religious adherence were not well accepted, particularly in Scotland. Charles was a very keen advocate of the concept of the Divine Right of Kings. This is a most objectionable idea to us today. It was the monarch's way of trying to grab back rights lost at various stages, starting with The Magna Carta in 1215. The idea was that the King was appointed by God and so could not be questioned. This meant that Charles challenged Parliament's authority continually. In fact, he tried to do without that institution for long periods. However, money was hard to collect without its approval.

In October of 1641, some Irish chieftains decided to rebel. In doing so, they set in motion a pattern of activities that has maintained until today. The plan was to capture Dublin Castle and then turn on the colonists, as they saw them, mostly in the North and to massacre or expel them. In one of those patterns for the future, the move against Dublin Castle was betrayed. However, the attacks on the Protestants went ahead. Londonderry became a particular place of refuge and, to some extent, so did Belfast, Carrickfergus and Enniskillen. While there was much bloodshed, the targets set by the Irish were not met. Again, in a foretaste of the future, drums and bonfires were used to warn the Protestants to defend themselves. We shall come to the events in Donegal later.

The attacks on the planters, the stories of dreadful death and destruction, were widespread enough, and in large enough numbers, to add to Protestant mistrust and tension for centuries. That, unfortunately, is how these things work. It is important to keep in mind that the uprising in Ulster was also influenced by events in Great Britain, as well as by the Thirty Years War (1618-48) raging in Europe, whereby nearly half the population of Germany perished. It was the final fling of the anti-Protestant Counter-Reformation. Its horrors spread throughout Europe and haunted it for centuries.

Many senior historians will suggest that the rebellion of 1641, on the island of Ireland, played an important part in the run up to the English Civil War. However, when one considers the events that year, it is no wonder opinions were sharpened, as well as swords. 1641 was the stuff of which legends are made. Facts are not so important; that year informed Protestant opinion for decades to come.

In nationalist circles, an equally dangerous mindset was developing, centred on events such as Cromwell's campaigns on the island of Ireland. I would suggest that much has been made of the sacking of Drogheda, a town just north of Dublin. The truth is not so important as the enduring effect upon Irish opinion. Legends were created that have informed nationalism right up to today. There is a modern idea that history is written by the victors. That, in my view, does not fit on the island of Ireland. There, history is many-sided and likely to be written by everyone, including future generations, sometimes to fit new circumstances.

The scene is now being set for one of the great battles of Irish, British and European history. The Battle of the Boyne on 1st July 1690 has gone into folklore on the island of Ireland and has come to mean different things to different communities ever since. In February 1685, Charles II died and his brother James II succeeded to the throne. Charles, the son of Charles I, who had been beheaded in 1649 by Oliver Cromwell, was appointed King when the monarchy was restored in 1660. The strongly Protestant nation, which had developed during the period without a King, was under attack. English Protestants became alarmed when sympathetic Charles died and his staunchly Roman Catholic brother James took over. In an attempt to force change, William, Prince of Orange, was invited to come to England and to replace James as king.

William, James's son-in-law and Stadthalder of the United Provinces of the Netherlands, landed on the south coast of England. James fled with his supporters. There was a bigger picture to consider. The French king, Louis XIV, was trying to unite much of Europe in what might be described as an early version of the European Union, with him as the Roman Catholic head. Clearly, William could not have this. Neither could the Pope, but for different reasons. Towards the end of the 1680s, James and a small army arrived in Ireland. After some manoeuvring, they ended up trying to take the walled city of Derry in the north west of the Province. But, in an act of unbelievable defiance, thirteen young men from the city closed the gates and, against the judgment of senior figures, prepared to defend their position. Thus was started the famous siege of Derry of 1689. This event, known for its cry of 'no surrender', is of importance to the Protestant, or planter, thinking.

The siege lasted for one hundred and five days before relief arrived up the River Foyle in a ship called the Mountjoy. The inhabitants had almost been starved into submission. Many had already died of hunger or related causes. The whole of the Protestant community revelled in the lifting of the siege and thus in the failure of James II. To this day, these events are celebrated all over Ulster, Scotland and further afield. To the good people of north Tyrone, east Donegal and west Londonderry, the Siege is part of their family histories. Many still tell of the part the local countryside and its people played in the event. For us, the homestead, at Ballyskeagh near Artigarvan, had a series of old broken muskets and horse-riding gear. All these were treated with reverence. 'They had been inside the walls during the Siege.'

James left the northwest and took his army south, collected more troops and received funding and other support from Louis. William, with a collection of units from many parts of Europe, mustered between Belfast and Carrickfergus. He stayed in a bawn, or Scottish style small castle, which is still there today. Indeed, because it was painted white, it gave its name to the area – Whitehouse.

In due course, William made his way to fight his father-in-law north of Dublin. It is remarkable that, on his journey south, William seems to have stopped at almost every modern lamppost, gate-lodge or even Chinese carryout. The route down is still a trail of places where he stayed, ate, drank or fed his horse. Fields, houses and lanes are named after him. Anyway, his army of highly trained soldiers met the smaller army of James at the river Boyne outside Drogheda on the first day of July in 1690. The battle lasted all day. By evening time, William was victorious. James and his supporters had fled, again.

The events of the siege and the Boyne were imprinted on my mind from a very early age. The very words 'the Boyne' have a magical feel about them. They conjure up an idea of always having to be on our guard, lest we are the generation to lose that for which our forefathers died. The times recalled were inspirational and we were not going to let them down. Looking from an adult perspective, it is clear that similar, but opposing, feelings were stirred in the Irish community. They are the building blocks of Ulster.

We now come to one of the most misunderstood events in the history of the island of Ireland. I refer to the 1798 United Irishmen Rebellion. It is only in the last twenty or so years that I have come to terms with these activities. In the family and community circles, it seemed that the Turn-Oot, as it was called, was given little space. Yet the Presbyterian rising in Ulster helps to explain much about both Presbyterians and their recent history. Today, there is a growing acceptance of 1798 inside the Unionist community and, in particular, the Ulster Scots section.

In the final quarter of the 1700s, the events leading to unrest were beginning. The Dublin Parliament was in a degree of control, when supported by the British authorities. But for the Presbyterians it was unsatisfactory. It included only those who were Church of Ireland, which was, at that time, the established church.

Those who were not of that denomination, such as Roman Catholics and Presbyterians, were clearly second-class citizens. Our rights were diminished, our churches' marriages were not recognised, the land laws were difficult for us and we had to pay taxes to the Church of Ireland. And that was only some of the grievances.

Belfast, at the time, was a centre of Presbyterianism. It was to become a battleground between those who followed the bible in all details, the Old Light, and those who embraced the new sciences and logic, or New Light, and it had helped to develop the Scottish Enlightenment. Indeed, its founding father was an Ulsterman – Francis Hutcheson. Even in the late 1790s, the city was considered, like Edinburgh, to be an Athens of the north. Much new thinking was taking place and an important contribution was made to the Scottish New Light movement. This, in turn, led on to the Scottish Enlightenment.

Just outside the County Down town of Saintfield in 1694, Francis Hutcheson was born. He was appointed the Professor of Moral Philosophy at Glasgow University in 1729. He became known from an early age for his political ideas, which, in those days, seemed revolutionary and out of place to many. Francis Hutcheson taught that slavery was wrong. He promoted the idea of the equality of men, to be administered by assemblies elected by all people on a regular and secret basis. His influence was to spread far and wide. One of his best-known pupils was Adam Smith, the author of *The Wealth of Nations*, whose impact on politics is still felt today. I consider him to be one of the most important Ulster Scots figures and one who is badly under recognised. Too many people look at the events of the past forty years and forget Belfast's free thinking and liberal past. The more that I learn about the liberal past, the more I identify with it.

Francis Hutcheson's ideas were the seeds that grew into the United Irishmen. That title can be misleading; the name was adopted to match the United Scottish Men of the same period, whose goal was for similar advances in that land. The united bit refers not to uniting the island for at that time it was administratively united, but the concept of bringing all people together, as individuals, to seek their human rights. Presbyterian groups were formed in and around Belfast. Contact was made with people of a similar view in the Roman Catholic faith, mostly in the South. In May 1798, the 'Turn-Oot' began, firstly in the southern counties of Wexford and Waterford. Small uprisings went on for weeks all over the area. But one event was to put a totally different slant on the entire rebellion.

On 5th June, a Roman Catholic mob herded over one hundred Protestants into a barn at a place called Scullabogue in County Wexford, set it on fire and all were burnt to death. At the same time, other sectarian acts were carried out against Protestants, which clearly ran counter to the ideals of the rebellion. The effect on Protestant opinion, when word spread, was understandable and was devastating. On 7th June, when the news was still on its way towards Belfast, the Presbyterians donned their good Sunday-best clothes, said goodbye to the womenfolk, formed up and marched to confront the Crown forces. Sunday-best clothes were worn just in case they were required to meet their maker that day; they had to be dressed for the occasion. Skirmishes took place in County Antrim, near Antrim town and Ballymena, as well as in County Down at Saintfield and at Ballynahinch.

The problem with anything to do with Presbyterians is that nothing is ever straightforward. Members of that faith called Laird, fought for the Crown forces outside Ballymena. Coming from that area, they could very well have been ancestors of mine. The only place where the Presbyterians won a battle was on 9th June at Saintfield. There, they defeated a detachment of York Fencibles in a battle remembered to this day as the Battle of Saintfield. And that brings me onto another important aspect of my make-up.

On the first Wednesday in February 1965, I, along with my brother Jimmy and a school friend, John Tinman, was initiated into the Orange Order in Clifton Street Orange Hall in Belfast. I feel at home in this organisation, with its camaraderie, support and belonging. Orangeism runs very deep in the lives of many Protestant families in Ulster. In the case of my family, it was not on the Dunn side directly but on families who married into them and, to an extent, on the Laird side. Few dates in the calendar were as eagerly awaited by a young John Laird as the start of July. Bunting went up in loyalist streets, wood was collected for the eleventh night bonfires and my father, as in a kind of religious ritual, positioned a large Union flag on a pole from the spare bedroom window.

For many Protestants, the Twelfth of July, when the Battle of the Boyne is celebrated, is their only bit of holiday and of colour away from the grinding job of raising and feeding a family. For example, the Shankill, which to this day is regarded as a loyalist heartland and where my father had been reared, is full of brightness and spectacle from the week before the day itself. You may have noted that the Battle of the Boyne was fought on July 1st, so why is the Twelfth the date associated? Simple! In 1752, for reasons too long to explain, even if I knew them, the calendar was changed. This caused all dates to move by twelve days. So Pope Gregory had decreed. Interestingly, those who considered the battle to be of Protestant significance went with the Pope's dictates. In 1965, it was time to join the family lodge. It was called York Loyal Orange Lodge 145, now sometimes known as Royal York. My father had been a member for decades, if not a regular attendee. There was only one lodge that the Laird boys were going to join and that was York.

York LOL 145 had been formed almost at the start of the Orange movement in 1795. The first members were from the city of York and were all part of a Fencibles Regiment, which carried the city's name. They had been sent to Ulster 'in case of unrest', which was becoming a possibility, as we have seen, during that decade. The York Fencibles' history of the lodge has given me a useful insight into the 1798 Rebellion. The York men were the only Crown forces to be defeated by the rebel groups in Ulster. Or, to put it another way, the Presbyterians won the day, on June 9th 1798. It was only when I examined those events, and matched them against my inherited yardstick, that I realised that had I been available for service the chances are that I would have been a rebel.

The cause was one almost tailor-made for those of my background: fighting for equality for all people, against hopeless odds, but fighting anyway because it was the 'right' or 'natural' thing to do. We would stand up for individual rights and justice and the liberty of belief and freedom of conscience; all essential Reformation and Enlightenment values. For Ulster Scots, the odds take a lesser place than the issue of being right or wrong. Acting according to your conscience comes to us as naturally as breathing, or so I felt and feel. These events became hard to explain down the years, in particularly during the Home Rule crises and the setting up of the Ulster state. Nationalists have tried to make links to the people and events of 1798, mostly because of the use of the words United Irishmen. But I have explained that origin. The Presbyterians showed a generous hearted spirit during this time. Despite the knowledge of the dreadful events of the burning to death of over a hundred Protestants in a barn in Wexford, the rebels demanded equality for all. The difficulties of 1798 were dealt with in a particularly Ulster Scots way, as we are about to see.

Robert Stewart came from Mount Stewart, a large estate just outside Newtownards. Under the courtesy title of Lord Castlereagh, he played a part in the history of these islands that makes him one of the most important Ulster Scots figures. Courtesy, in this context, means that, as the elder son of a marquis, he was able to call himself a lord while still being a commoner. Castlereagh decided that the way to satisfy the demands of the rebels was to disband the Dublin Parliament and so curtail the influence of the Church of Ireland. This had guaranteed an unequal place in society for their members. On 1st January 1801, the Irish Parliament ceased to exist and the United Kingdom of Great Britain and Ireland was born. From that date, around eighty Irish Members of Parliament attended Westminster, along with an appropriate number of peers. It is believed that Castlereagh's tactic to get the Dublin Parliament to dissolve itself was bribery.

Castlereagh went on to the larger national stage where he played an even more important part. For a time, he was the Foreign Secretary. It was he who, at the discussions leading up to the treaty of Vienna in 1813, successfully negotiated a period of peace in Europe; no mean feat in that cauldron. From the historical perspective, after he inherited the title of Marquis of Londonderry on his father's death, he was to fall from favour. In the early 1820s, in a fit of depression, he committed suicide. And within the British Establishment, after you commit suicide, there is no way back.

By joining York LOL 145 I had placed myself into a historical frame heavily coloured by the events of 1798. By definition, all Orange lodges have a sense of history. York, being one of the oldest, was no exception. Members, mostly over the last two decades, have explored their roots and have become intrigued with the Battle of Saintfield. Over fifty of the York Fencibles who were killed, on the fateful day, on 9th June 1798, are buried at the bottom of the graveyard attached to Saintfield First Presbyterian Church, in an area now called York Island. We went much further, under the leadership and hard work of senior brother Kenneth Latimer. Kenneth is also chairman of the lodge's support group, the York Island Historical Society. For many years, he organised the Liberty Days Festival. This was a celebration of our Ulster Scots culture that included an annual re-enactment of the battle. In this way, we played a part in the massive Ulster Scots revival that encouraged such educational events all over the Province. Now it was to be my turn to play a part in, and to observe, a real life rebellion.

On 1st January 1974, to take the place of the former Northern Ireland government, a new executive (or cabinet) was formed. It came about as a result of discussions at a beautiful place called Sunningdale, just outside London. The problem with that conference was that only a minority of Unionist members of the Northern Ireland Assembly were invited to take part. People like me, for example, who were critical of Her Majesty's Government, were not included. On the agenda was the creation of a local administration that would represent the two traditions and would have institutionalised links with the Irish government. To some, in today's climate, these concepts may seem totally reasonable after the 1998 Belfast Agreement. In 1973, when the negotiations were taking place, they did not. Some who were at the negotiation on the Unionist side, later related that their leader, Brian Faulkner, had gone too far in conceding to nationalism. They, it is claimed, could not make him hold back and think of the reaction at home. Whatever is the case, the Sunningdale Agreement was most unpopular amongst the Unionist people.

It must be remembered that tension was very high, security issues were a main concern, and people were dying almost every day. Inside the Unionist community there was no desire to reward the Republicans for the death and destruction. Deep inside, I could have sympathy with the idea of power-sharing on some basis, but the thought of creating any form of executive link to the Irish government was against everything my inherited knowledge had instilled in me. 'You can never trust the Irish with our culture, our wellbeing and our future' echoed down the years. In the nineteenth century, the Roman Catholic Church had become an implacable opponent of everything for which the Enlightenment stood, especially liberal democracy, science and industry. The cry that Home Rule would be Rome Rule, which had haunted the earlier part of the century, still resonated. Held up at many gathering of Unionists were examples of how our kith and kin had been treated in the Republic, both in the 1920s and up to that date.

Power-sharing might have taken hold then, when it involved the Social Democratic and Labour Party, but not for the Unionist community, when they saw how it was worked out. Human nature has always a part to play. When the new SDLP ministers took up their offices, mistakenly, if understandably, they were triumphant. Their chauffeur-driven cars took them, several times a week, to Dublin to meet their counterparts. Their language was of impending so-called unity. In my experience, I have never seen a period of such total Unionist discontent as the first month in 1974. The Irish Dimension, as the Council of Ireland and all associated with it became known, brought people together in a community feeling that I had never felt before. It was not the anger of those near a bombing, or the sorrow of a funeral; it was the sheer determination that 'up with this we were not going to put'. Just then, one of those events in history happened, which was unexpected but which had an effect in the province forever.

On the national scene, the Conservative government, with Edward Heath as Prime Minister, came under pressure from the trade union movement and, in particular, the miners. That group was striking for more pay. Mining is a stinking job; underground in restricted space, dust everywhere, digging for dirty coal. I and, I suspect, many others felt they could hardly be paid enough in such conditions. But the Tories took on the strikers and tried to bring public opinion with them. At the beginning of February, Heath called a general election, to clear the air. While that proved to be a political miscalculation on the mainland, in Northern Ireland, a problem that Heath thought he had solved at Sunningdale, the effects were earth-moving.

The election, which was held on 28th February, almost ran itself. At that stage, I had ceased connection with the bank, which had employed me and was, on a voluntary basis, running the media side of the Unionist Party from Unionist Headquarters in Glengall Street. That location was handy; it was on the edge of West Belfast, the area that I represented at that time. There was no shortage of willing canvassers and no shortage of resources and help. In putting together election material, I took an idea from my brother, and turned it into an election poster, which all Unionist candidates who opposed the Council of Ireland quickly adopted. I took the slogan: 'Dublin is just a Sunningdale away.' The word Dublin was shown written in a traffic sign pointing one way. Underneath, I placed the word Sunningdale, with the words 'Vote Unionist' inside a road sign pointing in the opposite direction. In some ways, people felt that this summed up the message that we wanted to put across. In later years, political commentators and local historians wrote about that poster. They were kind enough to say that it was one of the best in decades of elections and was a part of the success of that campaign. Whether that is so or not, the election was a landslide. Our brand of Unionism won eleven out of the twelve seats then available. But importantly, for us in Northern Ireland, it was with almost fifty two percent of the votes cast. Harold Wilson, the Labour leader, two days later formed a government with only thirty six percent of the popular vote.

From that point on, the writing was on the wall for the Irish Dimension executive. A clear majority of Unionists were having nothing to do with it. But the new arrangements were supported by the Westminster government, which was very busy dealing with the aftermath of the miners' strike. Loyalist groups in every part of Northern Ireland were asking why our mandate was not heard and why all Unionists were not allowed to have a say in future arrangements. I cannot excuse the actions of Protestant paramilitaries but was it any wonder that they just grew and grew? What were we, as public representatives, to do? Alongside the violence, this was the nightmare scenario.

With the support of my colleagues in the Unionist Coalition, I took the initiative. The Unionist Coalition was the grouping in the Assembly that opposed the Council of Ireland arrangements. On 19th March, as a rebel to the Westminster government and just about everything else except Unionism, I stood up and proposed a motion which said:

> *That this Assembly is of the opinion that the decision of the electorate of Northern Ireland at the polls on 28 February, 1974, rejecting the Sunningdale Agreement and the imposed constitutional settlement requires re-negotiation of the constitutional arrangements and calls accordingly for such re-negotiation.*

I did not speak many times in the Assembly, but, with all the passion that I could muster to befit the situation and the political climate, I managed to put the case clearly. I include some extracts:

> *'The General Election of 28 February was not called because of anything that happened in Northern Ireland or by the whim or desire of any section, party, body or individual here. A specified range of candidates with clearly defined policies on the one emotive issue of the Sunningdale Agreement and the concept of government that has been proposed for Northern Ireland, were given an overwhelming mandate.'*

'As you know, Mr Speaker, the electorate gave them nearly 52 per cent of the total vote cast. One of the operations that have gone on since that date is an attempt to say that 52 per cent of the electorate is not great; it is not putting forward a clear demand, it is not putting forward a clear voice; it does not represent a mandate. Let us be clear what sort of vote is represented by 52 per cent of the electorate. In the general election of 1964, the Labour party was swept into office, getting only 44.1 per cent of the votes cast. In 1966, the Labour party renewed that mandate and got a much larger majority of 100 in the House of Commons. On that occasion, it had 47.9 per cent of the vote. In 1970, the last Conservative government had 46.4 per cent of the votes cast.'

'Let us not equivocate. The eleven people who were elected out of the twelve candidates stood on clear, specified policies in terms of the Sunningdale Agreement. Why is that agreement so emotive? I believe I have said this before in the House; certainly it has been repeated outside the House by many people. In the latter part of the 20th century, nobody can deplore co-operation between two civilised countries bordering on each other. Co-operation is the acceptable thing. What you, Mr Speaker, may agree is repugnant to the people of Northern Ireland is that there has to be the setting up of formal institutions to secure this co-operation. Why is it necessary to have a system of chambers, a system of structures with roles and functions, simply to get co-operation between two countries which happen to border each other?'

The final section included a timely and, as it turned out, correct, analysis of the short term future:

In the Constitution Act we had the fact that there had to be wide acceptance of any new constitutional arrangements for Northern Ireland before they could really be put in motion and the brakes taken off. Is it any wonder that we, on this side of the House, think that we are like a team playing a ball game, when the referee and the other side are in collusion? Every time we look as if we are about to score a goal, they change the rules.'

'I should like to fire one warning shot. I should like to say with all the sincerity that I can command that we have come to a very serious situation. This could very well be the most serious situation in what has been a succession of nothing but serious situations. The Ulster electorate have spoken. They have used the election of February 28. They have spoken clearly. They have spoken loudly. They have made their demands known. They have said: 'As far as we are concerned Sunningdale is finished. There has got to be some further look at this so-called package.' They did that by use of the ballot box. By the use of the proper parliamentary democratic machinery provided to us.'

'What is the implication if 'the powers that be' do not listen to that democratically expressed wish? I wonder what conclusions the people, for instance, I represent come to when they see the results of the ballot box pushed to one side? What conclusions must they come to? That is a very serious state of affairs. I should like the cry to go out from this Assembly today. Beware; you tamper with something, the exact import and the exact consequences of which you do not understand. Do not meddle with the democratically expressed wishes of the people of this province. In all honesty, in all sense of decency, fairness, and fair play, there has got to be some further looking at, scrapping of, re-negotiation, further discussion, call it what you will, on the Sunningdale Agreement; otherwise we are far, far away from getting this country back to any form of normality.'

[Honourable Members: 'Hear, hear.']

Incorrect use of English, but, nevertheless, it was from the very heart and soul of an Ulster Scots rebel.

One day every week from 19th March, the debate continued in the Assembly. A lot of words were used up and outside the political temperature rose and rose. A group called the Ulster Workers Council (UWC) came to the fore. Made up of employees from all the major industries and, importantly, the power workers, the Council claimed to speak for all loyalists. There is little doubt that it had links to the paramilitary side as well as to the political one. Uncomfortable as we publicly elected representatives were, the general view was that we had failed in the use of our political processes and had little ground with which to argue. Another view was that we could add a moderating hand to any actions which the Council might consider, if we kept in close contact.

The UWC issued a statement at the very beginning of May, which said that if the Assembly would not take the position seriously and was not to pass my motion, then there would be a general strike until they did. Fighting talk! This meant taking on the entire world; the army, the political machine, the media, the Republicans, the bosses and any one else who could get in the way. To the democratic world, the liberal media, some of the middle classes and to the government, this seemed like a declaration of rebellion. So what? It is nothing more than what Ulster Scots do when confronted with a decision they think is unfair. Besides, there were those who thought that the whole thing was bluff.

On 14th May, in the Assembly, the vote was due to be taken at the end of business, at around six o'clock. The vote was to be on my motion. My actions were to start the rebellion! The 'Rebel Laird' was to have his fifteen minutes of fame. I arrived at Stormont at around four o'clock, to be met by a very angry senior member of the Democratic Unionist Party who was talking in an incoherent manner. By now the whole media speculation centred on how the vote would go, and would a strike be the result? Calming the DUP man down, I learnt that he and some other politicians had just been visited by several members of the UWC. They had taken cold feet and were asking the politicians to get them off the hook, concerning the impending events. We politicians had suffered weeks of pressure and discord and were in no mood to placate the strikers who had made our lives so uncomfortable. My friend, the DUP Assembly Member, had told them in straight language, for which Ulstermen are noted, that they had got us all into this position and we were not going to help to save their bacon. I have rarely seen someone as angry as he was that day. He could hardly speak, which, for a DUP man, is hard to believe.

Events in the Assembly chamber moved on and came to a conclusion at around six o'clock. A combination of Unionists, who supported the Dublin Dimension and all the nationalists, defeated my motion. It seemed that through the due process, there was to be no reconsideration of the dreadful agreement and so the views of the electorate, as expressed in the February election, were to count for nothing. The teatime radio and television news programmes carried the result, along with an announcement from the Ulster Workers Council that the strike had started. The rebellion was underway.

I left Stormont and went home to the nearby Belmont Road, not knowing what was going to happen next. I watched the news. Things began to seem unreal. Was this a film? The traffic outside seemed normal and people still walked the footpaths. But now a strike had been called, which was designed to bring the entire country to a halt if the UWC's demands were not met. However one looked at the problem, the fate of the Unionist cause seemed to hang on this action. It was a family habit that I did the weekly shopping. Carol, at that stage, did not drive and could better spend the time preparing meals and cleaning. So it was decided that, although the day was not the usual shopping one, I should take my car to the nearby supermarket, and purchase anything that I could. After all, there was a strike, who could know what would happen? We needed to stock up.

I was definitely not looking forward to meeting my fellow east Belfast people at that shop. It was clearly understood through the media that it was a vote on my motion that had started the strike action. I arrived at the supermarket and the whole area was overflowing with shoppers. Everyone was determined to stock up and so see out the siege. Would my good middle class neighbours turn on me and blame me for the perceived hardship ahead? By any standards, I was a well-known figure, especially in that location. I was a regular sight on the television and, as I had learnt, it is the media that make a person seem familiar. People sit in the comfort of their own rooms and study the face of any one on the television. In real conversation, an individual looks into your eyes when conversing with you. But on television, the viewer can study your clothing, your nose, and your ears. You are there for them, warts and all.

I parked my car, collected myself and entered the arena of the supermarket. People were everywhere. Several points struck me. Everyone was quiet, acting with great courtesy and I was totally accepted without any problems. This was the first example for me of a spirit in the Unionist community that I had never seen before and which was awe-inspiring. That night, the shopping took much longer than usual. People were carrying out massive loads of tinned food and almost anything they thought they would need. But the point was that there was no pushing or fighting. If the item that you required was finished you bought something else. There seemed to be an acceptance of the situation. I really did not know what to make of it. Was this how it was going to be? Would this be the spirit of the next few weeks? Or was it the quiet before the storm?

It was clear that the next day, when people were considering going to work, the strike was going to bite or to fail. I have no doubt that, going by the reportage and people's experiences, there was a level of intimidation around the country. While this is to be condemned strongly by all law-abiding people, I am convinced that it was on a small scale and not centrally organised. In some areas, folk looked out, checked what others were doing and made their own calculations. Employees of vital services went to work and continued to do so for the duration of the strike. Schools, in the main, opened and began the process of calculating what to do. Up in a large old house in east Belfast, the UWC, and others, including politicians, came and went. Decisions were made about the day-to-day running of the country in that former residence, which, at other times, would have seemed surreal.

Over the next three to four days, the size of the exercise, which had descended upon us, came home to all. Government, army, police, workers, businessmen, politicians and others were all wondering how to respond. It was the middle of May and the weather was typical of examination time. The sun seemed always to shine; people spent most of their time, off from work and school, outside. If you are thinking about going to have a general strike, then pick a month like May! The atmosphere, which had never been hostile, began to change to one of determination to win, at any cost. Help came in the form of most unfortunate decisions and statements from Merlin Rees, the Secretary of State for Northern Ireland, and the rest of the Irish Dimension-supporting politicians. The world's media were flooding into the province, in full measure, and staying at their favourite haunt, the Europa Hotel. This large, modern construction was right beside Glengall Street, the site of Unionist Headquarters, where I was located.

William Sanderson, known as Billy, lived in Frenchpark Street, in the heart of the Village area of my constituency. Why the area of five thousand voters was called the Village is not clear to me, but, to this day, the strongly Unionist area is called by that name. Billy, who worked for many years in the aircraft factory, called Shorts, had been off work with a serious internal condition. He was a faithful, willing and hard working supporter of the Unionist cause. Many long days and evenings, without regard for his health, he had canvassed, given out leaflets, put up posters and generally carried out any task asked. William Sanderson, a loyalist from the Village, was to play an important part in the worldwide hearts and minds media battle which opened up.

Due to the location of Unionist headquarters, I was the first port of call for the press, including television crews, when visiting Belfast. All were keen to cover the story of the mighty British government having its tail twisted by a bunch of nobodies who called themselves workers. Many of the reporters could hardly speak English and would approach me with a card, which they would either try to read out or would show to me. The card would say something like: 'What is going on here?' From that start, a whole television interview or newspaper article could be built. The way into Unionist HQ was like a swing door. All that I had to do was to sit and wait. So my part of the strike was handling the external image. I was delighted.

Glengall Street, as members of the party call Unionist headquarters, was an old building with many offices and several halls. In 1972, it had been bombed, with most of the back part destroyed, and so was open to the street. With little resources and having to wait for compensation, the back had been boarded as best we could manage. One morning on arrival, I discovered that someone had broken in through the back way. Nothing looked missing or even disturbed. However, on one desk was a note that said: 'Sorry, I did not know it was Unionist HQ.' Some people will do, or not do, anything for our cause!

Outlining the background and underlying reasons for the UWC strike was a problem. So I had to create what is now called a creditable, visual narrative. On the Donegall Road, near the Methodist church, there was an empty house. This was taken over as the welfare headquarters for the area – Village and all. At that stage in the strike, bread, milk and other vital items were not being delivered to shops, which were closed, anyway. Instead, the bakers and milk-distribution people were still working but, to show support for the cause, gave away their produce without charge. Across the road was a petrol station that was being 'supervised' by some strong-armed men. One, clearly a candidate for a front row forward in rugby, would put his head to the driver's window of a car and say: 'Youes are nay gating petrol unless youes are vital services like a doctire.' One man responded from his large machine: 'My good man I am a consultant in the hospital.' To which he was told: 'I do not give an f.... Unless Youes are a doctire Youes is nay gating petrol here.'

I arranged with the ladies looking after the welfare house that they would tell a good story about hardship and the determination of the Unionist people, were I to bring foreign journalists around. I then enlisted Billy Sanderson. The system was that a media person would visit me in Glengall Street, hear the story of aspiration lost by my community and then I would point out that, instead of me, ordinary members of the public should inform them. The media person, without fail, would say that was a fantastic idea and would I come along to show them the appropriate area. I would check with the young secretary, who knew exactly what to say. She, in turn, would consult a diary and inform me that I had a series of important meeting in the next few hours. I would then appear puzzled and seem like someone torn between activities. I would say to the young girl that I thought that I should go with the media because I did not want them to end up in danger. The journalists were so delighted and grateful that I was allowing them precious time, as well as looking after their safety. We would leave in my car and head to the nearest point of interest, which happened to be the Donegall Road. Meanwhile, the secretary would phone Billy and let him know that I was on my way.

Billy Sanderson was a natural performer. He knew all the main arguments and I had schooled him in the sort of information that an American or Japanese journalist, for example, might require. He rushed across the road, warned the ladies in the welfare house of the impending visit and then took up position to walk up and down the footpath outside. I would arrive and take the visitors into the welfare point; there they saw what was going on. I would suggest that perhaps they would like to interview an ordinary passer-by on his feelings about the political position. Out on the footpath again, Billy had been parading up and down. I would say: 'Oh look, what about that man there?' I would stop Billy, ask him his name and go through the whole exercise of explaining that these media people wanted to know about the strike. Billy would always seem to be in a hurry but, because the interview was about the cause and because he was an admirer of Mr Laird, he would be glad to forego other activities and allow himself to be interviewed.

This pantomime went on for days. On one day alone, I think, I had six visits to that 'randomly' selected location near to Unionist headquarters. On each occasion, Billy backed up, as it happened, the points that I had made earlier. It is my view that Billy Sanderson from Frenchpark Street appeared on television screens all over the world during that period. And there was no better man to talk about the wholehearted commitment of an entire community to win political objectives. The community support was not just talk or the outcome of revisionism. Those who did not experience the shutdown from 14th May 1974 will always be hard to convince about the atmosphere. Everyone in the Unionist community worked together, from the richest businessman to the most humble lowly paid worker. There were no divisions; no going back; no surrender. For Unionists, the die was cast.

Merlin Rees MP, the Secretary of State, was a decent, honest man. He took over in early March, just after the general election. The Conservatives had lost ground. After a few days' delay, during which Heath had tried to stitch up a deal with the Liberal Party in Parliament to allow him to govern, the Queen asked Harold Wilson, the Labour leader, to form an administration. Edward Heath's actions, at that period, had caused a major rift between the Tories and the Ulster Unionist Party. The two parties had been locked together as one since 1921. Now Heath, who thought that he had settled the Ulster question at Sunningdale, was angry that, at a most inconvenient moment, the Unionists were not taking to the idea of the Irish Dimension. For the eleven MPs elected on the Unionist ticket in February, the price for supporting the potential Heath administration was a scrapping of the Sunningdale Agreement. He refused and went into opposition.

The post of Secretary of State for Northern Ireland is not regarded as a plum job in the British establishment. The actual work is not rewarded with acclaim in the London-based media. Nor is it full of opportunities to made dramatic announcements that affect everyone in the United Kingdom. But it was a position where, if you did not make a total mess, you could collect sympathy and a more respectable job afterwards as a reward. Rees never looked like a man who was enjoying the job, or anything else for that matter. The Welshman with a Leeds parliamentary seat looked like a worried man, and he was. His problems during the strike were manifold. He had to try to keep order with a demoralised police force and an army that did not want to get involved in something that they could not win. The nationalist politicians were

Dr Norman D. Laird OBE, MP, JP

John Laird at two years of age

Inst; the Royal Belfast Academical Institution (Photograph: David Laird)

Cecil Bell, brother James and John, at the wedding of Carol and John

Belfast Telegraph

101st Year Friday, November 13, 1970 Price 7d [8d in Eire]

NILP candidate loses his deposit

ST. ANNE'S GIVES LAIRD DOUBLE-MAJORITY WIN

By our Political Staff

UNIONIST CANDIDATE Mr. John Laird to-day won the St. Anne's by-election in Belfast with a majority of 5,323 – almost double that of his father, the late Dr. Norman Laird, who formerly held the seat.

The Social Democratic and Labour Party, in its first electoral contest, pushed the Northern Ireland Labour Party into third place in the three-cornered fight.

There were noisy scenes at Belfast City Hall when the result was announced, with shouts of "Up Paisley," "No surrender" and "We are the people," from the Unionist supporters.

The full result was:

John Laird	**8,204**
Ge[illegible] Lavery (SDLP)	2,881
William Ritchie (NILP)	863
Majority	5,323

The front page of the Belfast Telegraph, Friday 13th November 1970

Stormont, Belfast (Photograph: David Laird)

Carol and John cutting a cake at their wedding on 24th April 1971

Councillor Mrs Margaret Laird with granddaughter Alison

demanding that the army was sent in to just about anything that was on strike; power stations; petrol stations; food factories; anything. The whole fabric of society seemed to be falling and it was Rees's job to make the system work. In addition, the members of the Executive, formed out of the Assembly, were at each others' throats, the mood in the rest of the United Kingdom was less than happy and there were adverse media reports around the world. The Secretary of State's plate was more than full.

By the end of the first seven days, nothing had gone well for the government. The Unionist community was as solid as it had ever been before. In those warm days in May, there was magic in the air. No one could be offended; everyone went the extra mile, if a neighbour required it. The nationalist community, cleverly, kept their collective heads down and got on with life. I am told that life was almost normal, in those areas. Well done them, for keeping it that way while we made our point. News bulletins are always well followed in Northern Ireland. During the strike they kept everyone informed. A feature of the BBC broadcasts was a gentleman from the local electricity board. Power was one of the main weapons in the UWC armour. Cleverly, they organised the power station workers to rotate supply around all areas so that everyone had electricity at some stage. As it was May, daylight was long and the nights warm. No one complained. Hospitals were given full power all the time and all other vital services were attended to in a similar way. But the screw was being turned, slowly but surely. The Ulster Scots people were at their work or not, as the case may be. They were doing that which they do naturally; making a stand for what they believe, against massive odds.

The trade union movement in Great Britain got involved. If this was a worker strike, then the people to sort out the mess were the Trade Union Congress. That body was outraged. Their good workers were being used, used indeed, for political purposes. The US Cavalry, in the unexpected shape of the General Secretary, Len Murray, was dispatched. I can imagine the scene in Transport House in London, as the comrades purred with satisfaction. They had the situation in hand, or so they thought. The hapless Murray was going to lead the misguided shipyard workers back to work with trade union banners flying and the soothing balm of worker solidarity rhetoric. The morning was picked and, down at the gates of 'the yard', about fifty others joined Len Murray as he led to work one of the smallest parades ever seen in the city. At that time, the shipyard employed many thousands. I am sure that most of the fifty who paraded were on first name terms with the trade unionists who organised the stunt. There, in full view of the world's media, and watched by several thousand interested and amused loyalists, the British trade union movement was humiliated. The TUC miscalculation just added to the general humour and disbelief of the strikers and the many thousands of supporters. If you take on the Ulster Scots people, it does not matter how important you are in your own circles; if you are wrong, you have an implacable enemy. Wherever Len Murray took his holidays from that day onwards, I am sure the Northern Ireland Tourist Board was not involved.

Strange things happened during the period. For one, the electricity board spokesman became very famous for predicting the total failure of the system at any time. This did not scare the Unionist community. They were fighting to the death. 'Liberty or death' was a cry used by rebels in 1798. In 1974, in front of a disbelieving world, on television screens all over the globe, against the might of the British government and its army, we stood alone. No one spoke of surrender. No one offered a word of complaint, just encouragement. Most surprisingly, part of the Protestant middle class, the so-called liberals, was now supportive of the strike. The mood was of determination. I now know that out in the country, as the second weekend approached, meetings were being held to plan the next stage. Merlin Rees considered the use of army technical staff to run the power stations. The idea was also floated of bringing submarines into Belfast Lough and running the electric network from there.

But out in the country, plans were being hatched to bring the power system to a total halt, in a way that would take months to repair. It was the UWC that was laying those plans. The concept of the total end to organised society, if we did not have our democratic request met, had no Unionist detractors.

On the second Saturday, 24th May, Harold Wilson asked the broadcasting networks for airtime to make a prime ministerial announcement. Rumours spread; what was he going to say? Was he going to threaten us? If so, with what? On that afternoon, I was a speaker at one of the many rallies that were held. This one was in the County Down town of Kilkeel. The centre of the town was packed. Bands played, lambeg drums beat out their rhythms and huddled groups speculated about the Wilson speech. It was timed for the evening. Information came our way that at the same time as the broadcast, an army squad would take over the east Belfast strike headquarters and arrest the strike leaders. At that time, in the old house, the only people to be found were the eleven Unionist MPs who were having a parliamentary party meeting. The sight and attendant publicity of eleven MPs being arrested by the army as rebel leaders, and carted away for questioning, was not to be. The army did not keep the appointment. Leaking, after all, is a two way process.

Wilson's speech was aimed at the people of the mainland. It was highly insulting to the Unionist and Ulster Scots community. There was a reference to us all as spongers. If there is one thing that the Ulster Scots people consider themselves not to be, it is that. The whole ethos of the ethnic group is of total individual independence, owing nothing to anyone. If there was one way for making the strike more solid, then Harold Wilson had found it. We were never going to work again. There was no pain that we would not bear, in order to win. There may be a view forming that I am dwelling too much on the atmosphere of the period and the solidarity of the community. That I can understand. Trying to explain the mood of an entire community, for someone who did not experience it, is almost impossible. Over the next four days, events were to come to a head.

The army, under orders from Rees, took over some petrol stations around the country. The response of the people was not to use them at all. Better no petrol than buy the stuff from a government-run station. Street parties became a popular activity. In the warm weather, in places like east Belfast, and in the part of west Belfast I represented, the adults began to keep themselves busy by running functions for the children. At least, that was what they said. The street parties interested the mothers and fathers just as much as, if not more than, the kids. The whole political class that supported the Agreement fell to fighting within itself. The Irish government, with the usual subtlety of a bulldozer, demanded direct military action against the Unionist people. That was strange, for at other times, when the lawless groups were nationalist, Dublin called for restraint and understanding. The one-sided approach of the Irish is always visible and remembered by Unionists. 'What can you expect from a cow but a kick?'

On 28th May, exactly two weeks after the start of the strike, the government gave in and the Executive became a failed entity and was no more. For several hours, groups of cheering loyalists paraded around the streets of their areas in a kind of victory dance. The Ulster Scots people had won. The rebellion, another in our long history, was a success. The next day, the factories and schools opened and the shutdown was over. Looking back, it was a time that I would not have missed for any money. The feeling, the very air, the excitement was a once in a lifetime experience. Even a democratically elected politician like me learnt a lot. I suspect the powers that be did also and that has informed their actions since. I hope so.

'The eyes have it' sounds like a parliamentary expression. It is, if spelt differently. But in the case I mean, they refer to The Right Honourable Enoch Powell. He had searing blue eyes that, upon making contact, dug into you like an electric shock. Powell was the Conservative Member of Parliament for a Wolverhampton constituency up to the first election in 1974. I suspect that his name would appear in many lists of people who influenced the lives of others. It does in my case.

Enoch Powell had been a cabinet minister in the 1960s. His right wing views had set him apart from most of his colleagues. I had instinctively not been able to agree with him on two large issues; his opposition to the European Economic Community (EEC), as it was then, and his opposition to Commonwealth immigration into the United Kingdom. On other issues, I was strongly with him; the maintenance of the Union and his opposition to capital punishment. Powell fell out with the Conservative leadership in 1973 and early 1974 on the issue of the EEC. As a result, he did not fight his Wolverhampton seat at the election.

In Northern Ireland, a problem began to appear in the form of the Unionist MP for South Down. Willie Orr was appearing to be unwell just after the February election and possibly unavailable to fight a second inside twelve months, as was forecast. In a clever bit of work organised by Jim Molyneaux (later to be the party leader and later still Lord Molyneaux), Enoch agreed to replace Orr. In this operation, Molyneaux had the support of other members of the Unionist leadership, Dr Ian Paisley and William Craig. The outcome of all this activity was that in the October 18th election in 1974 the Unionist candidate was John Enoch Powell, a nationally, if not internationally, known figure. I was working in Unionist headquarters at the time, while still being an Assembly member (MLA) for West Belfast. For a period of the election campaign, I came into close contact with Powell and he had an effect on my life.

The new candidate was something different. He was one of the cleverest people that I had ever met. His adherence to logic was legendary. In order to help ease him into the province, I spent much time with him. Trying to break the ice and lift the mood, I tried humour. Powell listened carefully to what I had to say and then proceeded to totally miss the point. He would analyse to death the punch line, much to my frustration. I organised his first news conference on his arrival in Belfast to take up his new task. He contacted me the day before and asked that I should have a particular scale map of South Down. At the press conference, which was packed with news people from all over the world, he was offhand and rude. At a debriefing after, I took my courage in my hands and asked the internationally known figure not to abuse our media. I had spent many years cultivating them and he was not going to arrive in my area and upset them. Thankfully, his wife, Pam, supported me in my difficult task. Powell thanked me for my advice and promised that in future he would 'pet my press colleagues'.

We settled down to an election campaign, the like of which I had never experienced before. Enoch taught me the importance of providing the voters with an experience that they will remember and talk about. At one meeting, in a packed hall, the usual format took shape. The senior Unionists, who had elbowed themselves into the select positions beside the speaker, were on a stage. Full of pride at first, they watched in horror when the candidate was asked to speak. Powell went to the front of the stage, took a leap into the air and arrived down in to middle of the potential voters. He said that he preferred to be on the same level as his potential voters. He had delighted them and amused all, including the large band of national and international media. Powell was a showman. Everything he did was different and new to the good people of South Down. When he became the elected member, he provided a different type of service to that of any other public representative in Northern Ireland. If someone approached him with a problem he would require them to convince him of the correctness of their case. When, and if, so convinced, he would take up the issue until it was resolved, no matter how long it took. The rest of us representatives just listened to the complaint and wrote to the appropriate minister. The rightness or wrongness of it was a matter for the higher authority, not us. But Enoch was right and I learnt.

In the middle of his election campaign, his police escort car, with supporting staff and a large fleet of media armed with cameras, swept into a South Down town. Powell directed that we stop outside the local public library. With his followers, he never seemed to 'travel' or 'go' to places. They swept! The candidate swept into the library, followed by his cast of hundreds, to the bemusement of onlookers, rushed up to the girl behind the counter and asked: 'How are things in Banbridge?' To which she replied: 'I do not know: this is Ballynahinch.'

CHAPTER FOUR

The Public Relations Consultant

PUBLIC RELATIONS IS THE CREATION OF A CLIMATE OF OPINION IN WHICH A CAUSE, PERSON, OR ORGANISATION CAN BETTER ACHIEVE ITS GOALS

THE AUTHOR

IN 1975, THERE was another election; this time, to a 'convention'. The idea was to decide a way forward, with as many people as possible involved. This was in direct contradiction to the settlement of the previous year. The constituencies were the same as the Assembly of the 1973 election. So once again I set out to woo the voters of the Donegall Road and Sandy Row areas. This time I had made my mind up that, come what may, it was to be my last electoral outing. I would have canvassed harder. The knowledge that it was my last election, which naturally I kept to myself, allowed me more freedom and also more of an overview of the whole process.

Election Day was set for 1st May, with the count on the 2nd, my wife Carol's birthday. Once again, I had topped the poll in West Belfast; the last time that a Unionist was ever to do so. I captured more than one and a half quotas and again became the first elected to a new institution. Despite a massive Unionist turnout and the submission of a report, after a year's work we were going nowhere. We all could see that. By the spring of 1976, the Secretary of State for Northern Ireland, Merlin Rees, was in no mood to accept a proposal that left out a role for the Irish government and we were in no humour to even consider it.

We were all paid off in May 1976. Each of the seventy-eight members went our own way. I clearly saw this coming and from the turn of the year had examined all sorts of options and ideas regarding the business of earning a living. One day I went down to the local social security office to ask about unemployment and other benefits. The office was on the Holywood Road. I went in and was so depressed, and felt so low at the atmosphere in the building, that I left faster than I went in. Ten years later, to the month, I was the proud owner of the office block next to the benefit building. All paid off and in my possession. There are a number of things of which I think I can be justly proud and that was one.

Luckily, I decided to try my hand at earning a living out of public relations. I had liked what I had seen in New York while working for the government and also after a period spent in a newly created Unionist Information Unit. I was thirty-one and married. My wife was eight months with child; our firstborn, Alison. In the bank and elsewhere, I had the sum of two hundred pounds. There were no proper fulltime, dedicated public relations agencies in Northern Ireland. The Troubles meant that most people in business kept their heads down. Besides, something as 'airy fairy' as public relations was not in the nature of Ulster people. 'If you cannot put your hands on it, it is not worth buying,' was the understandable attitude of my fellow country people. But I could not fail. The very word was unthinkable. Creating a living was the only option.

On Monday 1st March 1976, in my own front room I opened for business. Life was tough, very tough. To the public I had no standing in such a field. I was a former bank official, bank inspector, computer programmer, Member of Parliament, Member of the Assembly and Member of the Convention, yes, but nothing pointed to commercial public relations. In political public relations and media handling, you are in a sellers market. But in the commercial world you are very much in a buyers market and you have to get used to it.

There is a time in most males' lives when they feel strongly that they should start their own businesses. The age of thirty-one was my time. I was to learn that creating your own income stream is a feature of dyslexic behaviour. Dyslexics see the world differently to others. How? I do not know. As a dyslexic I have no idea of how a non-dyslexic thinks so I cannot compare. However, in ordinary conversation and in observation, it is clear that others seem to see a different world to me. One example is watching rugby or football. I have watched many matches of both types. My understanding of the rules of the games is better than average. I played both, to a degree. But I seem incapable of following the moves. Some think that dyslexics see an overview of a given situation. For me, that does not apply to watching those two games. Attending a match, I have found that there always seems to be someone standing near to me who is giving a running commentary to a third person within earshot. But their game bears no resemblance to the one that I see. They see more, much more, than I do. Interestingly, in the case of cricket I have no difficulties. The style of play is so different. Anyway, on visits to well-known grounds in England, the spectators around me seem only interested in reading the daily papers. I am usually the only one watching the game.

A disproportionate percentage of people who run their own businesses are dyslexic. In an organisation, as an employee, the dyslexic reaches a position where his, or her, coping skills can no longer hide the dreadful truth. You are outed in a most embarrassing way, with a consequent loss of authority or confidence. However, if you are the boss and running your own show, then being outed is of no importance. There is a maxim that says: 'The boss is not always right but he or she is always the boss.' I was very lucky. When I reached the position of employing staff, they soon began to work out what I had meant to write, and not what I actually did write. While making the point about dyslexics and the proportion who run their own businesses, it is interesting to note that my fellow sufferers make up thirty three per cent of the prison population. Clearly, this is a highly disproportionate figure.

I think that in March 1976, when starting my own one-man business (as it was then), I had a number of advantages. I had stared into the abyss of unemployment. I was dyslexic and I had to succeed: I was about to become a father, and had no reserve of money. Of course, I knew nothing about my dyslexia. It was not spotted until the late 1980s. I just thought that I had had a strange and disappointing educational career. Looking back, I can understand that my condition was an important part of my PR career. Some people think that public relations people do nothing all day but write press releases and shake hands. While this may be true for some, although those ones are called press officers, there is much more to the job, as I was soon to find out.

The making of a successful public relations consultant is complex. The consultant requires the ability to see the big picture across the wide screen. Also vital are the ability to explain concepts in words that are easy to understand, using as few of them as possible, and a knowledge of how the society in which you operate works. Add to that the importance of being able to work with anyone at any level, in particular at the very top of organisations. But I had to start small and almost learn the trade as I went along. None of this did me anything but good. The working days were long and the spare time at weekends short. However, the work was invigorating and exciting. The need to get out one month, sell the idea of some work, perhaps do the work in another month or so and then, several months down the line, lodge the appropriate cheque, was a challenge. To my delight, within a few years two things happened. I began to be taken seriously to the point of advising management at boardroom level and others were attracted into the market place. On the basis that if you need a solicitor then I need one as well, I encouraged potential competitors to join the trade. Today's Yellow Pages for Northern Ireland is full of public relations agencies. I take that as the normalising of the trade in the province. We had caught up with the rest of the Kingdom and, if I had played any role in that, then I was pleased.

For the most part, I had to leave politics to others. I had a living to earn. Besides, involvement with one section of the political sector, during the nervous time in the 1970s, would not be good for trade. It is one of the strange facts of political life that the public expects its politicians to be hardworking, dedicated, take little if any time off, be very poorly rewarded and then refuses to let them back into the employment market. I had thought that perhaps this trait had lessened in more recent years, but events of 2009 proved otherwise.

The period through which I developed and ran my own business was long and the work was complex. In common with all who start their own businesses and who expect to succeed, hard work, day after day, is required. For the twenty-three years in which I ran and operated the organisation, I felt that I spent almost half of the nights working. The rest of the time, at the start, I spent worrying. Again, this was the path that I had chosen and I had no complaints. Stress and, through it, the possibility of depression reared its ugly head. This time I was more prepared. I was going to fight it. Much of my difficulty was, as I was to find out later, the old problem of being dyslexic. In recent years while lecturing on the subject, mostly in England, I developed an understanding of the condition. Put simply, the problem is that a person who is dyslexic has his or her brain 'wired up' differently from those who are not dyslexic. There are different levels of the disability and that depends on the degree of difference in the wiring. When I am asked a question, for example, my brain considers the answer and passes it to a form of communication such as my voice. But, in the process, it sends the information up to twice as many parts of the brain as a non-dyslexic person. So, to answer the question, my brain uses twice as much energy as that of 'normal' people. But because the information is processed differently, the answer could be from an unusual perspective. The net effect is that I can see things differently to others. How different I cannot say, as I have only ever been dyslexic and have nothing with which to compare the condition.

The other major effect of the condition is that I feel twice as tired, mentally, as non-dyslexics who are asked to carry out the same tasks. The solution to that difficulty usually for me is rest, in the form of naps. Winston Churchill, the war leader, was dyslexic and was well-known for his ability to take short and refreshing sleeps. If I did not use the technique when I was under stress or mentally tired, which is almost the same thing, I would become depressed and find things getting out of proportion. Churchill called this condition the 'black dog'. For me the effect on the mind was physical too. When in the tired and distressed state, I felt as if there was a wet rag being pulled on and over my head. I never was a details person, which, at a certain stage, is bad for a PR person but at that those moments everything seemed unimportant except having a sleep.

In 1976, in starting my own business and having serious family responsibilities, I knew that I could not afford, in any sense, to fail. I developed the concept that I had started to use several years before. That was of self-taught positive thinking. The point was to control and focus my mind. I had heard about positive thinking as an American idea. But, being dyslexic, I certainly was not going to spend time reading the literature, which for me is exhausting and hard work. As a consequence, I could devote time, saved from reading, to thinking about everything and anything. It is my view that, compared to others, I spend a vast amount of time considering and analysing small amounts of information, usually collected verbally. But this theory remains, of course, untested.

For those of us who are dyslexic, the increased availability of verbal and visual mass communication has been a godsend. As a boy, I would join my parents and brother in our sitting room perhaps on a Sunday afternoon. There were comfortable chairs in each corner. I would take my place in one and watch in silence while the rest of my family were each engrossed in a book. Every now and again, I would try to engage one or all in conversation, but to no avail. Silence reigned and, without me, would only be broken by sudden and loud bursts of laughter from my brother. These regular occurrences made my parents, on occasion, invite Jimmy to remove himself to another room. Either my elder sibling specialised in books of a funny content or he had then a strange and all-embracing sense of humour. Whatever, I would leave the room and return to my world. Being part of a family who would read every thing from War and Peace to the label of a sauce bottle did not help my feeling of being inadequate. It seemed that unless you read and read and read again, your information was limited and your opinions not valid. Along came radio and television and a new world opened up. My mother, in particular, thought that the television was a threat to the reading classes. I did not.

Dyslexics are known for their communication skills and interpersonal abilities. While I think that this is true in my case, I feel that I could and did overplay this area and had the ability to become a bore. Whatever the position is and was, I am mid-range dyslexic and that is a major part of the making of me. Today, when I lecture on the topic, it is mostly to human resources groups who know little about the disability. I make the point that we dyslexics are the lucky ones in society. We can see the solutions to problems quicker that non-dyslexics can. Our skills can play a major part in the lateral thinking required today and in the future. I suggest that soon those like me giving such lectures will find themselves pleading instead for equality for non-dyslexics. Dyslexics will inherit the Earth!

The years when I ran the business were stimulating and, after several very hard years, financially rewarding. While I worked at home for the first ten years, I had the pleasure, not usually accorded to one running his business, of becoming an important part of my family's daily routine. Carol had kept her job at the Ulster Hospital after we married in 1971 and was of outstanding support and encouragement to me during the political period, darkness and all. At the start of what was to become John Laird Public Relations, she offered encouragement, even when it meant giving up a room at home. However, in March 1976, the month I started in business, Carol delivered our firstborn, Alison Jane Laird. The exact date was

24th March in the middle of a cold night in, appropriately, the Ulster Hospital, Belfast. I suggest that the birth of a first child is a life-changing experience for both mothers and fathers, but in different ways. Carol sailed through the pregnancy and delivered Alison, nine days overdue. While my wife was clearly more and more prepared for the new experience, day by day, I was involved in wrapping up my political career and preparing for commercial work. Cecil Bell claims that several months after I ceased to be a politician, he overheard two Sandy Row women in Great Victoria Street one day. One said to the other: 'Sadie, that's dreadful about your house, have you an MP to go to for help?' 'No,' said the other. 'We used to have John Laird, but I hear he is working now.'

I did not get to see Alison until the morning of the 24th. What was one of those experiences of a lifetime? To that point, I was rather matter of fact about the approaching event but when Carol placed the small bundle into my arms everything changed big time. I felt that I had been hit in the centre of the back by a cricket bat. I looked down to the helpless minute face and I knew from that moment that for the rest of my life I would worry about and feel responsible for this human being. I was a part of the reason she existed. I now had serious responsibilities from which there was no hiding, even if I had felt so inclined. The moment of seeing a firstborn must sink deeply into a parent's mind. For me, it was one of the most defining moments in my life. Suddenly, everything seemed to have a purpose and a meaning. It is important that I should point out that the fact that the first child was female or that it was Alison is not the issue. It was that I became a parent. The following year, on 18th October, I was to be presented with another child, this time a son, John David. The emotions evoked were just as strong for him but it is the firstborn who changes everything, by definition. If I had any ideas of not being able to earn a living and so support my family, they soon left. Thankfully, I think that I was determined anyway.

Domestic life settled in. Soon, Carol returned to her job in the hospital but now working two nights a week. I am full of admiration for my wife in her pursuit of nursing. I could not work with a daily diet of death and injury, in the way that she does. In the theatres of The Ulster two nights a week, Carol takes part in harrowing acts of mercy and compassion. Sometimes in earlier years, it fell to her to put right that which terrorists had inflicted on others. I could not do that work. She did and still does and, in my view, is one of the unsung heroes of society. Thank goodness there are people like Carol around.

The period when I was a public relations consultant and running my own business was demanding and very fulfilling. Every day I seemed to understand more about communication in all its forms. This allowed me to develop new concepts, unheard of in the local industries. Being a spin-doctor, a term about which I am not sure, was the perfect career for me. I have little doubt that my upbringing and experience to that point had fitted me for such work. By the 1980s, I was employing more and more people. That just made things more rewarding and interesting. In 1986, the business moved to a large house that had been converted into offices, at 104 Holywood Road. This was about a three-minute drive from my home, although the journey could take four if there was traffic about. John Laird Public Relations was long past the point of no return. Return business and referrals provided a major part of the business. All that had to be done was to service the client base well and with imagination and, it was to be hoped, the agency would continue. And so it did.

I was not involved in politics during the late 1970s and the 1980s but, like many others, I felt strongly about things and was affected by events. Two in the latter decade helped to define my political position today. By 1980, everyone could see that the IRA was getting nowhere with its policy of death and destruction. The IRA decided to enter the political arena. But to do so it needed a cause. The decision was taken by their Army Council to require their prisoners to go on a protest, which, for some, would include a hunger-strike. The main protest was to refuse to wear prison clothes except a blanket and to smear their cells with their own excrement. The result was horrifying and sickening scenes in the largest local prison, The Maze. Those sections of the world not peopled by Irish Republican extremists, stood back in total disgust and occasional ridicule. Many of my friends who were of the Roman Catholic faith, but not hard line nationalists, were appalled also. But this too was getting nowhere, so the focus was on the hunger-striking prisoners. Most people could not give a damn about the strike because it was self-inflicted. But I was very annoyed. I am totally against suicide in any circumstances. Having sampled depression, I felt I had a right to that opinion. Today, partly as a result of the adulation shown to one Republican, in particular, who took his own life in the hunger-strike, we have a disproportionate number of suicides in Belfast, compared to other UK cities.

Events were unfortunately to play right into the IRA leadership's hands with their policy to bring politics into their campaign. In the early months of 1981, the independent nationalist Member of Parliament for Fermanagh and South Tyrone, Frank Maguire, died suddenly. Frank had held the seat since the October elections of 1974, when he dislodged the sitting member, the Unionist party leader, Harry West. In 1974, the nationalist groups in that constituency wanted to rid themselves of the Unionist member and decided that if they put up one united candidate they could win the seat. A point that is mathematically correct, when based on a religious head count. At a meeting to select the person to stand, the view was that they should pick a total unknown. The idea was that no one would have anything against a candidate of whom they had never heard. The attendees at the meeting agreed with this policy and everyone looked round for a person. Someone said that over in the corner was Frank Maguire and he was a total nonentity. So Frank, a Lisnaskea publican, was selected.

In a marginal seat, like Fermanagh and South Tyrone, it is essential to ensure that your vote turns out in full. Cross voting and floating voting are totally unknown. On the day of the count, 19th October 1974, there was a recount, caused by some fancy work by a Unionist who had managed to move some votes from Maguire's to Harry West's. This was spotted and corrected and, just after six o'clock, as the last constituency in the UK, Fermanagh and South Tyrone was declared. Maguire had won by 2510 votes. The evening national news, broadcast from the BBC, was interrupted to bring the result. An out-of-breath young English reporter then asked Frank Maguire, live on television, what his policies were, given that he was now the new member. 'Policies,' Maguire spluttered, 'Policies! Look, son,' he said, 'I have been fighting an election for the last three weeks. I have not had time to think of policies.' While I knew the sense of what he had said, in the context of that area, I was often to wonder what the good people of England thought.

My old friend Gerry Fitt, the MP for West Belfast, had a particular dislike of Frank Maguire. Frank would never condemn any violence caused by the IRA. His major trick was to undertake radio interviews down the telephone line. When he was asked what he thought of a recent act of Republican violence he would respond by saying that the line was fading and he could no longer hear the question. Maguire hardly ever came to Westminster during his six and a half years as a member. He certainly never spoke except for one day when he shouted 'rubbish' while the Secretary of State for Northern Ireland was speaking. Enoch Powell, Unionist member for South Down, rather cleverly parodied the one word as a maiden speech. He offered all the usual congratulations to Maguire on the thoughtfulness and excellence of the maiden effort and expressed the hope that the House would be blessed with many more such contributions.

Frank Maguire was known as an abstainer in all votes, through his non-attendance. However, on one occasion he told the BBC News Department that he felt so strongly about an issue that he was going to London just to abstain in person. Fitt, never one to miss an opportunity to crack a joke, especially at the expense of someone he disliked, expanded the visit of Maguire. Fitt claimed that he met Frank outside the Palace of Westminster, trying to cross Parliament Square. He could see that Frank was in difficulties, so he approached and asked if he needed help. Maguire is reported to have said that the traffic was the worst that he had ever seen: 'Worse that the Main Street in Lisnaskea.' Fitt offered some advice, indicating that there was a zebra-crossing further down the street. Maguire is said to have responded: 'By God! I hope it is having more luck that I am having!'

Frank Maguire's untimely death gave the IRA just the opening it wanted. The first hunger-striker, Bobby Sands, was nearing death and so the decision was taken for him to stand in the Fermanagh and South Tyrone by-election. This was the first time that a Sinn Féin-endorsed candidate had stood for many years. The purpose of the IRA prisoners' strike was to obtain political status. The government's line, backed up by the Conservative Prime Minister, Mrs Margaret Thatcher, was that what the prisoners decided to do was their affair and only theirs. Besides, the inmates had been convicted of dreadful acts of terror and as such were common criminals. But making Sands a candidate put him in a position where he could not back down in the suicide. He had to die. More convicted terrorists were required by the IRA to join the strike and, in time, to die.

Just around this time, my wife's mother became very ill. Mary Kathleen, or wee Mary Kate, or Sadie, was not blessed with good health throughout her lifetime. Quite a number of times in Carol's youth, she and the rest of her sisters were sent off to stay with aunts and other willing relations, to allow their mother to undergo treatment. This is one of the benefits of a large family. For Mrs Ferguson, the main problem was her kidneys. In later years, she only had one that worked. Early in 1981, it became clear that her health was not good at all and that she would need yet more care and attention.

Mary Kate, as I think of her, was one of life's heroes. From my Belfast viewpoint, she held the farm at Dromore, Derrygonnelly, together. She worked night and day, seven days a week, feeding, cleaning and tending to the animals and, in the earlier days of her marriage, bringing up a family of six. She worked miracles, with never a word of complaint.

After Easter, in April, Mrs Ferguson was admitted to hospital in Enniskillen. In the traditional way in which families bind together at such times, we all knew that there was only one outcome. Carol's sister, Vera, was sent for from Vancouver Island in Canada. There, she and her husband, Terence, ran a store selling just about everything. In another one of life's uncanny turns, Mrs Ferguson, although seeming to be unconscious, remained alive just long enough for Vera to arrive from the airport, after a frantic dash around the world. On the 2nd May, which was unfortunately also Carol's birthday, wee Mary Kate passed away.

On 9th April, Bobby Sands was elected to the vacancy in Fermanagh and South Tyrone. In a by-election against Unionist leader Harry West, Sands polled 30,493 votes against West's 29,046; a majority of 1,447. This event had a very considerable effect on the politics of the province. The ramifications were, and are, felt in the nationalist community still, I think. But what I do accept is the effect it had on the Unionist community, including myself. In an act of unbelievable cowardice, the Social Democratic and Labour Party (SDLP) refused to put up a candidate. This point still grinds with Unionists to this day.

The big issue, which still is a talking point in Fermanagh and South Tyrone and which informs Unionist opinion, is that almost the total Roman Catholic community voted for an IRA terrorist in the process of committing suicide. Added to that, he was the leader of a group of criminals who were on a dirty protest, contravening most of the world's notions of decency. Through my Fermanagh connections, I have had it said to me by Unionist folk that they just cannot come to terms with the fact that their next-door neighbours, whom they respect and work with, could vote for someone like Sands. I, from the perspective of Belfast, felt full of mistrust and apprehension at the development. Despair was in the air everywhere. 'Who are we living beside?' was a question being asked around the constituency.

The election raised tension throughout April, the month in which Mrs Ferguson was in hospital. The funeral was held on a pleasant day, 5th May, the day Bobby Sands succumbed to the sixty-sixth day of not having food and drink. The picturesque home in its beautiful surroundings, outside Derrygonnelly, was packed with relations and neighbours. To the credit of the entire community in that area and due to the respect in which the Fergusons were held, many Roman Catholics from nearby attended. The atmosphere at a funeral can be sad and tense and this was no exception. Cecil Bell, who was well-known to the Ferguson family, was determined that the external events should not take away from the day. In typical style, on that sunny, warm day, Cecil was at his playful, if respectful, best.

Amongst the visitors was a tall blond clergyman wearing rather unusual clerical clothes. He was a fine figure of a man, whose very stature demanded attention. Cecil could be most understanding in such circumstances and, in a spirit of liberalism, he made a point of thanking the cleric for attending the funeral and, in doing so, showing solidarity across the religious divide. 'Particularly at such a time in our country's affairs, it is heartening to see one such as you here,' Cecil commented. I watched as, a few moments later, the cleric turned to the man standing along side him and enquired why a Methodist shouldn't be welcome at such an event. The gentleman of the cloth was a visitor from Sweden who was acting as a stand-in at the local Methodist church. All anyone can say is that Cecil's heart was in the right place.

The summer of 1981 was long and hot, not just in the climatic sense but also in the political and security arena. One further event was to have ongoing implications for my family and friends. In the tension of the Sands election and funeral period, the local Ulster Defence Regiment (UDR) units were working day and night, playing a vital role in keeping the lid on trouble. A story involving a family member came to light. A relation, who was a part time UDR member, woke an entire household one dark night when he cried out in a dreadful and scaring series of shouts. The family member was asleep but his outcry could only be as a result of the extreme tension of that period. In due course, I told Cecil about the incident and moved on to other topics. Cecil was to say later that it was the last straw for him. He realised that his duty, as a single person, was not to spend time on political activity, albeit of a liberal type. His duty was to join one of the part time security forces and to help protect the community. Being in Belfast, he opted to join the Royal Ulster Constabulary Reserve.

To cope with the security issues, the government had decided to Ulsterise the conflict. Certainly no Unionist could disagree with that. A special regiment was formed; the Ulster Defence Regiment. Trained to the highest standards of the British Army and commanded by locals, the regiment was successful in keeping the peace in almost all of the country area, but only at vast cost in human life and injury to its members. In all, 197 officers and soldiers were killed on active service. A further sixty-one were killed after they had retired from the regiment. Very many more were injured during the civil unrest of the period. The UDR did not detract from, but increased the effectiveness of the regular army in Northern Ireland. It was the only part of the British force that had its area of operation defined. It could only serve in Northern Ireland.

The Police Reserve was designed to act in support of the police force. The Royal Ulster Constabulary Reserve, or RUCR, as it became known, was also trained to a very high standard and was to be of considerable support, particularly in the Greater Belfast area. Many of the force also made the supreme sacrifice. The final toll for all grades of police was 303 murdered, with over 9000 injured. Both forces, following formation, developed sections which allowed their members to become full time employees and do duty as such.

Gerry Fitt, (Member of Parliament for West Belfast from 1966 to 1983) is one who came out of the whole dreadful Republican suicide campaign with greatly enhanced credit. (An extreme Republican might not, of course, hold that view.) Gerry, in a shock result on 31st March 1966, took the West Belfast seat from the sitting Unionist MP, James Kilfedder, by a 2011 vote majority. The shock was felt nowhere stronger than in the Laird household. As a unit, we had worked very hard for the return of the sitting member. Kilfedder was something of a Walter Mitty figure, but at least he was our Walter Mitty!

Gerry's career had begun in the City Corporation area of Dock. In the late 1950s, he became a Republican Labour councillor. He progressed in 1962 to win, from the Unionist Billy Oliver, the Stormont seat of Dock. Fitt had a persona that suited the Belfast residents of industrial areas. He was articulate, quick witted and young and, for many, a breath of fresh air in the City Hall committee rooms. My father disliked Gerry, regarding him as a 'corner-boy' and not someone to be in politics. My mother, I suspect, had a sneaking regard for Councillor Fitt. She had to deal with him on a daily basis, when she was a member in the Corporation for St Anne's. But she could never express that view while my father was alive. But when a widow, over the course of thirteen years, she changed her personality to a large degree and felt able to express her views more freely.

The general election of 1966 was a bitter affair in West Belfast. In terms of the running of a campaign, it asked many more questions than it answered. For months afterwards, my father spent time trying to understand what had happened and how. It seemed that everything that could go wrong, did. And the result was the narrow Fitt victory that dumbfounded the Unionist community.

Many years later, when I became a member of the Westminster upper house, and so joined the, by then, Lord Fitt, I sat one day on the terrace of the Palace of Westminster. As it happens, it was my birthday. There he and I discussed that fateful election in 1966. His lordship told me about his campaign and ours, all of which seemed surreal but never the less explained the events of that period. The experience was like finding the last piece of a jigsaw, after a long time lost. It fitted perfectly, when put in its place, but its inclusion caused the entire picture to change.

The story that unfolded is this. Early in the campaign, a senior loyalist figure from the Shankill, that traditional loyalist heartland, and a group of supporters, who would normally be regarded as Unionists, visited Fitt. They explained that they were extreme lefties and had joined the Unionist Party and the Orange Order on the well-worn basis of infiltration with a view to discrediting the organisations. They said they supported Fitt's admiration of the extremely Republican, but also left wing, James Connelly. As a matter of interest, Fitt always invoked James Connelly as his role model. I was to find out that his knowledge of Connolly was very limited. When asked a question about him, Gerry would change the subject. I think now that I knew more about Connelly than he did.

The group that visited that day seemed under the control of the well-known loyalist who had a connection to the very heart of the Unionist campaign. Quick thinking Fitt, feeling that he was being set up by the Unionists, told them to be very active in the Kilfedder campaign and report everything back to him. They agreed to this and then left to go about their work.

On the terrace, I put questions to Gerry, which he fully answered, and the fog totally cleared. I now understood why the Fitt camp knew all about our tactics almost before we had thought of them. Some points became too clear. One of the traditions of elections in Northern Ireland, which I am glad to say is no more, was the belief that democracy required every possible vote to be cast and if the voter was unable through illness or death to attend to the matter, then other helpful souls would. In order to undertake such work, it was necessary to have a 'flying squad'. This was a group of centrally organised people of all ages and both sexes, who had a supply of hats and coats into which they could change and so alter their appearance.

During the canvassing part of the campaign, those who could not vote were noted and appropriate arrangements made. This practice was not restricted to one side. Everyone was at it, all sides cancelling each other out. If we polled an extra thousand, they would poll an extra thousand. As the process had to be paid for, it was a waste of time but it was tradition and that goes a long way. There was only one method of ensuring that 'doing' votes would be a success and change the outcome of an election. That was if the other side's squad was also polling for your candidate. I discovered that day, on the terrace, that that was exactly what had happened. The Shankill group became our flying squad but they were polling for Fitt. In all the forty years between the election and that day, never in my wildest dreams had I thought of that happening.

Fitt gave me more than enough other information to assure me that the flying squad activity was true. He went into details about the Hibernians Hall of the Falls Road, in which his squad was based. It seems that part of our group was also using that facility. That explained why polling cards would appear in our tally rooms with the word 'plug' on them. Tally rooms were the local areas' headquarters in those days. I now understand that, in the 1960s, the nationalist word meaning to cast a personated vote was 'plug'. On the Unionist side, they talked about 'doing' a vote.

On polling day itself, the evening Belfast paper, the Telegraph, had, as the top front-page picture, a group of nuns from the Mater Hospital, having abuse and stones thrown at them by a group of loyalists, while they were on their way to vote for Fitt. For years, I wondered how this picture, which was a massive benefit to the opposition campaign, could happen. Who knew when the nuns would vote? Who would have told the loyalist mob to be there? And how could it be that the Telegraph would have a handy photographer available to record the event in time for the evening edition? All was now clear. Everything was set up by the Shankill group and, in the case of the evening paper, with the help of several supporters in the press. The unusual activity of an apparent drunk at the count was another indication of Gerry's thoroughness.

In the space between the final votes being counted and checked and the official announcement of the result, there is usually a period of anticlimax. In the early hours of 1st April at the count, during just that period, one of the Shankill group, full of drink, climbed on to the series of tables used by the counters. He proceeded to run up and down, shouting: 'Gerry we spend all day voting for you, hundreds we put in.' When my father returned home that night in a low mood, having just lost the seat, he did take some pleasure in regaling us with the story about the clever loyalist who tried to ruin Fitt's day by pretending to be drunk and then claiming that many of his votes were personated. I learnt, on the terrace, that it was no pretence. The gentleman was drunk. He had voted all day for Fitt and he did embarrass him. Had we looked through the wrong end of the telescope? In the version accepted at the time by my family, the flying squad scam had another interpretation that was counter to the former MP's. My problem is that the later story fits my understanding of the events more comfortably than any others. Perhaps history will unravel the actual events.

As the Troubles progressed, Gerry Fitt, who had played a part in supporting the early demands of the civil rights movement, began to feel alarmed by what was happening, as did many of the Roman Catholic middle classes. More and more, Fitt was distancing himself from the Republican element in his own constituency. He was a most likeable fellow; the more you knew him, you more you liked him. At least, that was how I found him, first on the streets of west Belfast and then in the Stormont Parliament. He had one major asset which came into its own in the tension between the communities from 1969 onwards, and that was a self-deprecating sense of humour. Time after time, I watched as he defused a difficult situation by making all present laugh, mostly at himself.

It was easy to see and to feel that Gerry was becoming more and more uncomfortable with the idea of violence for violence's sake. Whatever nasty traits he might have had, being a bigot was not one. Right from the start of the suicidal hunger-strike campaign, Fitt was totally opposed to it. He felt that a hunger-strike forced on young IRA prisoners by their leadership was immoral. I, and many others, agreed. But, representing the West Belfast constituency, his opinions were important. He became the subject of considerable abuse, organised by IRA Sinn Féin. Crowds would strangely appear wherever he went in the area and give him verbal abuse. Gerry told me several times in the 2000s, what hurt him the most was that when he looked at the menacing rabble he recognised very many of them. Over years, as their MP, he had helped them or their families through difficult periods. There is little gratitude in this world.

Respect for Gerry Fitt grew dramatically over that early 1980s period. While still retaining his Labour credentials, he realised that the united Ireland that he would like, at some stage, could not be the version on offer from the IRA. Killing and terrorising people of all creeds and classes, in pursuit of some Celtic myth, was immoral and nonsensical. Putting bread on the table, housing, health care and social injustice were always his concerns. Using guns to take control of entire housing estates, whether nationalist or loyalist, was the road to anarchy. I and the majority of people agreed with him.

In the 2000s, when we were both in the House of Lords, I spent a lot of time with Gerry. I saw how he fitted into that parliamentary life and how he commanded a great deal of respect. Many an hour he spent in one of the many bars, regaling any and every group of drinkers with stories about his career. Each tale was funnier than the last. At times, I would pluck up my courage and interject with a story of my own. Gerry would quickly slap me down. It was his show and it was only his tales. I did not mind. Gerry was in the swan-song of a long and distinguished career, which was full of threat and tension. No man deserved respect more than him.

It may seem strange that a former Republican Labour member should end up in the House of Lords, but that too owes its origins to the summer of the hunger-suicides. Tension ran high in West Belfast after Sands's death. A large Republican funeral was held in the area for him. IRA Sinn Féin kept up the heat until the 1983 general election when Fitt, predictably, lost to the IRA Sinn Féin leader, Gerry Adams. The Thatcher government offered Gerry Fitt a peerage to allow him to sit in the Lords and still take part in the affairs of Northern Ireland. Gerry told me several times of the difficult decision he was forced to make. Become a member of the British Establishment? A person with his background? But an incident was to make up his mind for him.

A Republican mob broke into his home on the Antrim Road one night, in the summer of 1983. At around four o'clock in the morning, Fitt, wearing only his underwear, held them off from advancing up his stairs and into his bedroom. He was holding a large government-issue revolver and was shouting for his wife to ring the police, the army, and the coast guard; anyone who could save the day for them. By staring into the eyes of what seemed to be the leader of the gang, he managed to make them reverse down the stairs, where they totally trashed the ground floor. Just then, an army patrol appeared and took control. 'Where are you from?' Fitt demanded. 'West Indies,' the senior soldier replied. 'No wonder it took you so long to respond,' Fitt joked. He was always able to defuse a tense situation. The next morning, on a wall near the Fitt home appeared the large words: 'Fitt – the fastest gun in the vest.'

In trashing the reception rooms in his home, the thugs had destroyed all his family photographs. Worse, they had stamped on them. Fitt was heartbroken. He was a family man or he was nothing. A sense of being totally let down does not adequately express Gerry's feelings, as he explained them to me in 2004. If that was how he was to be repaid for years of dedicated service to West Belfast, then he would continue the battle in the only place available; the House of Lords. The noble lord, Lord Fitt, soon felt at home in that part of the British establishment. When I arrived there in 1999, one topic still alive was: 'What did you do in the war?' On that issue, Lord Fitt could hold his own with anyone. Gerry spent most of the hostilities on merchant ships, bringing much needed supplies to the northern Russian ports. They were constantly under German attack and the sea itself acted as a death trap. If someone fell, or was blown, into the water, the best estimate was that he would die in nine minutes. The sea was cold and full of ice.

There is no doubt that Gerry Fitt played an important part in my life. I learnt much from him about handling people in difficult circumstances. I certainly learnt many outstandingly funny stories, with which I still bore unlucky people today. Gerry had the ability to see the funny side of almost any situation. In this, he was similar to Cecil Bell. In the mid 2000s, to my great pleasure, I was able to bring them both together for an entire day. Cecil acted as a driver and Fitt the passenger. Gerry, to my knowledge, never drove a car.

As I had expected, the two of them got on famously. The fun, or, as we Ulster Scots say, 'the crack', must have been fantastic in the car on that famous day. Above all, I learnt from Gerry humanity expressed with a sense of humour. That, I will always value.

In the fullness of time, in late 1981, the security position settled down again. But, for many, nothing could ever be the same again. A number of the convicted terrorists were 'persuaded' to die for their cause, before the whole strike folded in disarray. I, like the majority of people in Ulster, cannot remember how many more died. I cannot remember their names, or even from where they came. I just feel sorry for their families. A son or father committed suicide, recorded as such in official government records, and nothing was gained for Republicanism or for anything else, and few can remember their names. What a waste! The famous and witty writer on walls in Belfast summed it up with: 'We will never forget you Jimmy Mc Sands.'

Another event took place in the 1980s, which affected me profoundly, even to this day. Again, the area affected was County Fermanagh. On Remembrance Day in November 1987, at the memorial to those who had died fighting for freedom in Crown uniforms, mostly in two world wars, a group of ex-servicemen and others were blown up by the IRA while taking part in the wreath laying. Eleven were killed and sixty-three wounded that dreadful day. The country, not just the Unionist community, was outraged at such mindless, insensitive brutality.

'What sort of people have no respect for the dead of others, and for what sort of cause?' was a common sentiment. The world seemed to be stunned, almost unable to react to such horror. I wept openly every time I saw Gordon Wilson, on television, describe the last moments of his lovely daughter's life, as she lay injured in the rubble. He held her hand and just before she passed away she said: 'Dad, I love you'. As a father of a beautiful daughter, I found it too much to bear.

Even sections of the IRA began to feel that the Poppy Day Bombing, as it became known, was a step too far. But for some it was too late. They were dead. Sinn Féin members of the local council, including the chairman, ran for cover. They were unable, as a result of the organisation's strict discipline, to say anything against the deed. Faith was restored in humanity for many when, as a direst result, Sinn Féin lost control of the council at the next local government election. Many of those councillors who refused to condemn the death on the streets of Enniskillen, I am pleased to say, lost their seats.

As the 1980s progressed, I was able to take more time to do things that were not business-related. One was to examine history as it affected me. In 1989, a book was published entitled *God's Frontiersmen.* This was the story of the Ulster Scots people in Ulster and in America. You will remember that, almost as a matter of policy, I do not read books unless they are non-fiction and exceptional. This volume, by Ballymena man Rory Fitzpatrick, is one such book. As a matter of interest, I did read a few novels in my early teens. However, I discovered that the enjoyment to hard work ratio was stacked against reading; besides, the novels were boring. I decided that I would never read another one and would confine myself to necessary books of fact, like railway information. Life was much more interesting that any story could be. It struck me that reading a novel was like getting into someone else's dirty bathwater!

Rory Fitzpatrick had one great advantage. He was not from an Ulster Scots background but instead from an Irish one. In public relations terms, this would be called third party endorsement. If I compliment myself, that is not credible because I am naturally biased. If someone else takes on the task then it is credible. Subtitled *The Scots-Irish Epic*, the book was accompanied by a Channel 4 series. While the programmes will not win any awards for exciting television, they were interesting to me and many other Ulstermen. One Ulster Scots character who came alive out of the pages was David Crockett.

Crockett appealed to me because he had, like me, Tyrone origins. He had made good in America by becoming a very tough politician, before dying a hero's death while fighting for freedom. To us in Northern Ireland, Crockett is a Huguenot name. That means his family were French Protestants who were required to leave their country of origin through persecution. Large numbers settled in Ulster, many in the Lagan valley area of counties Down and Antrim. It was they who brought linen-weaving to Ulster. Irish linen is still world-famous today. The Crocketts settled in County Tyrone, in and around Ardstraw and Castlederg, both not far from Strabane or, as I feel, more importantly, near to Artigarvan. In the rush of Ulster folk who sailed to America in the seventeenth century was Crockett's grandfather.

Davy Crockett's father had fought at the battle of King's Mountain in 1780. Three Lairds had also fought and died in that battle. King's Mountain was one of a series of contests between the new Americans and their British overlords, on the road to American independence. As with events in 1798, I have no difficulty with the idea of my relations fighting Crown forces. Ulster Scots fought for what they thought was right, regardless of the nature of the opposition and regardless of the price. Crockett was a large, charismatic figure; the very sort that legends are written about. He had a successful political career, but only up to a point. Many felt that he was presidential material but circumstances were not to go his way. Like most in history, he had to be content with a supporting role.

From my Ulster Scots viewpoint, Davy Crockett's real claim to fame was his last encounter, the Alamo. After his political career fell apart, he went back to Tennessee, where he enlisted a bunch of men to go to Texas, to an old church building called the Alamo. The year was 1836 and there was discontent in Texas, which had become part of Mexico years earlier. That country's leader was General Santa Anna who was all powerful and, in common with most politicians in that position, thought that he could do anything. On this occasion, he was in the process of trying to put down a rebellion. The Alamo was strategically significant and its defence would slow down Santa Anna's advance.

Crockett reached the monastery with one hundred and ninety-nine other souls. There they determined to take a stand. The longer they could hold out the better, for, in doing so, they delayed Santa

Anna's army. Sam Houston, another Ulster Scot, was leading a force toward the fortress, but he needed time to get his troops into place. The men at the Alamo knew that their survival was impossible. They were all gathered and a line was drawn in the sand. Their commander told them that those who stayed to fight had no hope but glory. Anyone who wanted to go could cross the line in the sand, the gates would be open and they could disappear. Only one took that course. He crossed the line, left and lived to tell the tale. One hundred and ninety-nine, many of them Ulster Scots, chose to hold out to the death. That event is the origin of the expression, 'a line in the sand'. After a two-week siege, all one hundred and ninety-nine were dead and the Alamo had fallen. But the important point is that the great objective, that of holding up the general until Houston and his men were near at hand, was achieved.

Sam Houston, whose people came from Ballynure, near Carrickfergus, eventually confronted Santa Anna and decimated his army. Soon Texas was independent and free once again. Sam Houston was appointed president. Houston, who had been a successful lawyer, a Congressman and governor of the State of Tennessee, was to have his ambition fulfilled in 1845. That year, Texas became part of the United States. It says a lot about the Ulster Scots psyche that, in Castlederg and other areas, the Alamo is celebrated each year. Some may think that the Alamo was a battle lost but, to the Ulster Scots mind, holding out for so long, against all odds, it was a victory. To us, the battle for freedom from domination is vital. The Alamo was another step in our journey to who we Ulster Scots are today.

CHAPTER FIVE

The Inst Governor

INST, INST, ANCIENT AND ROYAL
INST, INST, GREAT IS THY NAME.

FROM THE SCHOOL SONG

ON A SOFT, still day at the end of October 1993, John Dunn passed away. He had been the fourth of that name to own and work the Ballyskeagh farm. Uncle Jack, as I knew him, had returned from hospital to the home of his forefathers, knowing the end was at hand. He was called Jack, to distinguish him from the previous two generations who, for a period, were all alive at the one time. It would be impossible to detail those who have helped to mould me, without spending much space on Jack. To me, he was the embodiment of an Ulster Scot and I admired and respected him for that. He was independent, hard working and would never ask anyone to do a job that he thought he could tackle himself. Even as a small boy, when I thought of the Wild West and cowboys, it was an image of him that appeared. Jack was the ultimate frontiersman. He would have been at home in the Wild West. His obituary in the local paper seemed to catch the mood of the local area when it said that his men did not work for Jack; they worked with him.

The homestead at Ballyskeagh was a typical plantation creation. The residence and all the outhouses faced inward to form a kind of safe fortress. It was only possible to see the classic view across the valley and into Donegal by going outside this fortress. Many a time I did just that. I stood and stared at the green rolling hills, the fields, the houses and the floor of the valley below. Nearby were the modern factory units of Leckpatrick Co-operative Creamery, started in 1902 on land donated by my great-grandfather. The creamery had been, and still is, the main employer in the area, as well as its pulsing heart. Around the plant is the newer section of Artigarvan, with the older part alongside Leckpatrick Presbyterian Church, or Kirk, as it is still called by some. The use of the words older and newer is relative, in the context of the village.

In the dip, past the church, was the course of the narrow gauge railway and the site of the local station, strangely called Ballyheather. Lift the eye further and you see the route of the main Strabane to Londonderry road. In later years, when old enough to know some local history, I imagined the 36th Ulster Division marching to the troop ships in 1915. The groups of people who waved Union flags and shouted encouragement must have inspired the young lads who, only a few years earlier, had been members of the Ulster Volunteer Force, also known as Carson's Army. Few could guess that many of these youths were spending their last days in their own beautiful Ulster homeland. On the continent, they would confront hell and, for those at the Somme, its very pit. Landscapes may not have ghosts to tell a story but they do speak of history.

Look beyond the bottom of the valley and the delightful county of Donegal is clearly in view. This is the land of my planter ancestors. The area to the north is called the Laggan valley and is not to be confused with the Lagan valley, which is around Lisburn. The Laggan was the scene of much plantation activity in the early 1600s, including that of my family. The area had been hard fought over and was still in considerable contention in 1641, the year of the rebellion against the planters. Thousands were slaughtered that year, along with homes burnt and cattle stolen. The Ulster Scots, to protect themselves, created two regiments that became known as the Lagganeers. They fought the rebels and chased them as far as Coleraine. While out of their home valley, a rebel army tried to take the castle at Raphoe, the unofficial capital of east Donegal. The Lagganeers heard of the attack and rushed back to defeat the invaders at a battle near Castlederg. In the following year of 1642, the rebels tried to capture the castle again but were stopped at a place called Glenmaquin, just outside Raphoe. The Lagganeers had a famous victory and 16th June 1642 was added to the roll call of iconic Ulster Scots dates. Today the battle is still remembered and local groups re-enact the events annually.

If your eyes turn left, away from the views over Artigarvan, they will settle on the local example of a gentle country residence. It is tucked into a forest and known as Adair's; the home is lived in today by my old friend Hammee, or Hamilton, Thompson. It makes spectacular viewing several times a year when it is open to the public. The area around Artigarvan is crisscrossed by many small lanes and roads. In early years, I imagined vehicles racing along these ways as they distributed the vital guns for the UVF on an April night in 1914. The whole area still has the look and feel of the plantation. The Dunns, my people, did not move directly into the area, but covered a route from Donegal to Donemana and district before obtaining the farm at Ballyskeagh in 1826. Donemana is the next town on a secondary road out of Strabane. Remember that much of the Strabane area was settled by Roman Catholic planters and the geopolitics, with an interesting historical background, takes shape accordingly.

The local landlords were the Hamilton family, who arrived in North West Tyrone from the lowlands of Scotland in May 1606. Hamilton is one of the major names of the area. They were Roman Catholic aristocracy, who converted to the Church of Ireland in due course. As with all landlord families, there were good and bad generations. But again, as with most landlords, they were not well liked in the Presbyterian stronghold of Artigarvan and the surrounding district. My great-great-grandfather was only able to buy the farm of Ballyskeagh because the Hamilton family, who by that time had been granted the title of Abercorn, lost large amounts of money while gambling. In Artigarvan circles, the concept of a title held no sway whatsoever. Presbyterians are like that. The irony is that many years later, and in order to honour my mother and her lineage, I selected the territorial title of Artigarvan and the village, without its consent or, indeed, knowledge, was turned into a barony. But I think that we should keep that point amongst ourselves at this stage.

I spent a lot of time in my youth at Ballyskeagh, although not as much as brother Jimmy, who was evacuated to the farm for the duration of the war. He was, for some time, to regard his Aunt Isobel as his mother and her brother, Jack, as a father figure. My time near Artigarvan was during the 1950s and the very early 1960s. Looking back, I think I was like Alice in Wonderland. I had fallen down a rabbit hole and embarked on strange adventures, exploring the area and meeting people of a type never encountered before. I might have been a city slicker, but these good Tyrone folk knew much more of life than I and could outwit me every time. It did take me a while to understand the local Ulster Scots language and the particular version that is used in that area. There are three types of the language, with slight variants. In North Tyrone, the version is called East Donegal. The two other types are known as Antrim and Down.

One other major influence on my life was framed in the setting of Ballyskeagh, although he lived near Donemana, at a place called Glenagoorland. My cousin was ten months older than me and had, confusingly, the same first name as my brother, James. It is my view, because brother Jimmy was brought up nearby, that the adults began to call him Jimmy, not James, to make the difference. As a youth, James Dunn was athletic and suave, with a presence for which I would have died. In a way, he was my second brother. At times, he was closer to me than my actual one, who is almost six years older. It might have seemed to me that James lived in the back of beyond, but I looked up to him and he did not disappoint.

My cousin was the necessary male every early teenage boy has, or should have, as a mentor. It was James Dunn who first introduced me to the delights of viewing the female form for 'interesting' bits. His descriptions used words that I had never encountered before in that context. However, they are not rude, just exciting. He described, with a loving care, the curves of young females he knew, the sort of words that motor enthusiasts use for their new sporting machine. At one stage, he introduced me to the idea of smoking. But that is one habit I cannot understand. The idea of paying hard earned cash to damage your health and to stink like a sewer is beyond me. The smell and dirt of the anti-social habit still haunts me to this day. He introduced me to pop music through Radio Luxembourg. For a while, we acted like Elvis Presley, but I was unable to perfect the wobble in the legs. James offered me advice on making myself look interesting. As a result, on the next visit to Woolworths in Strabane, I bought a tiepin for my school uniform!

My cousin and I spent many a happy Sunday afternoon walking the lanes and by-roads around Ballyskeagh. We just chatted the usual boys' talk, as well as holding conversations with any and everyone we met; if they were young and female, well and good. I watched the master at work. The young folk of the area could, and I suspect did, have me for breakfast any time they wanted. In particular, there were two young daughters of a creamery-worker called Herbert McLucas. These two, who I think still live in Artigarvan, were younger than I, but they had an understanding of the ways of the world that was beyond any city slicker. Herbie had been a prisoner of the Axis forces during much of the war. His brother Maurice lived and worked at Ballyskeagh during most of the 1950s.

William Anderson, known as Willie, was born in 1902 and died only at the turn of the century. He worked for my uncle for part of his life. Willie was a strong personality, with a ready joke and a fulsome laugh for all occasions. He lived, in his latter years, in a cottage on the lane up to Ballyskeagh. James, true to form, was more interested in the young female side of the Anderson connection. Other people came and went over the years in the area of the homestead. Grace McBride, from west Donegal, was Jack's housekeeper for his last thirty years. A more decent, honest woman could not be found. Her culinary repertoire may have been a bit limited but the warmth of her personality more than made up for any shortcoming in that direction. She was a fluent Irish speaker, although, even when speaking English, it was possible to miss a word or two. It was typical of the good side of community relations in the area that Jack would drive her to Sunday mass at the chapel in Glenmornan and return to bring her home. In fact, Jack the Presbyterian always looked forward to the regular visits by the local priest because, as he would say, 'the crack was good'. In later years, Jack held court in his kitchen with Grace, while a number of younger 'boys' from the area exchanged stories, mostly about local people.

A story that Jack loved to tell concerned his time in the Home Guard during the war. One moonless June night, the Germans were expected to try and take Northern Ireland by advancing up through the Irish Republic, a neutral country (in theory, anyway). The whole area was rife with rumour. The generally accepted version was that the Panzer, or tank divisions, as we call them, were to advance from the heart of County Donegal, from a place called Stranorlar. Taking the back roads, they were to advance over the hills into our part of the United Kingdom. There was a bridge near Castlederg, which they would use to enter Tyrone. The men of Artigarvan, in common with all other men of the area, were determined that they should not take our homes, cattle or womenfolk; perhaps even in that order. The local Home Guard had few weapons and so was armed with pitchforks, rakes and anything else available. The men set out that night to protect their homes. Road blocks were erected around Artigarvan and the men settled down 'to show those Germans what Ulster Scots men are made of'. All night they waited and waited. Six o'clock in the morning came and the demoralised Ulstermen realised that the Panzers were not coming. Besides, it was the morning milking time. They packed up their 'weapons', took down the roadblocks and, in low spirits, went home. Uncle Jack remembered giving his sandwiches back to his mother. The group's role in history was not to be enhanced that night. The general view in the area was that the Germans took fright, when they heard about the boys from Artigarvan.

It is in places like Artigarvan where you learn of the link between history and the local area. Although property has changed hands, and therefore family names, the background and the lineage of farms is intertwined with connections to people of long ago. Today, well over fifty years after becoming acquainted with the area, I can travel around and point to houses and land whose family names I can recognise and whose people are still there. On the main lane from Ballyskeagh, as it joins the road to Donemana, there is a cluster of houses, some very old and some new. The main name there, since I could speak, was Bertie McCorkall. He still lives there today. One of the old, unoccupied houses there in the area, Liscurry, was always known as Knox's House. It is only in recent years that I connected Knox with a very well-known cartoonist in Belfast called Ian. His work is much acclaimed, mostly for its inclusion on BBC television programmes, such as *Hearts and Minds*. I suspect, on closer inspection, I may have gone to school with him in Belfast, seventy-eight miles away. Northern Ireland is like that. Be sure never to insult anyone; they may be connected to you in some way.

The Knoxs were, like the Dunns, planters and for many years they lived in what is now thought of as the farmyard, in Ballyskeagh. The Knoxs and the Dunns lived side by side and never interbred, at least, not as far as I know. Wherever I turn, I can see reminders of my ancestors or memories of my childhood. One of the rituals, at Christmas in the 1950s, was to be given the wet battery from the farm's radio set and go down to Jim Donaghey's house, where he would charge it in time for the Queen's speech. Jim was the local motor mechanic and he lived in a house which would not have looked out of place in the southern states of America. Situated on the lane down to join a back road to Artigarvan, the house has a veranda and looked to be constructed of wood.

I feel that it is important to be an Ulsterman of my time. I like to think that I can understand my forebears. There is a responsibility with this desire. I hope that they would accept me as part of the family and that in no way have I let them down. The ghosts of yesteryear can feel like a critical jury.

In the early 1990s, a handwritten letter, with a handwritten envelope, arrived on my doormat. To make matters more interesting, it was from the respected Lord Chief Justice, Sir Robert Carswell (now Lord Carswell). I was most surprised. But also I was delighted. The communication was an invitation to join the Board of Governors of my old school; the many times mentioned, Inst (The Royal Belfast Academical Institution).

Schools all around the world have a board of management, or governors. But only one of them is Inst. Few who are not exposed to the old school mentality surrounding my place of learning can understand the importance of the invitation. By definition, because I have only been to one grammar school, I cannot compare the old boys' network with any other experience. I feel that I owe an intense loyalty to the place in the centre of Belfast. I have difficulty in expressing my views on this issue. I have little doubt that, being far from a star pupil, a major part in my development was attending the school. Inst had set me free. It opened my mind to question all and everything.

The invitation to join the select group was also important in helping me to exorcise the demons that were still in my mind, left over from the Inchmarlo experience. By this time, David, my son, had gone through the junior school and had enjoyed the experience. I was very pleased with every part of his school career. But even on my last visit to the junior school, as a parent, I felt uncomfortable. The remnants of a panic attack would appear. I had tried to be involved as much as possible to reduce the tension but was never totally successful. I find it interesting that I can now write about the place with no residue of resentment. Joining the school governors was the final step.

On the appointed day and after much briefing, I was to be introduced to the other governors in the school boardroom. Naturally, I had to go through the formalities of waiting outside until the chairman, Sir Robert Carswell, felt it was appropriate for me to enter. That day I joined many old friends. None was more important to me than the head boy in my last year at Inst, who is today a much respected figure in Belfast; Colin Gowdy.

The governors represented the old school's great and good. They sit in two clearly defined locations. There are the elder statesmen who, with the chairman and principal, sit at the board table. Then there are what they call the backbenchers; a title they use themselves. They sit on the closely packed chairs around the walls. Having been appointed to join this illustrious group, a range of thoughts came to my mind. They included the almost god-like esteem in which I would now be held by some Instonians; the very high attendance rate at all meetings; the very low participation rate amongst the backbenchers and the sheer volume of work carried out on a voluntary basis by the chairman and several senior members. As a boy at the school, when I saw the school governors on the stage at the annual prize distribution, they looked so old that I was convinced that they were the founding fathers of 1810. Now I was old enough to be one of them. Nothing could prepare me for the House of Lords better than my time on the board of The Royal Belfast Academical Institution.

I was grateful to Inst for allowing me a chance to join the inner circle and so be accepted. But, much more, it reawakened my interest in the school's history and its important place in that of Belfast. I began to look more at the importance of Presbyterian New Light thinking and its comparison with the Old Light version. I became more and more grateful to be associated with Inst. Someone once asked Michael Ridley, then the school principal, whether, as an Englishman, he considered our perception, that the Inst old boy network was stronger than any other in Northern Ireland, to be correct and, if so, why. He agreed at once about the strength of the old boys and he made a point about the particular nature of Inst boys' lifelong attachment to the school, which we had never heard before. Ridley pointed out that for parents to send their son to the school was not the easiest course of action. On his way to school, every pupil had to pass another grammar school in order to reach Inst, in the centre of Belfast. I considered this point for some time and I agree with it.

The name Ridley is from the Scottish and English border, not far from the area of the Dunns. The Ridleys were known to be a particularly nasty reiver family, but that was over four hundred years ago. Michael Ridley was, from my viewpoint, an outstanding principal. During his time, the school's achievements in both examinations and sport were of the highest order

The year 2010 was the two hundredth anniversary of the creation of Inst. Many events were held to recognise the significance of the year. One was a grand ball, in the school's common hall. There, with much entertainment, parents of current pupils enjoyed the evening while sitting at tables that bore the names of famous Instonians. I was both humbled and delighted to learn that one such table was called Lord Laird; that is what I call peer recognition. And I am not being sarcastic.

In early 1993, out of the blue, I was offered a Visiting Professorship in Public Relations at the Faculty of Communication Studies at the University of Ulster. I was staggered. I had been a regular lecturer at the university and had played a part in the development of the faculty's subjects. I liked taking time away from the PR business to discuss issues with fresh, opened minded young people. I am not sure what the students learnt but I certainly picked up some useful ideas. The public relations industry in Northern Ireland was growing fast. As an employer, I could see only advantages in developing a stream of interesting new recruits. I had previously been a computer programmer. That industry was moving so fast that it seemed impossible to draw up academically meaningful curricula for potential employees to follow. The result was that a whole race of alleged programmers could move from job to job before they were caught out as having only a limited knowledge of computing. This mushrooming of a profession was happening again with public relations. Too many people with little experience of PR, other than being 'good with people', were on the rampage, moving from position to position and, in the end, only damaging the industry. No one would go to a medical doctor who had been a fitter the week before. The only way to upgrade the whole scene was through the academic route.

I enquired as to what a visiting professor was to do, in order to keep the title. I was told; continue lecturing, be available to advise on issues within the course and create your own special event, or events, every year. The interesting bit was that I was entitled to use the title professor when I wished; although in educational circles it was strongly suggested that it is used at all times. My father had been a doctor, my brother has that title also and our mother was a councillor. I was Mr Laird. Not anymore; the one not academically qualified could call himself a professor'. I felt that I had been upgraded from economy class to business. Was that a good way to look at the picture? I had discovered that I was dyslexic, just a few years earlier. Was this the time to come out of the closet and admit to this handicap? Even when you are running your own business that is successful, the idea of explaining your poor literacy skills seemed fraught with difficulties. My hope was that I would be offering support to the many similarly afflicted and thus be a help. But, who was I to feel that people would take any notice of me? I chickened out and kept my secret, at least for a while.

The whole area of communication was fascinating to me. This was no longer just a route to resources for my family, this was an important interest in which I could experiment and could examine the results. At the same time in Northern Ireland, society was developing at such a rate that advanced concepts in communication were needed. The caseload became more varied and absorbing. It was the golden era of John Laird Public Relations. Many new recruits came to the agency and even more on work experience. Public relations is considered to be a female profession, unlike advertising. The thinking is that a PR person is required to undertake many tasks to a high degree, at the one time. An advertising executive generally carries out one job at a time, to the highest possible degree. These differences in the approach to work seem to be expressed in the different sexes.

I regret that my dyslexia was not discovered and managed in earlier life. Had it been, I might have taken a more academic path. Then again, perhaps what I did suited me perfectly. Anyhow, I developed a thirst for learning which sent me, night after night, to part-time courses. Initially, I attended several art-related courses in oil painting. In one, I was the only male; that is, until one week, when it had been announced that a nude female would appear to act as a model. On the session in question, I seem to remember noting males whom I had never seen before, carrying in cases full of painting gear. Several of these males looked as if they had appeared straight from the bookmakers. At the appointed time, the nude female model casually appeared and took up a pose. She had long, flowing red hair, dark red lipstick and nail polish, and she looked every inch her age; somewhere in her mid-seventies. Behind me a male voice unkindly said: 'They should have ironed her before putting her on display!'

In the 1990s, and after becoming a visiting professor, I was hardly at home in the early evening. I was mostly attending classes or, sometimes, taking them. I learnt about European history, aspects of British history and of the same periods in America, car maintenance, the Ulster Scots language and its culture, philosophy and, with Carol, German. The least successful was car maintenance of which, despite the best efforts of my teacher, I can remember nothing. My most successful courses were those concerning Ulster Scots and philosophy. My thirst for knowledge grew and I began to explore the world of Ulster Scots history. The role of my ethnic group in the creation of the world fascinated me. It was as if many pieces of a jigsaw began to appear and form themselves into a picture. The key point was that I was comfortable with that resulting picture. In some way, I expected it to be there. As with every other decade, this one was to be life-defining and different from all the rest.

One Ulster Scots person who took my interest at that time was a Limavady man called William Ferguson Massey, and nothing whatsoever to do with tractors. Ferguson is a consequence of the Scottish tradition of using a mother's maiden name as a middle name. A part of east Belfast at the top of the Belmont area is named after Massey. Outside the Limavady borough offices, there is a statue of the gentleman.

William Ferguson Massey, it could be argued, was the most successful prime minister of New Zealand in the twentieth century. His reign started in 1912 and lasted until 1925. William was born in March 1856 near Limavady, of planter stock. In common with many of his community, his father was attracted by the prospect of a better life elsewhere. In 1869 the family farm was sold and all headed for New Zealand. On the other side of the world, the New Zealand nation was beginning to take shape. The first European name of North Island was New Ulster, reflecting the number of people from the province who went to live there. William was a strong Presbyterian, along with the rest of his family. Throughout his youth, he became imbued with its values. After his education, he worked on the family farm, before taking an interest in politics of both his new homeland and that of Ulster.

Massey won a seat in the New Zealand Parliament in April 1894 and remained there for the rest of his life. In the initial years, he was in the National Association, or Conservative, opposition grouping. There, his Ulster Scots background made him strong in support of the underdog and gave him a view of the wider political picture. He wanted to open the country to the new world. He knew that many felt New Zealand was at the end of the earth, so he was a keen advocate of his new country becoming part of Australia. I have visited the beautiful islands of New Zealand and discovered that many now think that they are at the centre of the world!

William Massey was a senior member of the Orange Order and a declared Unionist, when it came to Ulster politics. While prime minister, he visited Europe in 1916 to show support for the New Zealand troops in the First World War. During that visit, he also returned to his hometown. There he received a hero's welcome. He offered support to Sir James Craig (later Lord Craigavon) during the third and final Home Rule crisis. Massey was determined that the establishment in London should not forget the dominion of which he was the political leader. In 1921, after the creation of Northern Ireland, he returned to his native land to endorse the new Northern Ireland state. He died in May 1925.

The exploration of Massey's story was only the start. I had a rough understanding of the Ulster Scots in America. Family history was peppered with interesting facts, such as the two brothers reared on the Artigarvan farm at Ballyskeagh, who fought on opposing sides in the American Civil War. I suspect that is not unusual. The Civil War has been described as an Ulster Scots (Scots-Irish) battle. I would go further and think of it in terms of Presbyterian Old Light against New Light, the north being the New Light. There were stubborn folk on both sides. I will mention just two on the Union side.

Ernest Everrard Burnside was the commander of the Northern Army of the Potomac. Lincoln, the president, considered him to be lacking in leadership and so he was replaced. Burnside was known for his whiskers, which he grew out from his cheeks. As a result, that type of facial adornment became known as 'sideburns'. One of his descendants is my friend David Burnside, who was the Member of Parliament for South Antrim from 2001 to 2005. In Ulster Scots, Burnside just means someone who lives on the riverbank. Burnside was replaced by another Ulster man; General Hooker. Hooker took over a demoralised army. With a flash of inspiration, he came up with a cunning plan. He sent all the wagons down to the local town to collect working girls and bring them back to entertain the men. Thus we have, to this day, the word 'hooker'. It makes you proud to be an Ulsterman.

With a bit more time on my hands, the blossoming interest in Ulster Scots, and the Presbyterian desire for betterment through education, I commenced on a campaign to find out about those from my background who became presidents of the United States. I wanted to understand their backgrounds and what drove them, and to see how that fits with today. The material is not difficult to uncover. What I was to find was a tale of men with whom I could identify. It is for this reason that I propose to take time to explain the beginning of the Presidents' Trail.

Andrew Jackson, the seventh president of the United States of America, was an archetypal patriot. His life and ancestry bear out some of the apparent paradoxes of the Ulster Scots in America. I will dwell on Jackson. He was the first, and possibly the greatest, of the Ulster Scots presidents.

Jackson was born in 1767 in the Waxhaws, in South Carolina. His family were Ulster pioneers from Boneybefore, near Carrickfergus in County Antrim. His father was a weaver who, along with his wife, had moved to America only eighteen months before boy Andrew's birth. His grandfather had fought for King William at the Battle of the Boyne in 1690. The grandfather's brother, another fighter, was the great-grandfather of Thomas Jonathan 'Stonewall' Jackson, the Virginian Confederate general of the American Civil War. This was a fighting family.

It was no coincidence that the Jacksons moved to the Carolinas. The first settlers had moved to Massachusetts and the Quaker colonies of Pennsylvania, named after its founding landowner, William Penn. The dream of a Presbyterian utopia had spurred many to leave Ulster for a new life and the fertile valleys of Pennsylvania did not disappoint them. Settlements spread along the great valleys, from the Octorara Creek, to the Susquehanna and into the Cumberland Valley, which was also accessed from the Delaware ports. Down the Allegheny mountain range, pioneers moved through the Great Valley and across the Potomac River into Virginia. The mighty Shenandoah Valley, celebrated in a great deal of Appalachian folk music, was populated by Scots-Irish, as the Ulster Scots are known in America. Their descendants are prominent to this day, especially in the counties of Augusta, Rockbridge and Tinkling Springs.

Settlers to the Carolinas, south of Virginia, tended to come through the entry port of Charleston. The Ulster Scots who came to America were, in comparison with many poor immigrants of their day, well educated. Personal improvement was a key feature of the Presbyterian ethos, as I have already suggested, and it was necessary to be able to read in order to engage in home Bible study. Many early Protestant settlers also kept journals, in which they documented the trials of the voyage westwards, as well as the demands of a life of hard work in a new land. This life was often disturbingly short.

The Declaration of Independence of 1776 can be considered to be a perfect specimen of Presbyterian thought. With its tradition of creating covenants, both with God and with their fellow man, the ideals of the pragmatic, tough and independent Presbyterian followers found shape in this singular document. It enshrined radicalism and the idea of justice for all. Personal liberty was something that could only be guaranteed, it was felt, by the ownership of land. Back on the island of Ireland, rent-racking and the continual threat of eviction was driving more and more to throw in their lot with fate and head across the Atlantic. It was natural that the right to carve out a life went hand in hand with the right to carve out a smallholding.

I often reflect that eight of the original signatories to the Declaration of Independence were of Ulster Scots Presbyterian stock. Charles Thomson left Upperland in County Londonderry at the age of ten. His house is still there and still lived in. He was the secretary of the American Continental Congress from 1774 until 1789. It was Thomson who wrote the great document in his own hand and went on to create the Great Seal of his new country by incorporating an eagle. The order for the Declaration to be written was given by John Hancock from County Down and it was printed by John Dunlap from Strabane, near Artigarvan, as explained earlier. All three gentlemen were Presbyterians.

In his log cabin settlement in the Waxhaws, Andrew Jackson, just nine years old, was chosen to read the Declaration of Independence to his gathered compatriots. Jackson was destined to share the troubles of his nation from an early age. In 1780, when he was twelve, he witnessed the massacre of American patriots by British forces. The British were led by a man who could have been dreamed up by Hollywood as the archetypal English villain; refined, cruel and cold. Colonel Banastre Tarleton was dispatched into the rebellious countryside by the British commander, Lieutenant General Lord Cornwallis. The War of Independence was in full swing and the Americans were divided into patriots, who saw their future as purely American, unimpaired by the high taxation that Britain had decided was their lot, and loyalists.

Loyalists, as their name suggests, were loyal to the British crown and saw America as a subject colony of Britain. In this sense, although the long war was, in many ways, the world war of its time, played out in the theatre of America, involving Britain, France and, to a degree, Spain, as well as the new Americans, it was also a civil war. This schism was continued after independence was won, in the split between those nationalists who wanted America to carve her own path, and those who saw Britain as the originating motherland and, therefore, a good trading partner.

In 1780, however, trading with Britain was not first and foremost in patriotic American minds. While the loyalists were fighting with the British to subdue patriotic rebellion, the Ulster Scots of the Waxhaws were doing their best to promote it. 'Bloody Ban', as Banastre was known, had been delegated to further subjugate the locals, after the capture of Charleston and the resounding British win at Camden. When American soldiers fleeing the fighting took refuge in Waxhaws, they were pursued by Banastre and his men. There the patriots were butchered, before the eyes of the locals, including Jackson. Jackson himself was attacked sadistically. Seen as a mere boy, he was caught and ordered by an officer to polish his boots. When Jackson refused to submit to this humiliation, the officer slashed Jackson's face with his sabre, scarring it for life.

The lack of mercy shown contributed to the undoing of the British. The locals were not inclined to bow their heads in the face of such barbarity. Instead, they took up arms and engaged in a new style of fighting at the battle of King's Mountain at which, you may remember, three Lairds were killed fighting for freedom against the British. What they lacked in soldierly experience, the rebels made up for with stealth, determination and common sense. The patriots' win was convincing and Lord Cornwallis was forced back to Charleston. A second win at the battle of Cowpens effectively finished the British off for good in America.

Later, Jackson trained for two years as a lawyer in Salisbury, South Carolina. It might be considered that a natural desire for justice drove Andrew Jackson to pursue this career. However, accounts suggest that the young Jackson was headstrong and rowdy, and inclined towards womanising. He moved to Tennessee, to the Cumberland River, where he was able to make a good living for himself. Here he met his future wife, Rachel Robards, who was then inconveniently married to another man. After her separation from her husband, she settled with Jackson and the pair stayed together for life.

Jackson thrived in Tennessee and had a hand in making it the state that it became. He drafted its constitution and was elected to serve as its first representative in Congress in 1796. He later served in the Senate. In 1812, Jackson had another dose of the British. This time, he was a grown man and a major general. His antipathy towards the bullies of his youth had not faded and he had the satisfaction of leading the defeat of their army at the Battle of New Orleans. This win made him a national name and lined him up for his later presidential career. Only a year previously, he had won his first major battle of Horseshoe Bend. Those fighting under him included two others who were to play their own parts in American history. One was Sam Houston, also of Scots-Irish heritage, from the Shenandoah Valley in Virginia. The other was Davy Crockett, frontier scout and identified elsewhere as an Ulsterman. Jackson, pugnacious and determined, was a natural contender in politics. He had done well in his career, building himself a mansion near Nashville. His key political rival was John Caldwell Calhoun, although the two were initially colleagues. Both had suffered under the British and both had their own vision of America's future. Jackson believed in a unified nation; Calhoun championed the rights of the individual state. When 'Old Hickory', as Jackson has been known, finally made it to the White House in 1829, Calhoun was his first vice-president.

Jackson's most obvious legacy was the Democrat party. One of his first concerns as president was the democratisation of the political process. He targeted the system of patronage that tended to determine the outcome of a political career. He looked for straightforward dealings in government and opposed the retention of power by elite factions. His approach polarised the American

Republican party into the Democratic Republicans – Jackson's party – and the National Republicans, or Whigs. These became known as the Democrat and Republican parties.

Jackson was prepared to fight for what he believed in, and to fight hard. To counter his national appeal, his Whig adversaries looked for a similarly gifted heroic figure. They chose Davy Crockett. Crockett's own exploits with frontier wildlife was promoted as a counter to Jackson's more straightforward success on the nation's battlefields. However, his career in Congress was short-lived. Whatever his success rate with grizzly bears, he was no match for Old Hickory. It was Crockett's destiny to achieve his enduring place in his nation's roll of heroes as the defender of the Alamo, not as a president.

Andrew Jackson never bowed to Congress. As president, he held power of veto and he used this effectively. He opposed what he felt was the undue power of high finance, in the form of the Second Bank of the United States. In this, he had the support of a majority of the American people. Validated by his citizens, Jackson had both the moral and political authority to impose his will on his nation. Keen to ensure his legacy, he put not only his immediate successor in place, Martin Van Buren, but also recommended those who should succeed him.

Martin Van Buren's name does not spring to mind so rapidly as Jackson's in the list of all-time great American presidents. Neither was he of Ulster Scots descent; he was from a family of Dutch immigrants. However, Jackson's last designated successor was Scots-Irish; James Knox Polk. He became the eleventh American president in 1845, the year of Andrew Jackson's death.

Polk was born in 1795, near Charlotte, in Mecklenburg County in North Carolina. His great-grandfather, Robert Bruce Pollock, came from Lifford in County Donegal to America in 1680. Pollock is a familiar name in that area, which is just six miles from Artigarvan. Indeed, I have relations of that name in my background. For reasons unknown, in America the name Pollock was shortened to Polk.

I have taken some time considering the life of America's first Ulster Scots presidents. They pioneered high ideals of freedom. If you are interested in history as much as I am, and you would like to read more on the history of the Ulster Scots and leadership in America, then please turn to the back of this volume. There you will find a highly edifying appendix; the Presidents' Trail. But remember to read the rest of this as well.

Also around this period, I became aware of the importance of the work of the 'Bard of Tyrone', W. F. Marshall. The Reverend Mr Marshall was the Presbyterian minister in the County Tyrone area of Sixmilecross, not far from Omagh. When two or three Tyrone people get together of an evening, with a few drinks, one of the Bard's poems, usually 'I was living in Drumlister and I'm clabber to the knees', is sure to be invoked. For me, one of his poems sums up our Ulster Scots relationship with the early times in America. 'The Ulsterman was there' places the role of Ulstermen into context.

Hi! Uncle Sam!
When freedom was denied you,
And Imperial might defied you,
Who was it stood beside you,
At Quebec and Brandywine?
And dared retreats and dangers
Redcoats and Hessian strangers
In the lean, long-rifled Rangers,
And the Pennsylvania Line!

Hi! Uncle Sam!
Wherever there was fighting,
Or wrongs that needed righting,
An Ulsterman was sighting,
His Kentucky gun with care:
All the road to Yorktown,
From Lexington to Yorktown,

From Valley Forge to Yorktown
That Ulsterman was there!

Hi! Uncle Sam
Virginia sent her brave men,
The North paraded grave men,
That they might not be slavemen,
But ponder this with calm;
The first to face the Tory
And the first to lift Old Glory,
Made your war an Ulster story,
Think it over, Uncle Sam!

These beautifully framed lines express the role of the Ulster Scots in the creation of modern America. But it makes the point that we Ulster Scots are prepared to take on all who would stand in our way, regardless of the odds, in order to obtain freedom. A strong message which cannot be repeated enough. Note that by 'all' we *mean* 'all', if necessary.

CHAPTER SIX

The Noble Lord

THE LORDS IS A DROP-IN CENTRE FOR THE ELDERLY

ANONYMOUS

THURSDAY 26TH MAY 1998 was a typical day in May, a warm, pleasant day when it is just good to be alive. I turned my car into a road that bordered Downpatrick Cricket Ground. I was on my way to address a committee of Down District Council at their office about half a mile out that road. The mobile phone rang and I slowed into the Cricket Ground Entrance to answer. It was my very old friend, Jim Nicholson who, for the previous ten years, had been one of the Members of the European Parliament (MEPs) for Northern Ireland. Jim was a member of the band of Young Unionists from the 1960s who seemed to graduate through all the stages of Unionism together. Each went on to play an important part in local politics. Others included Dennis Rogan, Reginald Empey, Dermot Nesbitt, James Rodgers, Fraser Agnew, David McNarry, Clifford Smyth, Roy Garland, John Taylor, Jack Allen, David Burnside, James Stewart, James Speers, Raymond Ferguson, Kenneth Latimer, Mervyn Bishop and Edmund Curran. The latter's fame came not through politics but through journalism.

I first met Jim in 1966 one Saturday afternoon at an obscure Orange hall somewhere near Markethill. Unionists in County Armagh were different. They still could be today. I suppose every area has aspects that make its political people view life differently. The Armagh folk hold their meetings on either Saturday afternoon, if not so important, or in the evening time, if important. At this stage, I was a senior young Unionist, if that is not an oxymoron. I was an office bearer of the Ulster Young Unionist Council and we thought we were important. The officer team attended meetings all around the province and, pompously, lectured the membership on aspects of Unionism. We, as Ulster Unionists, were on the move at that stage and many meetings were well attended. Sometimes they were full of young female Unionists who were looking for young males or who were acting as a shotgun against any preying specimens of the first type.

Jim Nicholson is a farmer's son. Tall, at that stage very thin, wearing a too small jacket, he had blood on his neck and on the collar of his shirt. I decided that was from rushing to shave to attend the event after a morning on the farm.

Fast forward to 1998 and Jim Nicholson was asking me about the state of my health. Once that pleasantry was dealt with, he asked if there was anyone with me. I said there was not. He explained that because we were talking on a mobile phone he had to be a bit obscure. Jim assured me that he was phoning in behalf of the 'top man', if I understood what he meant. At the request of 'the top man', would I allow myself to be sent to where there were red seats?' I was aware enough about politics to put an interpretation on the words which, while seeming to be totally ridiculous, turned out to be correct.

I have a habit, which annoys even me at times, and that is to try and make a stupid remark that is intended to be funny. As an Arsenal supporter, I replied: 'why would Arsene Wenger want me to go to the Ritz Picture House?' At one time it had red seats.

Jim said he was not joking. He was never as serious as now. The MEP continued: 'I will ring you tomorrow morning from a land line and we can talk better.' We exchanged goodbyes.

What a way to end a phone conversation! Was I being invited to accept a seat in the Lords? If the top man was David Trimble, the Ulster Unionist Party leader, as I suspected, then what was it that was being asked of me? But I could be making a complete fool of myself. I could let my mind go haywire and end up as a laughing stock of my friends and family. What would such a misunderstanding do for my self-confidence if I acted upon it?

In a fog of excitement and disbelief, I finished my short journey to Down District Council office and had my meeting with members and staff. All day I had felt that the meeting would be difficult. But on my cloud of disbelief and excitement, I flew through all the difficult points about planning permission for a supermarket in the town, with the grace of a small feather being blown by the wind. And I was most likely as effective.

Next morning came the landline call from Jim Nicholson. He outlined a short series of events that had brought about the previous day's conversation. The referendum on the Belfast Agreement, which had just been signed in April, took place on 23rd May. David Trimble, the courageous leader of the Ulster Unionist Party was, according to opinion polling by the Northern Ireland Office, expected not to obtain a majority of Unionist votes for the agreement. That would be a disaster. I decided to support the agreement for reasons that I will come to. I was taking time away from my business to support the party's yes campaign. My deputy in the agency was Jane Wells, who was on her way to becoming one of the most outstanding public relations people ever produced by Northern Ireland; more of Jane later. In the meantime, she was 'on loan' to David Trimble for the election period. The referendum was followed by an election for yet another Northern Ireland Assembly; the third such institution. Jane had developed an interest in politics partly through working for John Laird Public Relations on behalf of Jim Nicholson every month in Strasbourg.

Through a series of clever electioneering ideas, when the poll took place, well over 50% of Unionists had voted for the agreement. I pay tribute to Tim Attwood, of the SDLP, who, in my view, produced the poll's winning event. He had the idea of running a concert in the Waterfront Hall with many individuals and groups playing music that would appeal mostly to younger voters. He enlisted Bono of U2 fame to take part in the event. The photo-call came when Bono asked John Hume, leader of the SDLP, and David Trimble to join him on stage. Pictures of the three holding hands above their heads ran round the world the next day. More importantly, the event and the photographs went down well in the province. Well done, Tim Attwood.

Most of the Ulster Unionist Members of Parliament were opposed to the Belfast Agreement and worked hard for the 'No' vote. The day of the announcement of the result and the victory of Trimble and his fellow 'Yes' campaigners brought much excitement and jubilation to the Unionist Party leadership, which had been under stress. At politically active times, usually on a Friday night, the boardroom in Glengall Street, Unionist headquarters, acted as a meeting place. The idea was to reflect on the recent events, consider future steps and to consume as much wine as possible.

On the landline, my old friend Jim Nicholson painted a picture for me of one such debriefing the night before. From memory, the gathering included David Trimble, David Campbell, a well respected party member, Dennis Rogan, the party chairman and a long time friend of mine, Jack Allen, party treasurer, and Nicholson himself. The mood could not have been better. One subject that amused them was the disarray amongst the MPs who had supported the 'No' camp. While toasting every possible cause, someone said that the party must be due some recognition from the Prime Minister, Tony Blair. After all, against the odds, the Trimble team had delivered a 'Yes' vote amongst Unionists. 'It is years since we had anyone appointed to the Lords,' someone added.

Trimble reflected, indicated he took the general point and that Blair could not refuse him any reasonable request. 'I think I should ask for two lords and two knights,' the leader is reported to have said. All knew that the lords, if appointed, would help to even out the Yes/No balance of the parliamentary party at Westminster. The saga continued. 'Who could we appoint to the Lords?' was the general question. I think that David had already decided on his selection for the knighthoods. Lordships were different because with that honour came an important job based in London. Somewhere in the discussion, Jim Nicholson threw in my name. My understanding of events, from Jim, is that there was a lengthy discussion about other names but at its end the only one which Trimble and his group agreed upon was that of me. If true, it is very flattering. We only gain a sense of worth from the members of the group in which we operate. The leader, there and then, requested Nicholson to phone me and ask my view. And that was the background to the mobile phone conversation on the outskirts of Downpatrick.

Following the landline call, which had confirmed that the House of Lords was involved, my poor brain went into overdrive. The implications of such an appointment would be massive. Being a political animal, the idea of being in the British Parliament with no elections to face seemed like heaven. It seemed unreal. The concept of a title, let alone of 'Lord' was secondary. I felt very pleased, but from the perspective of my family, living and dead. One of the very first things I did was to check what the title implications were for my close family. If I were to become a peer, Carol's title would be 'The Lady Laird' of whatever the territorial name selected would be. The use of 'the' in Carol's name is important. It denotes that she is the wife of a peer as opposed to a baronet or knight, in which case the title would be 'Lady Blogs'. Interestingly, our children Alison and David would also have titles, which, as for Carol, were for their lifetimes. Both the next generation would become 'The Honourable' Alison or David Laird. The peerage is one of the oldest institutions in the United Kingdom and so is based on tradition. The Lords itself dates from the early thirteenth century where a council of barons was created to check the activities of King John, following the signing of Magna Carta. The system of titles is still based on a tradition that gives precedence to males. Despite women being amongst the members of the chamber, since the mid twentieth century, the title system remains the same. I discovered in the frantic days of May 1998 is that while both my offspring would be called 'The

Honourable' only David, as the son, confers that title upon his wife through marriage. Daughters' husbands remain untitled!

Jim Nicholson and the events that he had outlined were flying around in my mind. It was even difficult to work. On a strictly confidential basis, I should now advise my family and close friends of this potentially life-changing option. Carol was away with friends on that critical day, so the first to be taken into confidence was Len O'Hagan. I had known Len about six years at that stage. He comes from South Down and has an impressive record at managing businesses and unusual situations involving business. Len and his wife Maureen have become close friends of Carol and I over the years.

On the 'telephone line day' I had lunch with Len to discuss client issues. Over the coffee, I explained the events of the last two days and Len listened. When I got to the point, he said, with surprise in his voice: 'You in the Lords?' Back in my office on the Holywood Road, I felt that I had to begin to look at the business implications. My number two was the previously mentioned Jane Wells, a former schoolteacher who had transferred to the world of public relations ten years before. Jane had also become a close confidante over the years. She is outstanding at her work and has a most engaging personality.

I went through the events again and, just when I was reaching the point, Jane said in a loud voice: 'You in the Lords?' At closing time, I went home and poured some refreshment with Carol when she returned from the social arrangements. For the third time that day, I went through the events. Just when the conclusion was in sight, Carol enquired: 'You in the Lords?' I may have been in a state of excitement but even I could see a pattern emerging. If I had not been so sure of my conversation with Nicholson, I might have panicked. Anyway; I understood the chorus: 'You in the Lords?' I felt like that too.

The next day, I met David Trimble in a corridor in Unionist headquarters. He said he wanted a private word. The only place available was a large stationery store. Amongst the paperclips, surrounded by rubber bands and with the smell of paper, the leader explained the request to allow my name to be submitted to the process that selects peers. Being a careful, thoughtful type, I pretended to consider the issue for point nought nought nought one of a second before I indicated that I consented to allow such a process to begin. Any doubt was now gone. Politically I could understand that the Prime Minister owed Trimble. Two places in the Lords was small beer to the government. Now began the process of waiting.

In May 1999, to the day, the very first anniversary of the phone call from Jim Nicholson, I received the following letter from Tony Blair:

IN CONFIDENCE

10 DOWNING STREET
LONDON SW1A 2AA

THE PRIME MINISTER

24 May 1999

Dear Mr. Laird

I am writing to let you know that I have recommended to The Queen that a Barony of the United Kingdom for life be conferred upon you.

Should The Queen approve this recommendation, your Life Peerage will be announced on Friday 28 May in a supplement to the London Gazette; details of the Working Peer List will be released to the press on Thursday 27 May, under embargo until midnight.

Your title would be settled on a recommendation from Garter King of Arms who will get in touch with you in due course.

Yours sincerely

Tony Blair

John Laird Esq

IN CONFIDENCE

The dye was cast. It was all official. My name and that of another member of the party had been accepted by the appointment process and we were to take seats in the House of Lords. The waiting was over. One of the most important events in my life, in anyone's life, was underway.

Things began to move fast after that slow endless year of anticipation. The other party member was Dennis Rogan. I had guessed at his involvement about six months before and I was proved right. I first met Dennis at the end of 1964 in Young Unionist circles. He was a leading part of the young Turks who thought that they should inherit the Unionist Party, and more if possible. Dennis is a Presbyterian, originally from Dromore in County Down. I am blessed with very good sincere friends. Dennis stars right at the top of such a list. I had the pleasure of being his best man in August 1968 when, in Woodvale Presbyterian Church, he married his longstanding girlfriend, Lorna Colgan.

Rogan is a typical Ulsterman. He is honest and hard working. As with many of his background, while being kind and generous, he has not been known to spend money without much soul searching and careful consideration. His many friends sometimes think that process also applies to the dispensing of semi confidential information. I was delighted to be going into such a strange institution with a lifelong good friend. When moving to a big school from a junior one, it is very reassuring to be with your best friend.

Dennis and I were called to London to meet senior Lords staff, see over the place and to be interviewed by Garter Principal King of Arms. I took my son David with me so that the day might live in family history. The Palace of Westminster, the grand home of the House of Lords, was intimidating. The whole place underlines the wealth of the British Empire in the mid-nineteenth century, when it was built. All tourists see the outside but the inside takes anyone's breath away. It is more than the building material. It is composed of history and atmosphere. It would be impossible to be a rebel in a place like that. The individual is weighted down by tradition and by history.

It is believed that the spot had been the site of Parliament since the mid-thirteenth century. A fire in 1834 had burnt down the original building, which Guy Fawkes had tried to blow up in 1605. The older version of the Lords Chamber was at right angles to the river Thames. The later format, with almost 1200 rooms and 100 staircases, is still in use today. It is of a much grander style, with the two chambers at either end of ornate lobbies that now run parallel to the river Thames. They are placed in such a way that the Speaker in the Commons can see the throne when the doors in between are open. Saint Stephen's Hall, the site of the old House of Commons, exists today as a passageway. The vast construction known as Westminster Hall was saved at the time of the big 1834 fire by the efforts of citizens and guards. While the two houses that made up Parliament were burning down, a crowd gathered outside and cheered! Could something like that happen today?

For Dennis, son David and I, the most interesting part of the London visit was about to take place. We hailed one of the many hackney carriages, otherwise known as cabs, and headed towards the Embankment to meet Garter Principal King of Arms. This is the gentleman who is responsible for peerage titles. His office dates back to 1415. His responsibilities include the creation and documentation of all official coats of arms. As at a dentist, I was taken first. So David and I were shown into an office that looked like something out of the Dickens era. Amongst the dust and piles of papers, some rolled up, some not, we located two chairs. Facing us was a most friendly and correct gentleman. 'Let me tell you about titles in the rank of baron'. He explained that he could change totally my surname by using the territorial title that all peers must have, as my family name. The system is that a peer has to be 'of' some place. In my case, because I was to have the rank of baron, the area must become a barony.

'Artigarvan is the location that I would like for my title,' I responded when asked. 'Artigarvan!' Garter shouted back at me. 'Where is that?' For a few moments, I considered doing one of my attempts at humour by commenting on the poor educational system in England, which allowed people to leave school without basic geography. Thankfully, I ignored my instinct and described the beautiful country of West Tyrone, with its rolling green hills and the small hamlet of Artigarvan slumbering peacefully in their midst. 'The area just cannot be a telephone box you know,' Garter observed. 'It must be a place marked as a distinct area on Ordnance Survey maps.' He dispatched his secretary to check, from the usual sources, the existence of the Tyrone location and, importantly, whether it was already is a barony, dukedom, or whatever. During the wait, he asked me if I had any questions. Wishing to take up some time, I asked about titles for Alison and David. The latter was sitting beside me. Garter turned his stare to my son and in a voice more suited to an army parade ground, enquired: 'Are you legitimate?' My stunned offspring turned to me and asked: 'Am I legitimate?' Even by the standards of the House of Lords, this was a strange question. I explained that in my opinion he was, but I was prepared to put the question to Carol! After a surprisingly short time, Garter's secretary returned. I was in luck. Artigarvan 'existed' and was available. It was difficult to understand why no one wanted the title before I did. There and then, in front of our eyes, Garter Principal King of Arms signed documents that started the process of turning the Tyrone area from a hamlet, or village, into a barony. And no one in Artigarvan was asked about the change of designation or even knew anything about it.

Anything to do with the House of Lords is steeped in history and if an event is taking place there, then it is carried out with military precision. The process of becoming a peer is a case in point. The events involved in turning my life upside-down were underway. After the selection of my territorial title came the decision that I was to be referred to in the House as 'The Lord Laird'. My actual name was to be 'The Lord Laird of Artigarvan'. I could have taken 'The Lord Artigarvan', or 'The Lord Laird of Artigarvan' for parliamentary use but I was happy with 'The Lord Laird'. As a courtesy, I am entitled to the prefix 'The Right Honourable'. That, I hardly ever use.

Right from the start, my basic idea was to make the Lords more accessible to the people of my native province. Up to that point, as someone interested in things political, I had not taken much notice of House of Lords activities. I certainly did not relate to it. To make the Upper House better known back home, I needed to retain the name Laird. This would help to make me seem like the ordinary person that I always hoped I was. I was conscious that some people might be jealous. Some might think that I had ideas above my station. Others might try to avoid me, perhaps out of a sense of misplaced embarrassment. I was not going to change. Why should I? The Lords was an important job and I was determined to do it to the best of my ability. Only in that way could I be fair to the many in Northern Ireland who are better qualified to be in the British Parliament and who could have been appointed instead of me.

The other place that I wish to make accessible to more people is Artigarvan. I hoped that by my use of the territorial title I would put my ancestral home area on the map. I hope, too, that the majority of people in Artigarvan are pleased with the use of the name. I feel that I have also honoured both my father and my mother. One of the disappointments of life is that successful developments tend to happen in later life when your parents are dead. What I would give to be able to tell my incredulous parents that, for all intents and purposes, Carol and I could be regarded as members of the aristocracy! What would my mother have said to learn that she had a son who was 'The Lord of the Barony of Artigarvan'? Would my father and his ancestors ever think that one of their Laird number could be ennobled? A strange point is that laird can mean lord in Scots or Ulster Scots languages. In the deferential Protestant community of County Fermanagh there was a respect verging on hat-doffing to those with titles. Carol and I were often to wonder what her parents, Willie John and Wee Mary Kate, would make of one of their daughters becoming 'the Lady', in this case, 'Laird'. Could they take it in? Anyway, the next job was to continue the process of being ennobled and this time my part was to be minimal.

The Great Seal of State is like a massive rubber stamp, but one made of metal. It is rarely used, except to indicate royal approval of something that has been conferred. Examples are the designation of city status, the conferring of the title 'Royal' on an organisation, or the granting of a peerage. Dennis and I were informed that on 16th July 1999 in the forenoon, in my case, and the afternoon in his case, our status would change to that of peers of the realm forever. On the appointed morning, Carol and I went about our business sorting out an apartment that we had purchased in Surrey Quays, as the London base. I felt nothing different but, as the clock announced noon, the Lord and the Lady Laird clinked two glasses full of white wine and drank to the future.

I am conscious that I have dedicated much space to my elevation. In any listing of things that have affected a life, I think it is not unreasonable to note a peerage. Because receiving one is not in the usual run of things, I hope that I can be forgiven for explaining the process and my feelings at the time. Being a member of the British Parliament is very important to me. Having a title is not. I am trying to be clinical about this point. As a human being, clearly I get pleasure out of being a lord. I am particularly pleased for my family, living and dead. I look upon myself as being family-orientated and so am delighted that Carol, Alison and David have titles for their lifetimes.

On 22nd July 1999, Dennis and I were introduced into the House of Lords. The ceremony takes place at the start of a sitting and only two newcomers are allowed per day. For the first time in the long history of that famous place, the same pair of supporters introduced two new peers. Separately, in full red ermine finery, Dennis and I were paraded into the chamber by Lord Molyneaux and Lord Cooke of Islandreagh. Both were members of the Ulster Unionist Party. Lord Molyneaux of Hillead had been its previous leader. I have known Jim, as I called him, since the mid 1960s. I presented my warrant to the Clerk. The warrant is sent on behalf of the Queen to summon an individual to Parliament. It was read aloud and so too was the Royal Proclamation; this is the nearest thing that exists to make manifest, in physical form, a peerage. Following this I took the oath, was paraded around the chamber, doffed my hat to the Lord Chancellor, was welcomed by cheers of 'hear hear' and then departed to the Royal Robing Room for the official pictures. My close family and friends, sixteen in all, watched the whole proceedings from the gallery. A day to remember!

Now I started the process of setting up arrangements to attend my new place of work on every possible sitting day. London always had a particular appeal for me. Like many throughout the land, we were brought up with pictures of the grandeur of our capital city. When the Laird family obtained a television in 1953, for the Coronation, the whole place seemed to come alive. Despite the very poor quality of the television picture, compared with those of today, I became familiar with all the main attractions. Buckingham Palace, Piccadilly Circus, Trafalgar Square and Parliament Buildings at Westminster all became recognisable at a quick glance. As a senior Young Unionist, and later as a computer programmer for my employers, I visited London on regular basis. Usually only for a day, but I found those trips exciting and magical. I suspect that I am not alone in this respect.

London is my national capital. I feel at home there. And I am not the first Ulster Scot to do so. Folks from my background have played their part in the development of the empire that was administered from the city on the Thames. Whether the British Empire was a good thing or not is a debate for another and longer day. It is a historical fact that the Ulster Scots role in it was disproportionate to the size of the ethnic group. One figure stands out when considering London. The name is Hans Sloane, after whom Sloane Square is named.

Born in Killyleagh in County Down in 1660, Hans was the son of a planter transferred to Ulster by King James I in the earlier part of that century. He was imbued with the Scottish desire for education. Sloane's early travels took him to London and on to France. There he qualified as a physician. Later the County Down Ulster Scot travelled further afield, including to the West Indies. His main interest was in the collection of all things that nature could produce. On returning to London, his collection expanded vastly. He was a colleague of Sir Isaac Newton and he became a Fellow of the Royal Society. Another of his claims to fame is that he invented drinking chocolate, something for which many people still thank him. Sloane died in 1753 but not before he had donated his huge collection of nature's creations to form the British Museum. I often wonder if many people from Northern Ireland, when visiting the British Museum, know that it owes its foundation to an Ulster Scot from Killyleagh.

The House of Lords, and to an extent the Commons, are run in a military fashion. The majority of peers have had some kind of military experience. But more than that, the historical pictures and busts provide a militaristic atmosphere. I am not opposed to such things. My part is in the present and, it is to be hoped, in shaping the future. However, the toughness engendered by the Ulster Scots background has been used to the nation's advantage for many centuries. Just as in the American War of Independence and the War of Northern Aggression, also known as the American Civil War, Ulstermen played a vital leadership role in Britain. It can further be argued that the Ulster hand was to the fore in the development of the British Empire.

Whatever the imperial role of the Ulster Scots, they certainly played a role in defending the United Kingdom. Of Britain's generals during the Second World War, quite a number had Ulster Scots origins. And of these, the most famous was Field Marshal Montgomery.

Bernard 'Monty' Montgomery was born in London in 1887, the son of the Right Reverend Bishop Henry Montgomery, of Moville in County Donegal. By the time war broke out in 1939, Monty had already served in the armed forces for thirty-one years. As was true of many officers of his day, his early career was forged in India. The Great War saw him posted to France, where he was seriously injured in 1914. Although he did not return to duty until halfway through the war, by 1918 Montgomery was Chief of Staff of the 47th London Division.

By the beginning of the Second World War, Montgomery was a major general; again, he was initially sent to France. By 1942, he was commanding the South Eastern army. The Germans, however, were closing on Alexandria, a key Egyptian port in the eastern

Mediterranean. This situation was so urgent that Winston Churchill himself, the war leader and the most famous Briton of the century, travelled to Egypt to consider his options. His solution was to appoint Montgomery commander of the Eighth Army. This decision was to lead to Erwin Rommel's defeat at El Alamein; a defeat that was to turn the tide of the war. In Churchill's words: 'Before Alamein we never had a victory; after Alamein we never had a defeat.' It was the outcome of this battle that made such an impression on my mother, back in 1942. 'The Germans are in full retreat.' Do I owe my existence to Bernard Montgomery?

Despite being born in London, Montgomery's roots were very much in Ulster. Just after the end of the Second World War, a small group of young men wrote to the Field Marshal to ask his permission to use his name for their newly formed pipe band. Monty gave his blessing to the Field Marshal Montgomery Pipe Band – and sent them a ten shilling note towards band funds. Today this band is a world leader in Scottish piping circles.

Interestingly, Montgomery's fellow general at El Alamein was also blessed with an Ulster Scots heritage. Harold Alexander's origins were aristocratic; he was the third son of the Earl of Caledon. Again, he was born in London, but raised in Ulster; at Caledon, County Tyrone.

Commanding the British 1st Division in 1940, he oversaw the evacuation from Dunkirk, being the last man to leave the beaches. After the North Africa Campaign, he led the invasion of Sicily, before becoming Commander-in-Chief of Allied forces in Italy. After the war, as Field Marshal Earl Alexander of Tunis, he served as Governor-General of Canada, from 1946 to 1952. He then became Churchill's Minister of Defence in the early 1950s.

In my view, Rudyard Kipling was the most famous British poet of the time. In his history of the Irish Guards (in which his son fought and died), he wrote of Alexander: 'It is undeniable that Colonel Alexander had the gift of handling the men on the lines to which they most readily responded; as the many tales in this connection testify. At the worst crises he was both inventive and cordial and, on such occasions as they all strove together in the gates of Death, would somehow contrive to dress the affair as high comedy. Moreover, when the blame for some incident of battle or fatigue was his, he confessed and took it upon his own shoulders in the presence of all. Consequently, his subordinates loved him, even when he fell upon them blisteringly for their shortcomings; and his men were all his own.' (From The Irish Guards in the Great War, Vol. 2)

Popularity amongst fellow soldiers was not enough to further an officer's career, however. Prime Minister Churchill himself took an active interest in the deployment of his generals. If he didn't get along with you, you could find yourself with a very distant posting, as Field Marshal Sir John Dill discovered. Nicknames for officers not tending towards originality, Dill was known as 'Jack'. Born in 1881, he hailed from Lurgan, County Armagh. His career took him to India and Palestine, as well as including time as a staff instructor at military colleges; Dill became commandant of Staff College Camberley. Eventually, in 1942, Churchill posted Dill to Washington as his personal representative, where he became head of the British Joint Staff Mission. This was his position when he died of anaemia in 1944. So sorry were his American colleagues by his death that the American Chief of Staff to the Commander-in-Chief of the Army and Navy composed the following memorandum, for delivery by President Roosevelt:

> 'I am deeply distressed to learn of the death of Field Marshal Sir John Dill whom I regarded not only as a great soldier but as a most important figure in the remarkable accord which has been developed in the combined operations of our two countries.'

Another Ulster general had the misfortune to be replaced in his post by two of his above-mentioned countrymen. A third approved his replacement. Auchinleck, 'the Auk', earned his stripes in the Indian army. He was a fluent Punjabi speaker, known for his affinity with his Indian soldiers. The Second World War saw him relocated to Norway, then back to India, before becoming

Commander-in-Chief of Middle East Command and Temporary General Officer commanding the Eighth Army.

Auchinleck's popularity in India was not matched in Downing Street, however. Churchill decided to install Bernard Montgomery in his place. Very senior officers, however, were not disposable; they were merely transferred somewhere considered less critical. In 1941, Auchinleck was made Commander-in-Chief of the Indian Army, a post he held until 1947, when he became Supreme Commander in India and Pakistan.

Auchinleck was succeeded as Commander-in-Chief of Middle East Command by Harold Alexander. A Lieutenant-General Gott succeeded him as Temporary General Officer commanding the Eighth Army. Gott was killed before taking command; the post then went to Bernard Montgomery. In replacing Auchinleck in Egypt, Churchill relied on the advice of the Chief of Imperial General Staff, Alan Brooke. (Brooke, in turn, had replaced fellow-countryman, Sir John Dill!)

'Brookie', the man who became Field Marshal Alan Francis Brooke, 1st Viscount Alanbrooke, was born in 1883 in France, and raised there. His father, however, hailed from County Fermanagh and his mother from County Louth. As a fluent French speaker, a great deal of Brooke's early soldiering career took place in France. He also served as an instructor in army training colleges, which was effectively a great networking opportunity. In the selection of his peerage title, he chose to include his first name as part of this new surname. Much later, when selecting his title for the Lords, Merlin Rees, the former Northern Ireland Secretary, took the same course and became Lord Merlin Rees.

Brooke was offered command of British forces in the Middle East in 1942. In his diaries, which were published years after the war in the late 1950s, he made it clear that he felt it important to stay close to Churchill. The Prime Minister, stubborn and belligerent, needed handling as well as sound advice, and Brooke considered himself the only man for the job. And if Brooke was critical of his nation's leader, he was critical, too, of his peers, including Alexander. Churchill read the diaries years later; he is not reputed to have been a great fan.

Unsurprisingly, Brooke's political mind was well suited to life in peacetime. Brooke retired from active service in 1946 and served as a director of several international companies. He became Chancellor of Belfast University in 1949. In the 1990s, a statue of Viscount Alanbrooke was erected alongside one of Montgomery outside the Ministry of Defence in London, marking for posterity the contribution of two Ulstermen at their country's great time of need.

If these military transfers and replacements look like a high-powered game of musical chairs, it only reflected the degree of strategic thinking necessary at the time. What is truly remarkable is that so many of the key players in Britain's defence were proud to call themselves Ulstermen. Northern Ireland's part in the Second War was much more than withstanding the air raids and the full scale manufacturing of ammunitions. They were to be found at all levels in the forces, many serving with great distinction. Many volumes have been dedicated to them over recent years.

There can be no doubt that the House of Lords is a very odd place. There are around 730 peers who are known as 'peers of Parliament' and thus able to attend, take part and vote etc. Thank goodness only about 250 to 300 attend on the average day. A weakness of the system is that to be called a lord is considered to be a great honour. Thus too many people wish to be appointed and then run back to their professions, which include business, and become ever more successful. These peers rarely attend. I think that this approach is totally incorrect. If you have been accepted as a worthy person to be appointed a peer, then you should do the job as a member of the British Parliament to the best of one's ability, which includes attending on a very regular basis. The House bristles with experts on almost every topic of which anyone could imagine. Some of the experts are world famous figures in their sphere of activity. While I sit back and listen to them in awe, I am forced to recognise that my position on the existence of the House is compromised.

While the House was flooded with hereditary peers, it was hard to justify intellectually. Being appointed to Parliament solely on account of your father cannot be correct. I am conscious that I was elected to the Northern Ireland House of Commons on the death of my father and, it could be argued, on who he was. I accept the point but respond that at least I was elected in a full election in which anyone could take part. Today, all but ninety-two of the current House of Lords are appointed as life peers, just like me. The rest, non-lifers, are elected from their own number, in a fashion similar to the Irish peers at the time of the Act of Union, which became effective in 1801.

The main point to remember about the Westminster system of government is that, for the last hundred years, the most important chamber has been the Commons. This is because it is elected on a regular basis, with never more that five years from one election to the next. Since the early twentieth century, the House of Lords has had no role in the collection or allocations of taxes. Also, in the passing of bills (to become acts of Parliament) the Upper Chamber's opposition can be overridden by the Commons. On the positive side, experts in the Lords are able to contribute in an important way to debates on every topic. Unlike our friends in the other place, there is no way of cutting down a debate by not considering amendments. This means that there is considerable scrutiny to all proposed changes of the law. It is the belief of many, including myself, that the standard of debate is much higher in the Lords than in the Commons. The reason being that, with no elections and being in the place for the rest of one's life, rough issues of day-to-day party politics very rarely, if ever, intrude. Not for us the joys of cat-calling, interrupting the opposition and trying to get the better of a political enemy. Provided the eternal reaper is not too eager on our benches, the peer opposite will be in his or her seat again, when the dust settles after a general election.

Everyone in the Palace of Westminster is pleasant and helpful. The staff, at all grades, is made up of very fine people. In fact, I prefer the staff to the members, some of whom, while being friendly, are full of their own importance. I do my best to open the palace to anyone who is interested, in particular if they come from Northern Ireland. On a regular basis, I take parties around the historic main floor. This I enjoy. I like to see and hear the responses of those new to the building when they examine such iconic items as the throne, the Woolsack, the death warrant of Charles I and much more. Strange as it is, the building is where I work and it is important, every now and again, for me to see the place through someone else's eyes. New visitors are totally taken by the atmosphere and the sense of history. Of course, on a guided tour I do add some gossip, interesting stories and remarks that, I hope, are regarded as humorous. I think that I may have missed my true calling. I should have been a tour guide.

After several months, I completed the final part of the process of becoming a fully-fledged peer. I had a coat of arms specially drawn up to my specification, complete with a family motto. To undertake this task, I reported back again to the Garter Principal King of Arms. Under his direction, I learnt about the method of developing what is officially called the armorial ensign. In my case it was of John Dunn Baron Laird. For example, as a Baron, I had to have four balls on my coronet. I required two bearers of the shield, one for each side and I could place a special thing, or animal, at the top. I took a deep breath and really went for it. I selected six red hands for the counties of the political province of Ulster, green wavy lines to recognise the rolling hills around Artigarvan, two steam locomotive driving wheels, for my love of railway history, and seahorses to recognise Belfast and my old school of Inst. Topping it all was a cat to underline my love of the species; in particular, Ginger, the feline member of our family at that time. Of course, to underscore my Scottish culture and background, Ginger is holding a thistle. The best is yet to be recorded.

'Forrits wi Jonick' is the Ulster Scots language for 'into the future with justice'. This, I am proud to report, was added as my family motto. As far as I can understand, very few of the peers' armorial ensigns are not in English. Mine was the first ever in Ulster Scots. For that reason I am very pleased with it. But more, it sums up the political point that, I would like to think, has dominated my time in the Lords. Given my background as a Presbyterian, holding on to my people's need for freedom, my own problems with dyslexia and bullying at school and my natural dislike of authority, the motto reminds me always to fight for the underdog.

Over the years, well meaning people ask me: 'How did you become a lord?' Sometimes they have disbelief in their voices. I do not take it personally. But how do you answer such a question? An answer will sound pompous. So what do I do? If the questioner is from outside Northern Ireland, I have indicated that I was appointed because I was one of the few in Ulster who owned a suit. Or that I was awarded a peerage to make up for my disappointment in not being awarded the Nobel Prize for Poetry. The response that I use the most is to explain to the hapless enquirer that I thought the appointment was to Lords Cricket Ground. Then, I point out, I waited for two and a half years for Baroness Jay to open the bowling, before I realised that it was not a cricket ground. The problem is that some people tend to believe peers of the realm; even me.

Early in the year 2000, I tabled my first Lords parliamentary written question. 'What plan has Her Majesty's Government to celebrate the two hundredth anniversary of the implementation of the Act of Union in 1801?' I enquired. 'None,' came the single word reply of the Northern Ireland Office. I took serious offence. While in the Northern Ireland Parliament, I had become known as a scourge of the civil service. I was always asking questions or writing letters to ministers, in an attempt to hold the government to account. This process, I thought, was reasonably successful and I made some notable advances. But, in 1972, when the Northern Ireland Office came into existence, everything became different. During that period, a journalist asked me about something the NIO had said. I responded that I felt that we had not descended so low that we now believed statements from that office of government. Twenty-five years later, in 2000, I could see that nothing had improved.

In the offending Act of Union answer it was not that the Northern Ireland Office had not developed plans for a celebration. What upset me was the dismissive tone of that one-word answer; 'none'. I had never seen a one-word answer from an office of state to a parliamentarian before. The natural format, to which I believed I was entitled, would involve explaining the reason for the answer. But, instead, I got 'none'. Right, I thought, if the NIO was going to play silly with me, then I was the one who would put them to the test.

In terms of the wider Northern Ireland picture, David Trimble (the Ulster Unionist Party leader) was trying to set up a cross community executive in the new Assembly. As predicted, the Sinn Féiners were playing games. They refused to decommission their weapons within the agreed timetable of two years and used the extra space to obtain extra goodies from the Labour government. This caused considerable upset in the Unionist community, which is still visible today. One of the effects of the ongoing crisis was that Stormont was suspended on several occasions. All the devolved matters were handed back to Westminster to control. This meant that, as a member of the Lords, I could raise any issue that was administered by any Northern Ireland Department. Add to that list the power over policing and justice as well as the political activity of the NIO, and I became very busy. For the record, it took Sinn Féin/the IRA seven and a half years to decommission their arms.

In general, I have a high regard for Northern Ireland civil servants. The vast bulk of them are hard working and impartial and very courteous in any dealings. It is fair to point out that, at times of direct rule, the civil service can claim to have run the place. However, over the years there has developed a mentality that is almost impossible to understand. Some locals from 1972 onwards, who are only interested in their careers at any price, felt that the establishment was the Westminster government and I could see their point. But support for the new management led some of them to act in a fashion that those on the Unionist political side felt was not even handed. Then, in later years, when the meddlesome fingers of the Irish government got into the affairs of our part of the United Kingdom, another group of senior figures seemed only interested in appeasing that country's wishes. At this stage, let me outline one such organisation.

The Northern Ireland Office is a very strange animal. At times, most of the senior employees are from Great Britain, while the hapless operatives are local. This mixture is its undoing. The NIO has an inbuilt inability to answer most parliamentary questions correctly, in full and on the first time of asking. In some of the more contentious areas, I estimate that it takes up to five tries to obtain a satisfactory answer. This means that for years I have had to put questions down on the order paper time after time. On three occasions I offered the appropriate minister a deal to cut down this process of asking the same question over again. If they would answer a question on the first time, I would only have to ask once. This should cut down the time and work for both sides. But here an interesting thing happened. The appropriate minister in the Lords, who was usually a cabinet minister, could not deliver. Whatever power the NIO officials had in its political activity, surely it was not to be told what to do by outsiders?

I am not trying to be destructive in asking so many parliamentary questions on a daily basis. Every question asked has been asked for a reason and represents a part of an ongoing campaign, however big or small. The weekly routine of preparing the questions is slow and requires research. I am grateful to those many people all over the United Kingdom who supply me with ideas and information. The process has become almost self-generating now, with answers providing further questions. I am entitled to six written questions on each sitting day. In many weeks, I have many more questions than the allocation allows. Some of my interests lie outside the province and only every now and again are questions asked for disruptive political reasons.

Kevin McNamara was well-known for being an Irish Republican-supporting Member of Parliament for a Hull constituency, and before he retired I would do political battle with him. I should point out that, in common with all other members, he did not take anything personally and I retain a pleasant one-to-one relationship with him. Kevin used to ask copious questions about Northern Ireland. I felt that this was unfair to his voters in Hull. In an attempt to redress the balance, I took to scanning his local papers and asking questions about the city of Hull. I became quite knowledgeable about the place and appeared on local BBC radio and television making points about schooling and hospitals. The constituency has one of the worst records of poverty and decline in the United Kingdom. On occasions, I was asked live on air why I, from Belfast, was so involved with Hull. I explained that over the last forty years their MP had taken an interest in my area and during that period his city had declined. So I thought that it was only fair that I should, in some way, pay back the debt owed to him. I did not confess, until now, that I have never been near to Hull!

If one gets oneself into the position of having a reputation for taking up almost any issue anyone raises, then one becomes the target for leaks. In the case of the NIO, I was, and still am, the receiver of at least two types of such information. The main type is from officials who can see what is going on politically, and who have a sense of fairness and want the one-sided approach of Irish-only policies exposed. In most cases, leaks appear without any indication as to the source. But there are times when I know only too well who it is. These leaks come from those political insiders who wish, for their own reasons, to throw light on a part of the NIO or its associated bodies. To date, this has always been from government members in or around the NIO, who think that, in some limited areas, my aims and theirs are the same. This type of information, which could be in the form of a pointer in a particular direction, is usually supplied inside the precinct of Westminster. There are also times when the leak is contained in the answer to the question! This does not happen often, but if you are used to scrutinising parliamentary answers, it is possible to read between the lines.

There is a higher than average rate of sickness within the NIO. When I discuss this point with officials, on an 'off the record' basis, they point to stress. In many cases, local officials know that what they are doing is not fair to one community. This causes stress and then sick leave. At one stage, some in the NIO tried to fight back against me. Leaks and briefings began to appear from the unofficial dirty tricks department. However, this backfired. Within days, I knew who had organised the briefing and on whose authority. I understand that the officials are aware that I know who they are. Some have moved on to other departments. They are rather sorry about their actions now. Thank goodness for honest civil servants! There is still a pattern of low-level briefing against me, but the media keep me informed. The political section of the Northern Ireland Office is a part of the problem, if you are a Unionist and an Ulster Scot who simply asks for equality. Rather like a sniper in a gunfight, I keep this section pinned down with the search for information. This means that their resources get rather tied up. Besides, I understand that the office has a policy of openness and transparency. I am only helping with such a policy. They really should be grateful to me. Perhaps, deep down, they are. The NIO has a competitor in one of the Northern Ireland departments, when it comes to unhelpfulness in the provision of information. But I will arrive there in due course.

Another side affect of having a reputation for taking up issues to the extreme is that many people read about this activity and so pass cases on to me. Sometimes these end up in parliamentary questions and sometimes in open debate. In the time that I have been in the Lords, I have used one of its more interesting privileges to good effect. During the course of a sitting in either chamber, a member can make use of information that could, if used elsewhere, become the issue for a libel case. This activity can damage a person, people or an organisation. While I have made use of this notion of parliamentary privilege four times, I feel that there is a duty to ensure that the information used is as correct as possible. One of the most interesting cases was that of the barbaric murder of a young fellow on the Armagh-Monaghan border in October 2007. The circumstances were such that hardened police and press were sickened. A large group of IRA men took the youth to a lonely farm-shed where he was beaten to death. For political reasons, Sinn Féin had to claim that the 'execution' was not officially sanctioned by their army council and, in effect, should be brushed under the carpet.

I began to receive information from folk with South Armagh Republican backgrounds. They had expected me to make the issue public. I carefully checked it out with some other locals and media people. I had two feelings at the time. Was I being set up? Perhaps that was an unworthy idea. Or should I be flattered by being trusted in this way by people who would not accept my politics? With regard to the latter, I felt a weight of responsibility. A number made the interesting point that they felt no longer frightened by the IRA and were prepared to speak out. This is a sentiment I was to hear on an increasing scale over the following years.

I took up the issue. The Queen's annual speech is followed, in each house, by a week-long debate in which almost anything can be raised. I never miss such an opportunity. I outlined the case and named those involved; this was published in Hansard (Parliament's official report). There was considerable publicity. The main reason was that the police, on both sides of the border, seemed to have been instructed to 'go easy' in the investigation in order to not upset the peace process. I even had members of both forces complaining to me that the 'go easy' policy existed. If murder is the price then it's some peace process. The following months were full of members of the 'nationalist community' offering me thanks for taking up the issue and naming the thugs involved. This sort of thing is very heartening to one like me who believes passionately in a shared future for everyone everywhere. The 'go easy' policy also affected many other cases, including the IRA's raid on the Northern Bank in 2004 and the brutal murder of Robert McCartney in the Markets area. The policy's origin is believed to be with Mo Mowlam, the Secretary of State for Northern Ireland in the mid 1990s. Mo may have been popular on the mainland but, for many, that popularity did not extend to Northern Ireland.

Of the many issues that I have followed since taking my place in the Lords, several serve to illustrate particular points. 2007 was not the greatest year for me. On January 19th, I was admitted to the Ulster Hospital in Dundonald, with a heart attack. While an interesting experience, the attack and its aftermath have never been far from me since. Anyway, I am lucky and, soon after, was able to return to my work in the Upper House.

In August of that year, an Ireland international rugby team played at Ravenhill, the home of the sport in Northern Ireland. This was a rare occurrence; 'internationals' have not been played at the ground since the upgrading of the Lansdowne Stadium in Dublin in the 1950s. I, in my younger days, had been a follower of the Irish team because it had its share of Ulstermen. But I had fallen away in more recent times. As soon as the match had been played, I began to receive messages from very angry Unionists about the decision of the Irish Rugby Football Union to ban the Union flag and the singing of the national anthem from the ground. I was outraged at this position because it was a clear breach of the spirit of the Belfast Agreement of 1998, which guaranteed parity for both major traditions on the island. But this outrage was being aired in all the local papers, the talk radio shows and, as far as I could see, in every club, pub and meeting place where Unionists got together.

Upon research, I discovered that there was an agreement between the rugby authorities in both parts of the island in the early 1920s to have, at such games, the anthem appropriate to that political area. The Unionist and nationalist leaders of the day had endorsed this arrangement. Clearly, given the current climate, this scrapping of the agreement was deeply offensive to the majority of Unionist people, which included many rugby supporters. For several decades I had attended a range of matches at Lansdowne Road, Dublin, where the Irish tricolour was flown and the Soldiers' Song was song. Both of these are deeply offensive to people of my background, but I was prepared to accept the position. The unspoken bargain was that in part of the United Kingdom, which was Northern Ireland, my symbols would be respected. But no, the Irish Rugby Football Union had selected to throw away the agreement and to insult thousands in my province.

Is it any wonder there was disgust? Of all the campaigns that I have undertaken, this issue has had the most response.

The leaks and the insider information began to flow. And not just from Northern Ireland Unionists but from all parts of the island. This made me go to the lengths of writing to all the major clubs asking for their opinions. I only had one response that agreed with the action of the IRFU. I wrote to the president of the IRFU but got no reply. I considered this to be very rude treatment of a member of the Parliament that had funded the organisation. I did learn much about the activities of the Ulster Branch of the IRFU. That body tried to blame the IRFU in Dublin for the mess, while its response was to blame the Ravenhill authorities. I did, however, learn a lot about the ownership of the Belfast ground; its past history and how public money was used to support activity in the strangest of places. It is very likely that at some 'inconvenient moment' I will use this material.

The briefing that was even more interesting, which came to me from several sources, was the background to the anti-British activities. The story centres on the desire of the Dublin-based IRFU to obtain more supporters from the Munster area, at the expense of the Ulster folk. Munster rugby is not known for its openness and enlightened approach to those with whom it disagrees in political or religious terms. This had become clear, even on the playing fields. It would appear that the ban was imposed at Munster's behest and in the full knowledge that it would upset most Unionists. I often wonder what some of the big names of the game in Ulster would think if they were around now. People like the late Ken Reid and Paddy Patterson, who, with others, recognised the need for an approach acceptable to all by introducing a Phil Coulter song, entitled *Ireland's Call*. While I, and many others, think this was the least successful of Coulter's work, it did make a point. Anyone looking at the Ulster players at Lansdowne Road when the Irish anthem is being played will see how counterproductive it is. In all fairness, during the debate, which lasted for nearly a year after the initial match, many people from the Republic (people I would consider to be Republicans) expressed their disgust for the IRFU's ban, both publicly and privately.

There is a footnote to this episode. In May 2009, one of the better-known members of the Irish rugby team, a Mr Ronan O'Gara, was introduced to the Queen at a reception in Hillsborough Castle, near Belfast. This fine specimen of Irish manhood managed to excel himself in a display of the worst type of nationalism. Flaunting extremely bad manners, he refused to shake hands with Her Majesty and instead kept his hands in his pockets. In this day and age, it is impossible to accept that someone of his international experience would not understand that when meeting any lady, anywhere, a man does not keep his hands in his pockets. The conclusions of those who reported or witnessed the event were clear. Mr O'Gara was making a political point, with which some in the Republic would agree. No doubt another blow for Irish freedom! How very sad that internationally recognised protocol was ignored, to make a point that is deeply offensive to many people in Northern Ireland and to some of his team-mates. Is it any wonder that a growing number of people in the province no longer have any time for the Irish team?

Perhaps the most disturbing aspect of the issue was the approach of the Ulster branch's top people, known locally as the 'blazers'. Anger was aimed at them in the letter columns of the newspapers, on chat shows and at club level. It was common for them to be described as cowards and lacking in backbone. The general view is that these gentlemen are more interested in their own careers – as rugby groupies – than in standing up for equality and parity for their own community, let alone for anyone else.

On several occasions, I tried to correspond with the appropriate blazer, but that was also to no avail. Their wagons were pulled tight around them and any idea of discussion, or even explanation, was not forth coming. Is it any wonder that I did not have much time for the middle class? The greed amongst the blazers was such that they showed no principles and, in my opinion, they have done the cause of rugby on the island considerable harm. I, in common with many others, will never support Ireland's team again. If its administrators do not want the likes of me as supporters and instead insult my political background, then I deeply regret all the time I wasted, in previous years, at Lansdowne Road. The blazers exemplify the sort of middle class people who are only interested in themselves. Such people will always find some allegedly liberal excuse to turn a blind eye to wrongdoing. Until, that is, somebody starts to take away their rights as well and then it is too late. Self-promotion and greed are strong motivators. The blazers knew that they were guilty of inequality and that was why a collective decision was taken to ignore any criticism. John F. Kennedy once said: 'Forgive your enemies, but never forget their names.' Many have taken that advice.

Another one of the many issues that I helped to expose is the work of the human rights industry. The legislation surrounding the Belfast Agreement asked the Northern Ireland Human Rights Commission to provide advice about special elements that Northern Ireland might require. But our human rights industry, always on the lookout for an opportunity to keep itself gainfully employed, took over. In fact, they went into overdrive. Considerable amounts of money were spent flying 'important' people in and out again, holding meetings, and visiting almost every part of the world, seeking ideas. On several occasions, the commission produced its shopping list. It was laughable and out of this world. An example is that we, in Northern Ireland, were to have the right to happiness. Yes, happiness. The American Declaration of Independence, written by an Ulster-born Presbyterian, required all to have the 'right to pursue' happiness. But we were told that we were to have it as a right. Is this what is meant by special circumstances in Northern Ireland? Issues like abortion and the right to fair employment in the Roman Catholic school system were not even mentioned. But there you have the heart of the issue.

This band of human rights folk seemed not to be interested in genuine rights for those in Northern Ireland. Rather, they were more interested in making our part of the United Kingdom unworkable. Human rights, yes, as long as it did not offend the

Roman Catholic Church. This human rights commission supported religious discrimination in the selection of recruits for the Police Service of Northern Ireland. For any of us who are actually interested in human rights, it is hard to take them seriously. At a human rights seminar in 2002 or so, I was confronted by what I took to be a Republican. He asked me why I was attending such a seminar. 'You are a Unionist,' he said. 'What has this seminar to do with you?' And that is the problem summed up.

Thank goodness, their views were so extreme that even the Northern Ireland Office revolted. Letters have flown between ministers and the commission, pointing out their remit. I do not expect that, as an organisation, the Northern Ireland Human Rights Commission will last much longer.

One quiet day, while sorting my usual post, the telephone rang. In fact it seemed to do more than just ring. It jumped off the hook and ran around my office, screaming at the top of its voice. I picked up the irate instrument and was confronted with the equally irate caller, demanding that I take note of a crisis of equality and 'do something'. While I paint a cartoon picture of my telephone, I do seem to think that calls about a major problem have a different ring tone. This may be down to a revisionist mindset. However, the call was from a Unionist student at Queen's University in Belfast.

The problem is that the local branch of the Bank of Ireland, in the Queen's area, was allowing its customers to carry out transactions at their outside cash-machine in the Irish language. The choice was between Irish and English. Having spotted the problem, is it any wonder that the young student was outraged? A ten-year-old child in a Unionist area could explain the problem. Following the Belfast Agreement and its promise of equality for the two cultures on the island of Ireland, here we had one of the institutions of the Irish establishment acting in a purely sectarian manner. Worse, the discrimination was being shown against those who were not Irish but who were customers of the Bank and were therefore paying to be offended. My informant was a customer of the Bank of Ireland and he was determined to close his account at the first possible moment. As someone who is known to be a champion of equality for the individual, I said that I would take up the case at once.

I contacted the bank's authorities and drew their attention to the inequality. I suggested that the solution was either to remove the Irish option or to include the Ulster Scots language as well. The response that I got was certainly curious. I was informed that Irish was only available where there is a demand! So I investigated several other branches; Connswater and Castlereagh, both in the heart of Protestant East Belfast, Holywood and Bangor, in North Down. It is my view that these were not known as major Irish-speaking areas and that the point of 'by demand' could not apply. I contacted the bank authorities again but a response seems to be a long time in coming this time. So I began to co-ordinate with the angry students from Queen's, who, by this time, had become quite a number, and with some Unionist members of the Northern Ireland Assembly. We had placards made up, pointing out the inequality of the bank's treatment of its customers. We picketed several of the East Belfast branches and so created publicity. Mention inequality and there is always media interest, and rightly so.

I never did get a reply from the bank, which just goes to show the extent of their bad manners. But I did hear from an insider that the management had conceded my point, and within a few weeks all of the inappropriately Irish-speaking cash machines were replaced with monolingual English types. This is only one of the many cases that I have taken up while in the Lords, but I outline it to make several points. The Irish establishment seems to think that it is disconnected from the Belfast Agreement, and it is not. The voters in the Republic were asked for a vote of support for it and they gave it in full measure. When I enquire about the many incidents of unfairness in that country, or its internationally recognised lack of human rights, the answer is that the Belfast Agreement had nothing to do with them. It was 'about the North'. But the electors of France do not vote for political change in Germany, so why would the Irish think that their votes affected only another sovereign country? Anyway, I would invite them to read the Belfast Agreement, which I think few have. There they would see that their government pledged to introduce human rights measures to 'at least' the same extent as those in Northern Ireland! As the issue of equality is a basic human right, that must include their country too. Many of the more politically aware in the Republic retort that there was no possibility of their state making good on such a pledge. 'It is only words,' they would say, 'and our government is good on promises and short on delivery!'

I can at least give some credit to the Bank of Ireland. They may have been very rude to a member of the British Parliament, namely me, but they finally took my point and made the appropriate changes. But then why had they not seen the problem before I had to blow it up in all the local media? These are the double standards flowing from the Republic, to which many often refer. There is a part of me that is happy with this position. I can say that my forefathers were totally correct. The Irish will never do right by people of my cultural background. I have been proved correct in being a determined Unionist. If, for example, the Bank of Ireland had spotted its inequality and made the correction itself, in a blaze of publicity, then I would not have had my political position backed up.

There is yet a further issue concerning the Bank of Ireland, which interests me as a member of the House of Lords. On a daily basis, we are hounded with information on issues that are, or could be, interesting to Parliament. Throughout the banking crisis of 2008 and 2009 and when we had a major bill in front of us about banking, did we hear anything from the Bank of Ireland? No! In the forum that regulated the UK's banking and financial matters, in the middle of the worst financial crisis in modern history, why did this part of the Irish establishment choose not to keep us briefed? I know more about the views of hospitals' management in Somerset than I do about a major institution in my native province during a time of crisis. There are almost twenty members of the Lords from Northern Ireland, alongside other interested peers, but as far as I could see, this entire bunch was ignored by the bank's management. Organisations with few resources can keep us informed on a regular basis but not that crowd. Some day there might be a crisis that directly affects them. It will be interesting if, at that stage, members of the Lords become targets for a charm offensive from the Bank of Ireland. But what will be more interesting will be the response from those peers. Will it be a case of calling the insurance broker to insure your house when it has already caught fire? Most damning of all is the feeling in parliamentary circles that the banks have become arrogant. Is it any wonder?

The members of the House of Lords are a fascinating lot. All are strange in their own ways. Within my close circle, I have made several very good friendships, which have matured nicely. Dennis Rogan, or Lord Rogan, I have described already. Since being allocated an office in around 2003, I have shared with Dennis and one other peer. The first was Baroness Blood, who was in the 1999 batch of new members, which included us. May Blood is a highly respected member. She entered the House as a crossbencher but in recent years has moved to the Labour grouping. Her earlier career was as one of the many mill-girls in Belfast. As the Troubles increased and as the textile industry declined, May became involved in community activities. The baroness is held in much respect on the Shankill Road, a loyalist heartland, in Belfast. In her autography, May wrote of her time spent sharing an office with Dennis and me. She said that it was great crack but not much work was done!

Some years ago, Dennis and I were moved to another office-block and our third person became Alan Brooke, or Viscount Brookeborough in the Lords. Alan's father is the late John Brooke who had quoted a Kipling poem on the last day of the Stormont Parliament, recorded earlier. The Brookes of Fermanagh are a historic family who have never failed to do their duty and show leadership for the community.

Also near to our office is that of David Trimble, or Lord Trimble. Both of us owe David much, because it was on his nomination that Dennis and I arrived in the Lords in the first

Lifelong friends, Dennis Rogan and John Laird were introduced to the House of Lords in July 1999

Andrew Jackson's parents' cottage, near Carrickfergus, County Antrim (Photograph: David Laird)

The view from Artigarvan; Ballyskeagh Farm, home of the Dunns (Photograph: Pat McSorley)

David Laird on his graduation from the University of Ulster with an MSc in Computing and Information Systems

Alison and James after their wedding in Enniskillen in 2008

The annual Twelfth of July Boyne celebration parade leaving Carlisle Circus, July 2010 (Photograph: Fiona O'Cleirigh)

The annual Twelfth of July parade in Belfast, 2010
Photograph: Fiona O'Cleirigh)

John Laird in his traditional position on the Belfast annual parade, July 2010 (Photograph: Fiona O'Cleirigh)

place. Lord Trimble was awarded the Nobel Peace Prize in 1998 for his part in the negotiations that led up to the Belfast Agreement of that year. Trimble is a politician's politician. He has four main areas of conversation; history, German opera, law and, of course, politics. I do not think that he would be insulted if I pointed out that the Diplomatic Service was not in a state of meltdown when he decided to become a lecturer at Queen's University in Belfast. He has an ability to discuss matters in such a way that the other parties are left thinking that he knows what he is talking about. In 1999, the then Mr Trimble was a guest at a major rugby match in Dublin. On that day our beloved Ulster was playing a nameless French team in the final of the European Cup. The Ulstermen won. In discussions with David, several days later, he gave me a rundown on the match, with some detailed observations. It was only hours afterwards that I realised that he was talking total rubbish, such was his authoritative manner of discussion.

Also in the Unionist grouping, with Dennis and myself, is Lord Maginnis of Drumglass. Ken is held in very high regard in the Unionist community. For eighteen years, he held the parliamentary seat of Fermanagh and South Tyrone. Traditionally, that seat is considered to be a nationalist one. He won the seat in 1983 and held it again in the elections of 1987, 1992 and 1997, on split nationalist votes. On one occasion, he did poll over fifty per cent of the votes cast. In 2001, Ken Maginnis joined us in the Lords. He has an amazing ability for getting through a high volume of parliamentary work. And he is not afraid to tell anyone about his workload either. Such are the other peers, all 730 of them, that I sometimes think that I am the only normal one.

From my time as a public relations person through until today, I have been encouraged by many friends. Over the last thirty years, one couple deserve particular note; Brian and Elaine Templeton. In the use of lateral and other different kinds of thinking, I am indebted to Brian Templeton, known as BOT. He is one in a million. I first met him when he was a senior chartered accountant in a major Belfast practice. Accountants have an unflattering image, one that I sometimes consider to be fair; but not in the case of

Brian. As a square peg trying to fit into a round hole, he came up with an original solution. He remoulded the hole.

Brian has a memory that is full of inconsequential information. However, in his hands, the information is vital to develop, make or refine a point. I found his understanding of the importance of public relations to be non-standard for one in his profession. The world would be a different place if all accountants were like Brian. Carol and I have spent many a most enjoyable time in the company of Brian and Elaine. I am always delighted when he joins me at the Palace of Westminster.

North Down constituency is very middle class and Protestant. Over the years, it has gained a reputation for electing a maverick Member of Parliament; not just a maverick in terms of politics, but also in terms of personality. One such is Lady Hermon, the talented, hardworking widow of the Chief Constable of the Royal Ulster Constabulary, Sir Jack Hermon. Sylvia won the seat in the 2001 general election by beating the sitting member Robert McCartney QC. I attended the count on that fateful date, when she was declared elected.

Lady Hermon came off the stage, where she had given a victory speech. In a piece either of outstanding timing or its opposite, she confided to her supporters that she was nervous of flying. She had just been elected to a high profile office in the British Parliament in London. This required her to travel at least once a week to the capital. Being nervous of flying could have been an election issue, but she only mentioned it several minutes after being declared elected.

My public relations colleague, Jane Wells, organised matters so that Sylvia would collect some tranquilliser pills from the main reception in my office on the Holywood Road. Sylvia picked them up on her way to the Belfast City Airport, and so began a career travelling every week to the mainland. Several months later, while having a cup of tea with the North Down Member of Parliament, she suddenly said: 'I hope that you did not tell your staff that the pills I picked up were tranquillisers.' I said: 'Sylvia, do you really think that I would let you down? Have a bit more wit for god's sake, woman. I just told the girls at reception that they were morning-after pills.'

CHAPTER SEVEN

The Chairman

THE CHAIRPERSON – POLITICAL CORRECTNESS!

THE NEGOTIATIONS LEADING up to the Belfast Agreement in April 1998 were long and complicated. At that stage, being only a party worker, naturally I was not involved. When published, there was much of interest in the document. At a general level, while I felt uneasy about the thrust of some parts, I was prepared to join the 'yes' camp. Much of this was out of respect for our leader, David Trimble. I still hold respect for his political brain and I think that the people of Northern Ireland owe him much for carrying out the heavy lifting necessary for the creation of the modern Ulster. Upon inspection, there was one item that I did not expect to see and which caused me delight and proved to be a turning point in my life.

In the section concerning cross-border co-operation was an agreement to create a body to promote Ulster Scots culture and language. Later I was to understand that this proposal was attached during the latter part of the eleventh hour. I was also to learn that its link to the Republic's machinery for the promotion of the Irish language was to be regretted by that government. But there it was. It was not satisfactory for those of us who desired equality and 'parity of esteem'. But, nevertheless, it was there and could provide something upon which to build. The proposed Ulster Scots Agency was to be a start. But, first of all, the referendum for the Agreement had to be won and an executive set up.

Some of those issues have been dealt with elsewhere. Now we come to the creation of a new power-sharing executive, with ministers selected by the D'Hondt process. This rather complicated mathematical system is designed to select ministers according to the parties' strengths in the Assembly. Clearly, some of the departments were big spenders, with a major impact on the affairs of the Province. But, given the circumstances in Northern Ireland, other seemingly small ones could have an important role. One such was the Department for Culture, Arts and Leisure. Culture is vital to Republicans as a method for excluding others and for making a political point.

There is a belief that a section of the Irish-leaning senior civil servants had co-operated with Sinn Féin in the preparations for the department. It was to be a placement for Martin McGuinness, a senior member of that party. It is widely accepted that McGuinness has played an important role in IRA activity in the city of Londonderry, since the very early 1970s. It was expected, by clever working of the selection process, that this iconic Republican figure would be in charge of the department. Special selected officials would be appointed to enhance Irish culture, more than likely at the expense of Ulster Scots. This is also how some of the senior officials of the Dublin administration saw the position. An interesting feature of that period was the manner in which the Republican facilitators worked. On many occasions, one or more of their number would leave the negotiation, shake hands with all the local parties, including Sinn Féin, set off in their cars and stop at a nearby car-park and hold a further meeting with the extreme Republicans. If the Irish thought that we did not know that was going on, then they are even stupider than we supposed.

On the day the selection process was run, David Trimble surprised everyone by selecting the Department for Culture, Arts and Leisure ahead of more obviously important ones. Sinn Féin was appalled. It looked as if their plan, so carefully put together with the help of supposedly impartial civil servants, had collapsed. The Minister of Culture was to be Michael McGimpsey, an Ulster Unionist. It was only some time later that I fully understood the importance of his appointment and of Sinn Féin's failure.

Subsequently, a cross-border body was established, one that would administer the Irish-language and Ulster Scots agencies. I was surprised to find out that I had been chosen from the Northern Ireland members to chair it jointly. The Irish version was to have a board of sixteen members, with eight from each side of the border. The Ulster Scots Agency was made up of eight, with four from each part of the island. At the time, this made us look to be lacking in equality, as did the totally disproportionate allocation of funding. My approach was to take the offer and to work for more, which I assumed, in the new spirit of parity, would not be long in coming. I calculated without the Irish-led stone wall, off which I was soon to bounce, time and time again. I was about to come face to face with those in authority who felt entitled to hold imperialistic aspirations over my part of the United Kingdom and over myself. I was about to understand why my forefathers believed that Ulstermen could not trust the Irish with our culture, or to treat us with fairness. I was about to cease being a paper Unionist. I was about to become a practical Unionist, acting upon my own experience. Hold on to your kilts!

The first meeting of the new Ulster Scots Agency took place in a South Belfast hotel in December 1999. The event was an experience for all eight of us. The Northern Ireland people I knew. They were well-known members of the community; Dr Philip Robinson, the much recognised linguist, John Erskine, a Presbyterian historian who was well-known for his language skills, and John McIntyre, a well-known and dedicated activist. I did not meet the members representing the Republic of Ireland until that day. They are also an interesting and dedicated bunch. Dr Linde Lunney was a much recognised language expert who, although from Northern Ireland, was living and working in Dublin. Patrick Wall was a most likeable lecturer at Trinity College Dublin. No previous interest in Ulster Scots was recorded but he always acted as the very best kind of regular citizen of the Republic. He was uncomfortable with any criticism of his country but, after some short reflection, was able to agree that it may be due. The final members, apart from myself, were Lynn Franks and Jim Devenney. Lynn was a most helpful and conscientious teacher in a Protestant school in County Cavan and Jim Devenney was an Orangeman from County Donegal. Lynn and Jim were examples of people within the Church of Ireland who were born in the Republic. More on that Protestant community will appear later.

The new venture was heralded with publicity. As I did not know the members from the Republic until that first meeting, I tried to use humour to relax everyone. This was one of those occasions when my attempts fell flat and the atmosphere changed dramatically. I asked each person to introduce himself or herself. The last to do so, at the board table, was Jim Devenney. Jim explained in a shy but appealing way that he was glad that he had lived long enough to see the day when his community, the twenty-five thousand or so Ulster Scots who lived in the Republic, was recognised. For the first time, he was officially looking towards the capital of Ulster, Belfast, for help and support. At once, a pin could be heard to drop. Each of us seemed to be in our own thoughts as we digested his emotional words.

There, unexpectedly, in a meeting room in South Belfast, before Christmas at the ending of the century, I felt the breath of my ancestors on the back of my neck. I confess to wiping away tears as I, the chairman, tried once again to take control of the meeting by saying something appropriate. I was living through one of those rare, not to be forgotten, moments that help us in the search for who and why we are. As an Ulster Unionist, I had come face to face with the unacceptable part of my history. This kind of moment must come to us all, those who set ourselves up to offer guidance to our communities.

For some, an explanation is due. The seventeenth century saw the plantation of many of my relations in Donegal. Some moved eastward in search of better conditions. But many were to be found in East Donegal in the early 1920s, when the Irish State was set up. They were of the same people as those I described earlier, living a few miles away in Artigarvan. My relations in the Laggan Valley of East Donegal were just as much determined Unionists as those in Artigarvan. Their desire for freedom was just as strong. When resistance was generated to fight the Home Rule menace, the men stood shoulder to shoulder with those from Artigarvan and other places in County Tyrone. Carson recruited his army from their ranks. The South Donegal Ulster Volunteer Force was commanded by a James Laird, who had a brother called John, killed in the First World War. James Laird is commemorated by a plaque inside Ballyshannon Church of Ireland church.

In the year of 1912, when rallies were held in preparation for the signing of the Covenant, one of the most famous was in Raphoe, the unofficial capital of that fertile part of the beautiful country of Donegal. When the 36th Ulster Division marched from Finner Camp to Londonderry, to join the blood and thunder of the battles in France, it carried the flower of Donegal's Ulster Scots youth. No village or row of cottages was to be unaffected by the blood sacrifice of the Ulstermen at the Somme. Every part of the old province told the same story. And never to be forgotten was the bloody rebellion of Easter 1916 in Dublin, when, led by some who refused to fight for world freedom, eight hundred men defiled the name of the island around the world. It is estimated that forty-five thousand men from the island rallied to the calls of Carson and of responsible nationalist leaders. They joined the army and fought for freedom. Then, in 1916, at the very height of the war, a small, unrepresentative gang pulled the plug on the brave ranks of soldiers and banished their memory for eighty years on part of the island of their birth. Of course, in their usual bad-handed way, the London authorities made the Easter Rising rebels into heroes by executing them. Some never learn.

When, in 1921, the Irish Free State was formed, the many thousands of Protestants who lived in the new country felt the pressure. And nowhere was the threat felt more than in the new border area, in which Unionists had been so determined to hold onto their freedom. As explained, many were murdered, some were injured and many more had to leave their family homes at gunpoint. This affected my family in East Donegal as much as the next. Bitterness exploded amongst them; bitterness at their neighbours who had turned against them and bitterness at the Unionist people, now in Northern Ireland, who had abandoned them. In order to hold a part of the old Province of Ulster, the Belfast-centred Unionists had accepted the borders involving the five border counties of Londonderry, Tyrone, Fermanagh, Armagh and Down. The sixth county, which does not border the Free State, is Antrim. The anger in my family is a story that has been told many times over. Some folk tore up the Ulster Covenants that they had signed in 1912. Many fled to join their community in the new Northern Ireland. Others, who did not want to leave their farms, stayed, but ensured that all their offspring would relocate across the border, at an appropriate time in the future. Some packed and left the island altogether. Some, including close relations of mine, became bitter and refused to accept anything British again. The strain on the local communities was unbearable. Even in my time in Artigarvan, in the 1950s and 1960s, it was a fact of life. On one side of a line, people were living in an Irish Roman Catholic-dominated society. On the other side, the ethos was British and a different type of freedom was on offer. To this day, border Protestants in the Republic feel that the Roman Catholic majority cannot accept Protestants to be truly Irish. A cold wind made the Republic a miserable place for those who were not wanted.

For decades on the border, this was not a topic for general discussion. In dealing with family, or those who lived through those turbulent times, you kept your thoughts to yourself. It was clear to me that there was a sense of guilt on the British side of the border. 'How could we have let our people down?' Across the divide, our community looked at us with eyes that said: 'How could you?' I quickly came to the conclusion that, had I been about in 1921, then, as a Unionist, I would have agreed with the majority of my fellow party-members. But I still felt guilty. This is the type of question that history throws up time and again. The Second World

War was started over the issue of Poland's freedom. When it ended, in 1945, Poland was still enslaved. Unionists in the UK, including myself, had avoided the issue of those on the wrong side of the border; people with British backgrounds and from a mostly Ulster Scots community. That was my position until December 1999. Then the furniture moved. I could feel that. But on that day, at the first meeting of the Ulster Scots Agency, I was not yet to know the full extent.

For the first year, the Ulster Scots Agency was dogged by political instability. This was due to the failure of Sinn Féin to keep its side of the peace agreement and to decommission its weapons, according to the approved timetable. However, I used this period to try and establish what all the board members thought that we should be doing. Not knowing the accepted background of our mother department, that of Culture, Arts and Leisure, I felt that I would get considerable support. After all, the Belfast Agreement had promised equality and parity of esteem for the two major traditions on the island of Ireland. Why wouldn't the agency be well received and supported? I soon learnt that DCAL and its Irish counterpart were not there to help us. They were determined to stop, at all costs, the advance of the Ulster Scots language and culture, or so it seemed to me.

The Ulster Scots language, or Ullans, is an offspring of the Scots version, Lallans (or Lowlands language). Lallans is one of the languages in which Rabbie Burns wrote. Sometimes he scribed in a mixture of English and Lallans. Ulster Scots is not an extensive language and it is well-known for attributing totally different meanings to English words. In Ulster, if you say to someone 'I doubt ya may ware your coat,' the person is more than likely to put his or her coat on. But, if you were speaking English, the coat would be taken off. 'I doubt ya may be right', is Ullans for 'I think that you must be right'. To an English person it means the exact opposite: 'You are not right.' The whole range of intensifier words is interesting; 'powerful'; 'brave'; 'brilliant'. Again, in English, the meaning is different. We also use words that cut an object down to size. The word for mountain is 'hill'; hence the 'hillbillies'. The word 'billie', when spelt that way, means a friend. Hillbillies are Ulster Scots friends who live on a mountain.

The language has a complicated grammar system, which is well documented in the accepted Ullans grammar book, by board member Dr Philip Robinson. Interesting areas are the use, in Belfast, of the third person. 'Here's ma ta ma mouther, I'm gaing oot ta nicht.' Then there is the ability to add a tag line. 'I'm gaing oot ta nicht, sa a am'. I think that it is a friendly language. It represents the background from which I come. It is colourful and wonderful. I want it preserved. However, I do not want to ram it down anyone's throat for political reasons. I do not want Ulster Scots-medium schools or the requirement for all police and others to speak it. That would be a waste of money and effort. But, under the Belfast Agreement, Ullans was promised equality with Irish. I had nothing to do with the writing of the agreement. But I do want Irish to have the same status as Ulster Scots. It is in the agreement! And the people in the Republic voted for it to extend to their country, as well. So where are the road signs, for example, in the three languages of English, Irish and Ulster Scots? This is yet another example of an occasion where I was to learn that the Irish are not a people of their word. Their government signed up to an international agreement and, of course, did not keep it. And then some wonder why there are Unionists like me!

There is another debate, as to whether Ulster Scots is a language or a dialect. The Belfast Agreement, the governments of Eire and of the United Kingdom and the European Union all consider it to be a language. I was not appointed to be the chairman of the Dialect Cross-Border Body. Or of the Funny Speaking Agency. No, I was chairman of a language body. If someone is of the intent to call Ullans a dialect, I think that it says more about them than about Ullans. It usually means that they have a political agenda. Having similarities to another language does not make a language a dialect. At least, if it does, do not tell the Italians and the Spanish, or the Irish and the Scots Gaelic! Dialect versus language is a useless debate.

In 1999 many people in the Unionist community and a very few others had heard the term 'Ulster Scots'. But I had been brought up with it. I set about, with the support of the board members, on a fast moving campaign to explain the part played by the language and, importantly, the history and the culture. As I had expected, the interest was instant with Protestants while there was suspicion in the collective minds of the Roman Catholics and the Irish community. For years, Protestants had been challenged by their fellow countrymen as to the nature of their culture. For most of the middle class members, this was a difficult issue, which would make them mad with frustration. Many pleasant dinners in the tree-lined areas of Belfast came to an uncomfortable end when that point was put. Were we Irish? Were we British? Were we both? What was our culture? The Irish could produce a whole complement of music, written material, dance and so on. The well-meaning Protestants felt inadequate. Now we were providing them with a neatly packaged cultural background and a history. In addition, people would be able to relate Ulster Scots history to what they knew of their family. A gap had been filled. It is strange that more about our culture was not taught in schools in Ulster.

The political spin was not missed by the more politically minded of the Irish Republicans. Their main plank was to get the 'British' out of Ulster and then we would all settle down as happy Irish. But if a large section of the Unionist community declared themselves not to be Irish at all, but Ulster Scots and, importantly, their choice was supported by European legislation, then that argument was useless. In other words, being an Ulster Scot was another line of defence against Irish imperialism. It seemed that all the politically aware in the Republican camp had thought that Ulster Scots did not exist or, if it did, that it was nonsense. They were in for a shock; none more than the Irish government itself.

Again, it is at this point that my old friend the unofficial briefing, or the leak, comes into play. In fairness, I must always point out that I have met many in the Irish community who may not agree with me politically but who respect fairness. Such people did not like what was being levelled against us in the cultural battle.

I also met many Irish language supporters who were most helpful in the early documentation of our language. Without their help we could not have been as successful as we were. It was not long before the information started flooding in. It was clear very early on that the Irish government had quickly realised that they had made a major mistake in both supporting the development of Ulster Scots and to place their language body into the cross-border arrangements. Led by Dublin, the battle started to confine, and seemed intended to stop, the development of our culture. However, in the type of climate that we have in Northern Ireland, the Irish attack on us suited us well. There were those in our community who could not decide whether to declare themselves to be Ulster Scots or not. Witnessing the Irish attitude convinced those people of the value of our position. We can always rely on Dublin to do the wrong thing.

The inevitable day came when I was, for the first time in my life, to attend engagements in the Irish Republic, involving local members of the British, Ulster Scots or Unionist communities. The first venue was in east Donegal, which had all the family significance I had avoided to date. To add to the experience, I was to be accompanied by Jim Devenney. Jim was now the vice-chairman of the agency, as well as the breathing manifestation of my political conscience, who had brought tears to my eyes at the initial board meeting. On the way I could feel the emotions rising. I did not know what was in store for me. Was I about to stir up people who lived in a different county? Was I about to do what I often accused Irish Republicans – those who came from the Republic – of doing in Northern Ireland? I could not avoid my responsibilities to the fifteen thousand Ulster Scots folk who lived in Donegal, outside the United Kingdom. It was a nervous John Laird who entered an Orange hall in County Donegal for the very first time.

I will never forget what I found that evening. The hall was almost full of men and women of all ages. The walls were decorated with Union flags, bunting and a picture of the Queen – more than I had ever seen in a similar hall in my part of the United Kingdom.

The meeting was to discuss the formation of an Ulster Scots group in that area. I gave my, by now, usual speech about the background of the agency and then spoke about the origins of Ulster Scots culture. Much of it was directed at the Laggan Valley and contained regular references to my family. They listened in polite silence. When questions came, they were subdued and very deferential towards me. It was as if I must not be offended at all costs. Until that stage in my life, I had never been in such a gathering, with such an atmosphere, before. But I was to be in a similar situation many times afterwards.

The important part of a meeting like that, as I was about to find out, was during the tea interlude or at the end. At those stages, individuals who wished to speak to me alone would approach me. They were so pleased that I had taken time to engage with them. They delighted that their identity was to be recognised. Some told me harrowing stories about how they, or their community, had been treated, over the last number of decades. The tales scared me. The tellers seemed to have a need to tell me everything, in the hope that I could help. This formula of a meeting was to become common for me 'over the border', over the next few years. And this is where I felt that the problems began.

For the next four years (and to this day, to an extent) I regularly attended many forms of gatherings, mostly in Donegal and, more recently, in Monaghan and Cavan. The format is very similar, no matter which county. The folk are close knit, full of community self-help, defensive and careful what they say and to whom. Early in my visits I learnt that they never criticise the Irish or the Republic to those they do not trust. A recent publication by the Church of Ireland, in Monaghan, about the plight of the border minority is titled: 'Whatever you say, say nothing.' This is a very good summary of the position. The problem for me is that I feel that I have a duty to help them if I can. But can I? In Monaghan, the point was put to me that there may be a Protestant Member of Parliament, but he has 'sold out'. I suppose there are not enough non-Roman Catholics to ensure his re-election and if he is seen publicly to support the Protestant community he will be in trouble, electorally, with his core vote.

Many decades ago, there was a Unionist member in the Irish Parliament (a TD). William Sheldon was his name. The authorities cut his Donegal constituency up so that the Protestant people could not elect their own co-religionist. In more recent times, a further example of gerrymandering was the dividing up of the local government ward that regularly returned the only Protestant to the County Council; Jim Devenney, the agency's vice-chairman. These are the kind of stories that are related to me on every visit. But also told were stories of a more violent nature. Things on the border are bad. As an Ulster Unionist, the first ever to have executive function in the Republic, I did not know what to do. That is, until I discovered that the Irish Minister for Justice was appointing an extra member to that country's Human Rights Commission, to represent the Traveller community, which numbered twenty-five thousand. It was our calculation that, in the three border counties, there was also a minority of twenty-five thousand that felt disengaged. So I wrote to the minister, Mr O'Donoghue, asking for a meeting to discuss the human rights of his government's Ulster Scots minority community. To my extreme surprise, I received a rebuff. The return letter said: 'It would not be constructive to discuss human rights of the Ulster Scots community with you.' I began to identify more and more with the invisible people along the border, as they called themselves.

In early September 2001, I noted that a delegation of the government of China was to visit Dublin and the Irish were proposing to raise issues of human rights in that country. What cheek, I thought. I cannot get alongside the Dublin decision-making process to discuss the human rights of a section of their population, let alone their appalling record to all its citizens. But I could, I supposed, ask the Chinese to raise these issues with the Dublin people when they met. I contacted the Chinese Embassy in Dublin to make arrangements. As a result, the following item appeared on the front of the Irish Times on 4th September:

UNIONIST PEER CALLS ON CHINA TO RAISE IRISH HUMAN RIGHTS ISSUE
By Paul Tanney, in Belfast

A UNIONIST peer has called on the Chinese government to raise the issue of Irish human rights abuses with the government.

Lord Laird of Artigarvan, the co-chair of the cross-border implementation body on Irish and Ulster Scots, said he was forced to appeal to the Chinese after his request for a meeting with the Minister for Justice was rejected.

Lord Laird said he had sought a meeting with Mr O'Donoghue to discuss the inclusion of a member of the Ulster Scots community on the Human Rights Commission but was told it would not be 'constructive'. 'The usual thing in politics is to meet someone and make a few sympathetic noises and then kick it into touch but they didn't even do that,' he said.

He said this was typical of the government's approach to human rights, with other examples being the fact that it had not changed the special place of Irish. He said the special place given to Irish was in fact illegal under international law.

If the Dublin government won't speak to me about human rights for Ulster Scots, I'll have to get the Chinese government to do it for me,' he said. Commenting on reports that human rights was to feature heavily in the government's discussions with the Chinese premier, Lord Laird said: 'The Dublin government's hands aren't clean. Their human rights record is extremely poor and they should spend less time criticising other people.

The whole ethic of the Republic is monoculture, and it must be multicultural to fit in with the European Court of Human Rights,' he said.

Lord Laird said the Chinese embassy in Dublin had been 'most interested' by his call but was not sure what steps it would take to raise the matters he brought to its attention. The Chinese embassy was unable to comment.

I was left with the impression that the Irish were not pleased with my intervention.

My problems with the Unionist or Ulster Scots population on the Republic's side of the border did not go away. They got much worse. As with all complex issues, the more that I looked into it, the less I seemed to understand. Here was a community that looked to its British cultural background, watched the BBC and was concerned about current affairs in Northern Ireland. Unless they were farmers, they could see no future in their current location and advised their families to take any opportunities to move northward. Should I take political advantage of them? Would that be fair? They had no spokesman who could take up their cases fearlessly. Anyone who might have done so also lived in the Republic and so would be under pressure. This was a community that was now down to its core, although in some areas beginning to show a slight increase in numbers. In Donegal, some people could have the same DNA as me. In any sense of the word, they were my people. I was invited to give the prize day address and present the awards to the pupils of the Royal and Prior School in Raphoe. I was very pleased to do so for many reasons, one being that my mother had attended the Prior bit of the school when it was a separate girls' organisation, located in Lifford.

I enjoyed the prize presentation on a dark night in the Donegal town. Out of interest, I noted that every child who received a prize had a Scottish planter name. In some cases, it was a name that I recognised and that could be related to me. The usual routine took place. After the event, as I was trying to get into my car to drive home to Belfast, I was approached 'off the record, you understand' about a grievance a Protestant resident had. And so it went on. But the next series of cross-border events interested me even more.

I can understand why, through family background, I was drawn to Donegal. However I have no known connection to Monaghan or Cavan, two other Ulster counties. I began to visit all sorts of Ulster Scots and Protestant events in those areas, on behalf of the agency and I was unnerved. Attendance at the meetings was much greater than in County Donegal. In some cases it was standing room only, full of mostly younger folk, and much more lively. Again I observed the red, white and blue in the halls. I attended services with poppy wreaths being laid to remember British soldiers killed in the two wars and in Iraq. At the end of the gatherings we all sang with great gusto: 'The Queen!' Where possible, I wore my kilt; some of them did too. When being introduced, or after speaking, I was treated as if I was a returning survivor from the Somme; perhaps the only one to survive, at that.

The good people of Cavan and, even more so, Monaghan were well organised, or that is how they seemed to me. There, again, I received the usual tales of woe. This was where the title of the 'invisible people' was explained to me. I would be shown streets, say in Clones, where in 1921 most of the shops were Protestant-owned; now, there may be only one or two. I remember my family showing to me a similar scene as early as the 1950s, in Raphoe. Standing in the Diamond, I had pointed out to me where almost the whole square was Protestant in 1921; little remained so, even then. One thing that I learnt early on was never to speak to another about someone's business in the Republic's Ulster Scots enclaves. It was also important to avoid identifying the exact location or nature of events taking place within the community. You will see that I have followed this rule within these pages. However I will make the distinction of the village of Drum, in County Monaghan. This reasonably sized village is totally Protestant and proud of its Ulster Scots culture. It was there that I came across an annual gathering and band parade held in July. In 2005, I attended this event and was totally taken with it. The small place was packed with folk from all over the area. A number of young groups performed Scottish dancing on a makeshift platform in the street. Bands, mostly from the surrounding area, with a few from Northern Ireland, paraded up and down the street. It was a joyful night out, full of young people, families with young children, older followers and those just there to see what was going on. The Irish police service directed the proceeding with four men and one car. There was no need for more. I talked to these worthy gentlemen during a lavish tea in the Orange hall, in which they were made most welcome. They are regulars in the area. They knew most of the people and always looked forward to an evening's entertainment and a 'full tea'. I rejoiced. That, at least, was the way that it should be.

It would be very wrong of me to give the impression that I thought that all the Irish in the border areas, and elsewhere, were difficult to deal with. By any standards, they were not. So what was the problem? Over the last ten years, there is hardly a day that goes by without my mind turning over the problems of the 'invisible people'. I have been in public affairs long enough to know that people like me are targeted by some malcontents who seek an opportunity to complain. Even if I were to consider that half of the issues raised to me were of that type, there would still be a substantial number of problems remaining. Also, any that I had investigated myself were mostly correct. A few might be overstated but that is what you get anywhere. The questions kept coming. Why were these people treated in this way? Most of them had relations and/or friends in Northern Ireland. A very monocultural picture of the Republic was being painted, instead of a positive, inclusive one. There seemed to be no moves being made to try and convince Unionists to embrace the Republic. Was I interfering in the affairs of a foreign country? Interestingly, I have been told on many occasions in Dublin, by members of that decision-making process, that the affairs of the border minority have nothing to do with me. Are those people who tell me that correct? The Unionist leaders of the early 1920s knew that they had let down their kith and kin: why did I seem to have all their guilt on my conscience?

Then there was the sense of responsibility for everything, which I had experienced back in the early 1970s; why had it returned?

The facts, as I saw them, were these. Even after what is now ninety years of the Irish Republic, here were people who seemed to have no sense of belonging. They existed, for the most part, around the border. The further one went into the Republic, the more the nature of the Protestants changed. I have had issues of discrimination raised with me by Protestants in Dublin, mostly about the discrimination in the Irish civil service, and from areas around Cork. These cases are nothing like the files that I have from the borders. How does the treatment of the 'invisibles' square with the decency of the ordinary citizens that I meet in the Republic? Why, when I visited the senior civil servants in Dublin, to raise issues of concern to their Ulster Scots community, am I treated like someone from Mars? I should add that I have always been shown the utmost courtesy, although mixed with disbelief. It is as if the 'invisible' do not exist. But then that is why they call themselves the 'invisible people'. Perhaps when a straight talking Ulsterman outlines their problems to those in Dublin, there is a communication gap. Why was I not allowed to meet a minister to discuss human rights for the Ulster Scots people? Should not the political class in Dublin have invited me into their den with open arms? After all, I was taking an interest in their part of the island – something they always seemed to want Unionists to do! And I was paying a political price with regard to my own Northern Ireland community, for doing just that. Why was there a lack of vision in the Dublin elite? Was it just me? Did they not like me? After several years of rebuff I was, of course, going to be robust. But I was not so robust at the start, when they first chose to ignore me.

In the Dublin decision-making process, words mean what the speaker wants them to mean at that time. Just as in Alice in Wonderland. I complained to a senior figure there, about an item of legislation that did not allow us to do what we thought we were required to do. He explained that: 'It is not what the law says that counts. It is what it is meant to say that counts'. I do not think that we would get away with that idea in the United Kingdom.

But perhaps I was looking at the question from the wrong end. Dublin's treatment of the border minority was allowing me to polish up my anti-Irish Republic beliefs. How would it have been if I had found that everything was as it should be and that the border Ulster Scots folk were content? Would I have been disappointed? Would I have changed my views? What would I have felt? I really do not know what I expected. What I found upsets me to this day. It has coloured my thinking and given me an insight into the life of a minority. It has given me an even greater fear of Irish control, if that is any indication of how we would be treated.

In later life, after I left the chairmanship of the agency and began to talk publicly about my experiences, more interesting things happened, which allowed the cloud before my eyes to lift. That is a story for later.

The agency's efforts to promote Ulster Scots continued. But, to my increasing concern, without any official help. I will outline one issue of the time that is worth recording. It came to my notice, through the usual leaks, that the Irish Foreign Minister of the time, Brian Cowen, was reported to be making fun of Ulster Scots culture and language at social functions in Dublin. While I am thick skinned, this, if true, seemed to show why we were receiving no support from either department. So I wrote to Mr Cowen, who has a very poor record amongst Unionists because of his extreme Republicanism, and outlined my concerns. I asked him to stop making fun of a racial grouping; in this case, us. As soon as it had been received, Cowen contacted the Head of the Northern Ireland Civil Service to complain that I was 'out of control'. The morning that this letter hit Stormont, senior civil servants, including the Permanent Secretary of the Department for Culture, Arts and Leisure, were summoned. The topic at the meeting was how to control Laird! I do not think that the meeting was a success. But that is not the point. This is a case where a minister from a foreign country had commanded the heads of another country's civil service to run a meeting about issues in his country. I learnt a lot from that experience. As usual, I knew about the meeting almost before it had ended.

Again, things just got worse. In April 2001, a reception was organised on Capitol Hill in Washington, to launch a network of Institutes of Ulster Scots studies from Canada, right down through many universities to the Southern States. One of the very first things that we did, when brought into existence in 1999, was to sponsor, in conjunction with the University of Ulster, an Institute of Ulster Scots Studies in Magee College in Londonderry. My old friend from the communications days, John Wilson, was its first director. John is a bundle of both energy and ideas. It was he who organised the Ulster Scots network down through North America. The concept was to make Ulster Scots studies available to students. It was a great success.

Professor John Wilson joined me, and a series of VIPs from the United States and Northern Ireland, at the reception. Amongst the guests was the Minister for DCAL, our sponsoring department, Michael McGimpsey. One of the main speakers was the Irish Ambassador to the United States of America. His remarks seemed to me to be totally inappropriate for the occasion. The ambassador referred to the forty million Irish who lived in America. The movement of the population from the island of Ireland to America, according to him, was due to the famine-driven events of the nineteenth century. I could feel the temperature of the event rising. The ambassador had a track record amongst Unionists. He was considered to be far too Republican. Clearly, that suited the Irish in the New York and Washington areas. But it always seems to us that the Irish claimed that the Scots-Irish were Irish, in order to make themselves seem more important.

I put away my prepared speech and delivered a polite, but, nevertheless, robust set of remarks that contradicted him. I pointed out that the Irish had only eighteen million, while we had twenty-two million Scots-Irish, in the States. I went on to outline the importance of the Scots-Irish to the creation of modern America. The ambassador left the reception early and, to the extreme anger of many Ulster Scots watching, gave an item of cut glass, that we had presented to him to mark the event, to the doorman! Worse, he took with him members of a small band we had brought over to provide background music for a dinner to be held afterwards. The group were composed of Irish people who could play Scottish music. So we adjourned to another room to have our dinner, with several gaps at the tables and with no music. We were all annoyed.

When I returned to Belfast, I penned another letter to Brian Cowen, complaining about the ambassador's behaviour. I also managed to secure media coverage of this outrage. I think that it is reasonable to describe Dublin's attitude as 'not best pleased' with me. That was fine. The reception of April 2001 taught me a lot. I think it also informed the Irish as to just how serious we were. We were not going to be mucked about. We have the capacity to disturb their cosy relationships in the States by clearly defining the Scots-Irish as totally different to the Irish.

After that incident, events changed for us dramatically. No longer were the Irish prepared to put up with us. They could see clearly the threat that we posed in the States. The forty million block vote that the Irish claimed was not so significant if it was reduced to eighteen million. Also, all the stories about the poor Irish and their plight, brought about by the English-inspired famine, would seem less viable when set against our seventeen presidents and very many other important American people. For the sake of Old Ireland, we had to be stopped. Forget about parity of esteem and equality of the Belfast Agreement: Ulster Scots could not be allowed to damage Mother Ireland. It took the Irish several months to develop a plan, but develop one they did. Pieces of loose wording in the Belfast Agreement, and its supporting legislation, allowed them to stop our funding for activities outside the island. This was in clear opposition to the activities we had already undertaken and placed us in a position of inequality vis-à-vis the Irish. Few things in this world are more determined and bull-headed than the influential Irish when the 'old sod' is under attack. And that knowledge helped to develop my understanding of what was going on. I will come to that point.

For us in the Ulster Scots Agency, from staff to board members, it seemed that the Department for Culture, Arts and Leisure

(DCAL) was not in any way interested in helping us. While I thought that they worked closely with their Republican opposite numbers, another interesting issue arose. In Dublin, they were taking decisions that affected DCAL and us but, not only did they not tell us, they did not tell DCAL. Is it any wonder that I refer to Eire as a nation with imperialist aspirations over my part of the United Kingdom? They behave as imperialists. It is not just that DCAL were difficult to deal with; they seemed to set out to disrupt us. Certainly, that was so after the events of the reception in April 2001. Examples abound; I will outline a few. When we were about to take decisions, as a board, we would get hand-delivered letters informing us of their concerns, just as the meeting was about to discuss the relevant issue. In stark terms, we would be told that because of some obscure point, what we wished to do was impossible. At one stage, the department required us to provide details of all our payments so that they could agree them. This messed up our bookkeeping. When we asked for decisions or advice, this would be slow in coming. Very slow; on occasion, it could take over six months. We once sent a form to the department to be signed. This was a standard procedure; it took fifteen months to return, completed.

On one occasion, I was informed that the Dublin minister, Eamon O'Cuiv, who had just been appointed to the cabinet, wanted publicity in order to get one over on his colleagues. So, at some political cost, I arranged a tour of Ulster Scots locations and meetings. It ended with him playing a lambeg drum at Stormont, as the major photo call. Then some of us sat down with the minister and requested extra funding for new projects. These included removing so-called Protestant paramilitary murals from walls, and their replacement by Ulster Scots ones, and allowing the opportunity for some parading flute bands to come off the streets and become concert-driven. This I thought would be both socially acceptable and good for society in general, including the tourist trade. O'Cuiv agreed and we were pleased. That was on a Friday. Not long after, I 'obtained' documents showing that, on the following Thursday, a meeting of the minister's senior officials took place in Dublin, to make arrangements to cut our budget.

Two points arose from that experience. Firstly, as an aspiring imperialist power, Dublin announced the budget cut in the Irish Parliament but had not informed DCAL who, in theory, should have had a say in the decision. It was me who read the appropriate item in the Irish official parliamentary reports and who had to inform DCAL's Permanent Secretary. She was amazed and thrown off guard. Within a short time, however, she came to terms with what her Dublin masters wanted. The second point was that I had to go back to the expectant groups and tell them that our budget had been cut by Dublin. It was at that stage that several members of the community told me words to the effect (if not as polite): 'Laird, you fool. You believed the Irish and, as usual, they let you down.' I had to admit I had trusted the Irish and now my friends were right. Looking back at the whole period, I did think that the Belfast Agreement was a clean sheet of paper. For the first time ever, it had seemed that the Irish could be trusted. I was wrong. This period of my life, as chairman of the Ulster Scots Agency, was supplying me with life-defining moments on a regular basis.

In the end, after several months and many tough confrontations, O'Cuiv agreed, grudgingly, to put back part of the funding. But we got no support or words of sympathy from DCAL on this issue. Having to act on an even handed basis, extra funding was returned to the Irish Agency as well, money that they had not asked for, but could use. I always got on well with the members and officials of the Irish Language Board. After the return of their funding, one suggested that they should use it to place a statue in Artigarvan with my title in Irish. He was only joking – I think. It is reasonable to say that true Irish Language people had, and, I hope, have, no problem with the Ulster Scots revival. After just a few years, this revival was being called by academics the fastest ever of its type in Europe.

In the early years, mostly when I was a Member of Parliament, I had been critical of the Irish language and its use in Northern Ireland. By the time I joined the Language Board, I had realised that I was wrong. In the 1980s, a Sinn Féin party member had said in public that every Irish word spoken was a bullet in the heart of a Unionist. That did not go down well in the Protestant community. But soon I began to think more carefully about this issue. It seemed that for me to be concerned about another culture said something about me. However, as I grew in understanding of Ulster Scots culture, I took a different view. I now had confidence in who I was, and the nature of my background. I felt that I could take on a discussion about history and culture with anyone. I had been wrong and not for the first time. In various newspaper articles and at a language reception in Dublin, I explained my case and my conversion to a more multicultural approach. I went as far as apologising for my former views.

It is that sense of self-confidence that I felt had to be instilled in the Unionist people who were Ulster Scots. But, to the politically minded Irish, this was a double-edged sword. On one hand, there is no doubt that the use of Irish is more understood by a better-informed Unionist community. But the very fact that there is now a well-informed and self-confident Ulster Scots community is going to play heavily against any suggestion of a united Ireland. Sinn Féin and the Department of Foreign Affairs in Dublin always believed that if they could drive out the British from Northern Ireland, the Unionist population would settle down as happy Irish people. But the resurgence of Ulster Scots was a further obstacle. A section of the population now referred to itself as Ulster Scots, and was protected in that choice of ethnicity by law. Gone are the stupid days when people were given a nationality, based solely on where they were born. Where you are born is a function of where your mother was on that day; nothing more.

Eamon O'Cuiv, the Irish minister, was, in terms of Dublin cabinet ministers, as honest as you can get. I think that he had a very poor understanding of Ulster politics and, in particular, of how Unionists think. He is, more than likely, a fair example of a decent Irish nationalist who cannot understand why anyone on the island would not wish to be Irish. My counterpart as chairman of the Irish board, Margaret Martin, was outstanding. She is a lady of great feeling, kindness and stature. Mrs Martin was the headmistress of a girls' school in Armagh and she lived in Dungannon. She did take flack from some of the southern-based groups for being a 'northerner'. That is partition for you. She was a great support to me at difficult times. Once she invited me to address the senior section of her school about my culture. This I was very pleased to do and was very well received. I feel it is sad that, while my wife Carol and I socialised with the Martins, neither party seemed able to leave their comfort zone for long enough to build a relationship.

While coming to terms with the Irish input, I came across a gentleman worthy of report; Dr Martin Mansergh. When I first met Martin, he was an advisor on Northern Ireland to the Irish Prime Minister, Bertie Ahern. He was of the old ascendancy background; born in Woking, outside London, and a member of the Church of Ireland. This was not a good start for an Ulster Presbyterian like me. Martin reminded me of a smoker who had given up and was now totally opposed to anything to do with smoking. He had become a nationalist of the most vocal type. To me, his knowledge of history was good but one-sided and his understanding of Ulster Protestants almost zero. He was unable to take any criticism of the Republic and could be overcome by his temper. And it was not just to me that he behaved like that. I felt that it was a great pity that I could not have a calm and considered discussion with him. It would have been worthwhile.

I could devote this entire book to the activities of the politically minded Irish in the Northern Ireland Civil Service. I have endless files and a long memory to support me. But I will resist that temptation. The promotion of Ulster Scots went well despite, or because of, all the harassment. After all, we are a thran (determined) race and, when obstacles are placed in our way, we get more thran. From what I heard and saw, local Irish people were amazed at the Ulster Scots revival. It seemed as if it had never occurred to some that we had a heritage, one which had helped to build the modern world. To some of the more political of their number, this seemed to be a disappointment. The image they preferred to portray of us was of a warlike, narrow-minded people, selected for those traits by the British, to hold a part of Mother Ireland. To find that the people with whom they shared Northern Ireland were people with a global vision, originators of human rights and fighters for equality, came as quite a shock. Then there were some middle class Irish who thought of the Belfast Agreement as a major step towards a united country; they could not understand why we were trying to swim upstream. This was said to me in my own home. Irish people have said to me: 'You cannot be serious about Ulster Scots language and history?' Others made fun and, on occasion, I had to suggest that they should not be racist. A few got very angry and called our language a 'DIY language for Orangemen'. It was rough for some years, in a way that I had not expected.

We took the battle for equality far and wide. The Irish government's television channel, TG4, was a great help. Then again, they are not a political but a cultural body and I had come to expect that support. The Northern Ireland section of the British Broadcasting Corporation (BBC) was different. Observing it over years, it was clear to see a heavy bias in favour of things Irish. In my opinion, this bias does not lie in the news broadcasts. Perhaps as a public relations person, I understood this type of programme. David Dunseith on *Talkback*, for example, had to be controversial to keep his listeners tuned in. If I could not compete with a professional like Dunseith, then I should not be either a chairman of the agency or a member of the British Upper House. Again, it was people from inside the organisation who were worried about the Irish bias.

Talkback is a BBC Radio Ulster programme, which invites listeners to phone in with comments about issues of current interest. For many years, David Dunseith was the presenter. David, for whom I have a great regard, had to ask difficult questions. But he was always fair. The Irish bias comes in the language and cultural programming. The Irish get considerable airtime and we get little. And this is despite the fact that all Irish speakers are taught the language and can also speak English. Ten of thousands learn Ulster

Scots at their mother's knee, at an early age. If a child has learnt Ulster Scots at home but has it knocked out of him at school, then that is illegal. Worse, it puts the child into a mindset from which they may never return. Would it not be more socially acceptable if the teacher told the child that they are bilingual? They could learn English at school and use Ulster Scots at home. I think that the youngsters would feel much more positive about themselves. They would come to understand that they were simply doing what a large number of other European children do, and that is to have more than one language. But then it is not in the interests of some Irish Republicans to build up the confidence and morale of the Ulster Scots. Some think that that is the problem with the BBC in Northern Ireland.

I had felt that a step forward for our culture would be a major movie or a show of some sort. In 2004, this came along in the shape of *On Eagle's Wing*. This was a large-scale musical telling the story of the Scottish planters coming to Ulster and then moving on to America. *Eagle Wing* was the first recorded boat to set out to take Ulster Scots people to the New World. The show cost a considerable sum. But, for reasons that I will spare you now and, of course, the usual harassment from officialdom, it ran out of funding. For me this was the very last straw. If the show was to succeed then I had to use community contacts to raise money. However, in order to do that, I had to set an example and invest in it myself. And if I did that, the Irish in DCAL would light a bonfire in celebration. They would now have cause to have me sacked, the reason being that the agency would have invested in a project in which I had a financial interest. So I packed my briefcase, settled my affairs and announced my resignation as chairman. The plan, which succeeded, was to highlight the unfair treatment of my culture. The morning's *Belfast Newsletter* led with the headline 'Betrayed', in very large black letters. All that day, I gave interviews to almost everyone who could speak. In DCAL, they pondered the news and were sorely temped to issue a statement refuting my points and attacking me. Wiser counsel stopped them giving me that ace. The date was Friday, 23rd April 2004; my sixtieth birthday.

Free from all official duties as the chairman of the Ulster Scots Agency, I could do other things to reveal the harassment against us, and also to further promote our culture. I had an idea. Just as an experiment, I would compare the way that the agency was treated against other organisations backed by DCAL, and to which it might be more sympathetic. In the words of Maggie Thatcher, in her final speech as Prime Minister in the House of Commons in 1990: 'What a good idea.' By this stage, there was an ongoing search for the moles in DCAL who were supplying me with accurate information. They never found any of them. In some official circles, certain staff would make fun of my passion for wearing chalk-striped dark suits. For some reason, this seemed to annoy them. Now I turned my spare time to trying to learn about DCAL and how it worked. One of the important weapons that I had was the ability to ask parliamentary questions about the department's activities. With these questions and the leaks, I was able, on occasion, to inform the Westminster politician, the minister in charge of DCAL, what was going on. Several agreed that I knew more about what the department was doing than they did. I am afraid that some senior officials did not get off on a good footing with their new masters. Some were even transferred to other parts, at the request of the minister.

My short-term future course was mapped out. I discovered some very interesting information, in particular regarding another cross-border body called Waterways Ireland, as well as some Irish festivals funded by DCAL. I had boxes of notes on both, but, in order to impart the flavour, let me record the activities of a House of Lords Committee of 2nd March 2006. You will have heard of the lord who was addressing the committee. It was I! Lord Rooker was, at that time, the Northern Ireland spokesman in the Lords.

Northern Ireland Budget Debate Ref. Hansard GC 222

Lord Laird: I have to say that I am slightly concerned about the value of debates in Committee. In July last year, I raised the topic of the funding of festivals in Northern Ireland, particularly in Belfast. The noble Lord, Lord Rooker, said;

'I shall not brook any cover-up or any funny-money fiddles that has my name on the end of it. I shall always want such things looked at. At the same time, I am looking at it purely on the merits of the case regarding what the rules are. If this is public money, the public are entitled to track it down; the auditors are entitled to track it down and know what is what (Official report. 4/7/05; col. GC 47)'

The noble Lord will remember that he was talking about the interim funding that was for use for West Belfast, Ardoyne, New Lodge and other areas. That was 7 July. I have a document here. Ardoyne Irish Festival 2005, which was signed off on the 29 July- some 22 days later. It was signed off by a gentleman in the Department for Culture, Arts and Leisure and the Department for Social Development, for a grant of £72,000. The report is for 2005, but when you read it, it is the same report as for 2004. In fact, it is obviously the same report as for 2004 because the whole way through it the dates are for 2004.

The problem with Northern Ireland is that it is a small part of the world and people talk to one another. The people who outlined the fact that they had used the 2004 report twice were actually the good people in Ardoyne. Just think of it – we on the Unionist side of the House cannot get money for our festivals and for funding our activities, and we meet people from Ardoyne who say: 'DCAL told us 'Send in the same report as last year and we will not read it. We might weigh it, but we will not read it.' The same report was submitted, but the bright spark who sent it in did not even have the wit to change the date. At least, in fairness to the people of New Lodge who sent exactly the same report in for 2005 as for 2004, they went through it and changed the dates.

That was 22 days after the Minister told me that he would not stand any funny money and that nothing would be done in his name with funny money. Only 22 days later DCAL is signing off £72,000 on the wrong year's report. I ask the Minister this: do we talk in a vacuum here? Is this a waste of time? Does information from these debates go back to the Northern Ireland Civil Service? Does it go to the departments?

The very document that was signed off by DCAL was signed off incorrectly under its own terms and conditions. The document says that it must be signed off on behalf of Ardoyne by a member of the board of directors of Ardoyne. Even that had not been done properly. How can DCAL, only 22 days after the Minister told me that there would be no funny money in his name, sign off a report for the wrong year which has not been properly filled in? I have raised this with the noble lord before, he knows about this. I raised it with him in December. I know that from December to March is not a long time for DCAL to answer queries. It is probably going through its book of weasel words.

................The only way we are ever going to get out of the mess that we are in, in Northern Ireland, is through fairness and not favouritism...

In this report in Lords Hansard is contained the details of outright one-sidedness to the Irish community by DCAL. I never got a satisfactory explanation from Lord Rooker, who attended the debate. As in earlier situations, it seems that an honest minister had been nobbled by some outside force, perhaps the Northern Ireland Office, and required to close his eyes to the unfairness. It did not stop there. Things were just as bad during the following period. The minister is reported to have been informed by Gerry Adams, the Sinn Féin president, that if the funding for the West Belfast Irish Festival was cut, buses would be burnt in the Falls area. Also, the rulebook for signing off these grants was reinvented to accommodate the Irish gatherings. Any other project had to be agreed in advance of the function if it wanted funding, according to a business model. A process called 'receiving a letter of offer' then followed. But in the case of these Irish festivals, the business aspect was sometimes only completed after the event, and then the letter of offer sent out by the department. I attended a meeting on this issue in London, where I witnessed the minister, looking very embarrassed, and the permanent secretary, both trying to defend this breach of procedure.

I am not against any of the Irish festivals receiving public funding. The organisers do a good job for their communities. In the case of West Belfast, I was a guest speaker at one of the events. I enjoyed the evening and, as I expected, was treated very well. What I objected to was that the non-Irish communities were not treated with equality. Why not? The figures are available. During one of those years, the Department for Culture, Arts and Leisure carried out an internal search into how much they allocated to Irish events and how much to non-Irish events. It soon became clear that the figures would be in the order of ninety per cent Irish, ten per cent non-Irish. In a fit of embarrassment, they stopped the search.

The other operation that I looked into in some depth, during that period, was Waterways Ireland. A long and complicated tale of mismanagement and bullying emerged. There were also appointments made for political reasons, something that is illegal in my part of the United Kingdom. To offer a brief explanation, I turn again to the report of the Lord's Committee of 2nd March 2006. The issue that I start with is of the purchase of bulk chocolates by the chief executive, John Martin, using public money. He gave these to his staff, as presents. John Martin was a Dublin-based senior civil servant who was well versed in the strange goings-on in the Irish government's system.

Lord Laird… '.the small matter of bulk purchase of chocolate for the staff. The justification is not clear. The chief executive lied to the Minister and Parliament about the approval to purchase it, and the noble Lord, Lord Rooker, reported to this House that the purchase had been approved by the senior management group on 3 December 2002 and 4 December 2003. The original minutes, of which I have a copy, show that to be a lie. This is the second time that the chief executive misled Parliament. The last time it was over the corruption surrounding the appointment of the director of marketing and communication. The chief executive appointed Martin Dennany without any recruitment process in a job-for-the-boys scandal. Yet the report made to the Northern Ireland Assembly in 2002 stated that the appointment was made through open competition. At least 21 staff have complained of gross mismanagement, corruption in appointments and bullying. In one case of bullying, the chief executive was investigated and the complaint upheld.

Very serious concerns have been expressed about appointments to two senior management jobs. Concerns have been reported about the culture of the organisation. There is a breakdown in confidence in the chief executive among middle managers and staff. The main reason is the growing concern and anger at the shift of blame for the dysfunction of Waterways Ireland, including financial matters, from the chief executive and senior management on to middle management and staff.........

Against that background, the Irish gave the chief executive a 35 per cent performance related pay increase between 2000 and 2004........ The right honourable Member for North Antrim has requested at Privy Council level to see the documentation relating to the affair, I was told that I could not see it since to do so would damage relations between the UK and a foreign country. The only explanation can be that the gentleman has political immunity. Did we vote for the Belfast agreement to bring in low standards of cronyism, jobs for the boys and low standards of Irish governance into our part of the United Kingdom... ......'

This is no more than a fleeting glimpse into the way the Northern Ireland Department for Culture, Arts and Leisure, deals differently with Ulster Scots affairs, compared with Irish ones. When it came to satisfying their Dublin masters, all doors were open. Every rule could be broken. No lie left untold. No Northern Ireland Office order left unanswered. But, when it came to considering anything that might benefit the Ulster Scots community, it was all about delaying, sticking to the rules and, if not hard enough, inventing some more. Whatever you do, smother this upstart culture that is not part of the Catholic Mother Ireland's script. Is it any wonder that many of us feel that Northern Ireland is now a cold place for us?

Chairmanship of the Ulster Scots Agency taught me a lot. It is a part of my life that has helped to define my political views. Other folk have changed by taking part in wars. For me, this period was similar. I can now talk about my Unionism in a new light. I am no longer just a paper Unionist. I have tested the Republican ideal and the world of Eire. What I found was worse than any Unionist could imagine. And there is more to come. From this period onwards I became a practical Unionist. I had been there, done that, and was not impressed.

On a soggy day in the early 2000s, I ventured down to the famous Boyne Valley to the site of the battle. A new organisation was being set up to administer part of the old site. The Irish government had purchased five hundred or so acres of the southern side, covered by King James and his forces as they fled. That day, I met the former Irish Prime Minister, John Bruton, for the first time. He and I were to head the new organisation. John is a very pleasant man. In common with politicians from the Republic, he showed little interest or understanding of the affairs of my part of the United Kingdom. Then again, why should he? But, standing out in one of the fields and soaking wet, I met a man who was to be of considerable help to me in later years, when investigating the affairs of the Republican movement's support groups in the Republic.

Kevin Cahill, as I soon learnt his name to be, is a most interesting person. Born and reared in County Laois with an average Roman Catholic, nationalist background, and fluent in Irish, his career took many turns. Following a period in the Irish army, he was enrolled in a church seminary to become a priest, but gave it up after several months to join the British army. Following that, Kevin read for a degree in English literature, at the University of Ulster in Coleraine. He later became a journalist and a researcher for Paddy Ashdown, who was then the leader of the

Liberal Democrat party. Recently, the gentleman in question has been writing books, usually about land ownership, both regional and global.

Kevin, in common with others from his community, has 'seen a shaft of light'. Until recently, he knew nothing about the Unionist case nor had he heard of Ulster Scots. But, being a fair-minded fellow with Liberal party leanings, he became very interested in the cause of Ulster's freedom. More than that, he had become disenchanted with Irish society and what has happened in the Republic. Through a complicated set of circumstances, Kevin owned the northern battlefield at the Boyne. Today, the twenty-seven acres are owned by a group of supporters and plans are in hand to rebuild an obelisk. This erection had been built in 1736, to mark William's victory, but was blown up by Republicans in 1921.

I am still heavily involved with the Boyne project, alongside Kevin and others. As an Orangeman, it is important that I should point out that we have received nothing but total support from the authorities in the Republic in planning and organising events there. The Irish Police Service has been particularly helpful. This is how things should be and I hope soon they will be, in Northern Ireland. I am totally against religious ghettos. We, all the taxpayers, own the streets and anyone should be able to use these communal spaces inside the law. The day must come when Sinn Féin can walk the Shankill and the Orange the Falls! Anyway, I was pleased to get to know Kevin and now regard him as a good friend.

The Ulster Scot

[illegible]

CHAPTER EIGHT

The Ulster Scot

THE ULSTER SCOTS ARE THAT PART OF THE SCOTTISH NATION WHICH HAS BEEN HARDENED ON THE ANVIL OF IRELAND

I AM NOT a grumpy old man. When you arrive in your mid-sixties, there is a natural tendency to make an unfavourable comparison between life in the old days with the hustle and bustle of today. I am sorry to report that too many of my friends have fallen into that pothole. As a result, their company can be difficult and even boring at times. To many, in every generation, past days always seem to be the best ones. The memory tells of sunny summers and a better quality snow during the winters. People in your childhood seemed more content and kinder. Elderly relations were a pleasure to be with, unlike their counterparts today, who seem demanding and time-consuming.

Logic demands that all this is revisionist rubbish! Memories of early childhood are the first into the memory and are thus of better quality. Also, the mind seems to retain only the extremes of good and bad. Adults remembering the same period as young ones have a different perspective on events. The greatest complaint of my generation is that time has speeded up – or so it seems. But that is an example of the law of relativity. And it is even more simple than $E=MC^2$. When I was five, a year was a fifth of my life. But, at sixty-five, a year is one sixty-fifth of my life. A day, when I am old, is bound to be comparatively shorter than when I was younger. So why complain?

Getting on in years must be taken into account when anyone considers their views and how they have changed since childhood. To me, there are more changes for the better than for the worse. Understanding that the world is a village community, the advance of science with all that has brought, and the drive towards equality. Even in my native province, things are, on the whole, better than in the 1950s or 1960s. Northern Ireland is a prosperous country, with a greater degree of contentment than before. In our particular case, the Troubles are over, with only a few head-cases wanting a strife-torn society to return. It is my view that all the important changes could have taken place without the civil unrest, which blighted several decades. But please allow me one substantial gripe. The main area of change, which is of doubtful merit, is the creation of a mandatory coalition at Stormont, as the result of the Belfast Agreement. My love for a local administration is known to be limited, but the concept of an enforced executive is madness and is not serving the people of Ulster. Each minister considers that their department is in their sole possession, to run as they will, without any policy agreements with other members of the executive.

The Sinn Féin Minister of Education has gone on a solo run, on purely political grounds. It is over the future of academic selection for children at eleven, to decide what type of senior school they will attend. As one who is dyslexic and thus failed the selection examination, twice, I hold no love for the current system. But it seems that where a pendulum swings, by definition, it swings too far. Other and more extreme examples exist, of Sinn Féin ministers pushing purely political decisions, against logic and demand. One, about which I feel very strongly, is the proposed new multi-lane motorway that would run from the border to fifty-odd miles away in Londonderry. This proposal, which I trust will never see the light of day, will make Northern Ireland the laughing stock of Europe. Do we really want to be the last place in the western world where a multi-lane motorway is being built, instead of using the existing track-bed of a railway line, which would solve the same transport problem?

On 14th February 1965, the last revenue-earning trains ran on the former Great Northern Railway line, from Portadown to Londonderry. The journey distance is of seventy-five and a half miles. The track bed is mostly still in place and, according to railway economists, could be reinstated, on an upgraded basis, for half the cost of the new highway. But there are other benefits. The land used up in the rail transport corridor would be only twenty per cent of the prime farming land required for the proposed multi-lanes. And, of course, most of the old line is still in existence. The amount of CO^2 emitted by a railway system is 60% less than that omitted by road vehicles carrying the same numbers. If that were not enough, a bus travelling from Londonderry to Dublin would take up to forty-five minutes longer than one of the high quality trains.

The Irish government claims that it has set aside many billions of pounds to pay for the multi-lane motorway, even though it is in a part of the United Kingdom. I do not get the impression that Dublin is awash with spare cash for this project. Besides, are we, in Northern Ireland, to become the carbon dioxide dumping ground for the British Isles? Irish citizens, driving through Northern Ireland and dumping the dreadful gas in the UK, will increase our emission levels while lowering theirs. It would be a burden for our tax system and the health service for decades to come, not to mention a permanent reminder of our follies.

Interestingly, Sinn Féin supports the creation of a new railway line from Sligo to Letterkenny, over ground in the Republic that has never had such a line. Yet fifteen miles to the east, in the United Kingdom, Sinn Féin supports the opposite policy; road before rail. Who wants a United Ireland? Is it the British government and the EU's policy to reopen railway lines, instead of building new multi-lane motorways? Direct rule would stop this rubbish. However, I feel that logic and common sense will prevail on this issue, even at Stormont.

If I have learnt anything in my life, it is a loathing for all forms of nationalism; not nationalists, but nationalism. Nationalism is narrow, inward looking and has shown a capability, over the years, to demand that people die in its name. In the wars of the last century alone, millions of people did just that. I am a proud Ulster Scot. I love the culture, the way of thinking, of speaking, its historical context and its worldwide perspective. But I hope that I am always careful to say that, while I am an Ulster Scot, our culture is as good as any other, but it is not better. An ongoing problem with the identification with one culture is the creation of the idea that your culture is better and has more validity than that of anyone else. Once that idea has taken root, it is not long before a group feels it has a God-given right to pursue its culture and identity, at the expense of all others. From that point, it is downhill all the way. A sad sight for me is to see some, in my own community, thinking that their background is better than others. Bearing in mind the decades of siege the Ulster Scots and Unionist people have been under since 1880, there may be an excuse. But we should rise above it.

One of the most pleasing things about being an Ulster Scot is the worldview that we share. This worldview contributed seventeen presidents of the United States, as well as many military, business, and church and entertainment figures. As you have learnt already, the history of that section of the Scottish people who were hardened on the anvil of Ulster, although they were small in number, has made a very significant contribution to the modern world. It is my view that they were right, with the correct ideals and a work ethic to match. But, and it is a big 'but', I must always bear in mind that my view is shaped by my background, one that was not available to those of other cultures. In the same way, I have not lived their lives or shared their history or experiences. While I believe strongly in my viewpoint, developed from the sum total of my reaction to my experiences, I must accept that other viewpoints are of equal significance to those that hold them. I fear for much of history. People seem to assume that those next door are wrong and must be brought to the truth and even, in some circumstances, to death. Correct or not, there is no hope for this overcrowded planet unless we live and let live inside a common code of individual human rights. One right that we do not have is to have as many offspring as we like. It is coming to terms with one's neighbour that is important.

In developing my thinking, I call up experiences of my homeland of Ulster and the events that have taken place there. I call also upon a combination of inherited knowledge and that insight I have gained from observing the culture in which I was reared. But one unfortunate side effect of the problem on the island of Ireland is the difficultly that people with my views have, when trying to interact properly with the Irish.

This is a two-way process; one side is the mirror image of the other. Again, this is understandable. The Irish, as a group, have inherited baggage and experiences that are all too alive. While I disagree with their understanding of events, I must have regard for it. The further up the political or religious scale my interlocutors are, the more they are likely to be objective and exchange information in a calm and meaningful manner. For example, I have talked at length to members of Sinn Féin, at all levels. My views are not a surprise to them, or theirs to me. But, in a clinical way, we can examine the factors involved. I have always found that rewarding. I have learnt much from listening to people of all backgrounds. In the middle ranks of Sinn Féin, there is an almost machine-like ability to outline policy and explain past events. Put them under slight pressure on a subject outside their comfort area and they feel unsafe. They are not trained for intellectual arguments. They are more at home on the constitution issues, but even there they can be rattled.

One of the major changes in Northern Ireland since 2000 has been the influx of other ethnic groups. As the Province became more prosperous and most locals had jobs, a labour shortage came about. This was gratefully filled by folk from Eastern European countries, recently freed from the USSR. The Polish were the main group to appear and to undertake the jobs, mostly at the bottom of the market. Northern Ireland is used to outside labour. For many decades, the hospitality industry and the medical sector were held together by good people from other parts of the world. Human nature being what it is, a section of the local population turned against the new workforce. Sadly, the protesters included some from the Ulster Scots or Unionist community. If only they knew the world vision of their forefathers and their role in developing the values of the modern world, they might well be ashamed. After all, we were the incomers once.

I am going to discuss the case against nationalism. In doing so, it is only natural that I use the example of the brand I know best – Irish nationalism. This is not meant to insult or demean anyone who holds nationalist views, but there are points that need to be made. On visits to the Dublin area for social functions, I have often been asked: 'What do Unionists have against a United Ireland?' Then, when I give the answer in detail, the questioners become deeply offended. This is an experience that is common to my fellow Unionists and causes us amazement and wonder. Why ask an Ulsterman a question if you cannot take the answer? People from my Province are known the world over for straight and truthful talking. If, in an attempt to humour our Irish friends, we softened or joked about the answer to their well-meant question, the result would be misleading, out of character and patronising. So why cannot the Irish take the answer to their question? The interchange is a partial illustration of the overall problem. Let us explore.

Ulster has rarely been a legislative unit with the rest of the island of Ireland. In less complicated times, geography defined areas of administration. The mountains south of Newry and the shortness of the thirteen-mile stretch of sea between Donaghadee in County Down and Portpatrick in Scotland dictated natural travel routes. When foot and boat were the only modes of transport, it was easier to travel from Belfast to Glasgow than to Dublin. In effect, the Irish Sea was the M1 of its time. The building of Black Pig's Dyke, underlines the distinction between the two parts of the island. This was a man-made border, not far from the existing UK border.

This defensive line is physical proof that Ulster regarded itself as a separate part of the island of Ireland. Instead, the area was Scottish in nature, along with its natural ally the west of Scotland. Running through the counties of Down, Armagh, Monaghan, Cavan, Leitrim and Donegal, the Black Pig's Dyke was built to keep out the plundering Irish. Although not a continuous dyke, it did cut off the two countries by being positioned to guard important routes. It is believed that its construction took place over many years, sometime during the period between 300BC and 300AD. In defending Ulster, it made good use of thick forests, earthworks and boggy country, to bolster the man-made parts. The dyke is of such historical importance that I contend that part of it should be recognised and preserved. But, in the age of Irish nationalism and its desire to ensure that all facts fit their narrative, there seems little prospect of this happening.

The Ulstermen, of Irish, Ulster Scots, English or any other ethnic group, all differ in outlook and values from the folk in the Republic. My Irish fellow Ulstermen will not only agree with this view but also will polish and refine my arguments. Paddy Kennedy was a young, vocal, Republican Labour member for Belfast Central when I was a Stormont Member of Parliament. He was a chartered accountant by trade and we spent quite some time exchanging ideas and stories about our backgrounds, during the long and boring sittings of the House. 'A Dubliner will urinate down your back,' Paddy once, alarmingly, said to me, 'but to your face he will try to explain it away as sweat.' Quite a remark for a nationalist! With the exception of Sinn Féin members, who came later anyway, nationalist politicians with whom I had a similar discussion would make the same point, although perhaps not so graphically.

While in the public relations industry, I made an interesting discovery. Particularly in the early years, I obtained a lot of well-paid work from Dublin. On several occasions, well-respected and senior PR consultants from Dublin made a similar point to me: In effect, they were pleased that they had assigned to my agency a difficult or complicated task. Because I was an Ulsterman, they could now relax in the certain knowledge that no matter what went wrong, the job would be done to the highest degree. Some would go further and say that getting anything done in Dublin by southerners was a nightmare. I have always pointed out that doing PR work for Dublin-based organisations was easy, interesting and financially more rewarding than working for my fellow Ulstermen. A large part of that is the natural inbred Irish flare for communication. I will give way to no one in my admiration for that group's ability to use language and action in a clever and creative way. In this area of activity, I think, I am more like the Irish than my own ethnic grouping.

There is a maturing and growing disconnect between those from Ulster and those from the rest of the island. For further proof, just look at the way Gerry Adams and company were like fish out of water, when fighting the last general election in the Republic in 2007. Adams was clearly seen as an outsider, a northerner, a blow-in, one who knew little about the system of administration in that country. Sinn Féin did very badly when all the votes were counted.

The Irish Republic is still a new country which has not yet come to terms with its past. It is only in the past ten years that I, as a Unionist, have taken to looking into the Republic. I am shocked with what I see. Until 1999, I could not have cared less how narrow, small minded and sectarian it was. I have plenty to do in the United Kingdom, which is very far from perfect. But my period as chairman of a cross-border body, where I had an executive role in the Republic, albeit a small one, opened my eyes and has given me a problem with which I struggle every day. Most of this you will have gleaned earlier, when I described my time as chairman of the Ulster Scots Agency. Unless, that is, you are just flipping through this tome, looking for interesting bits.

Looked at from a Unionist perspective, with Unionist values, the Republic is full of doublethink and double talk. Again, I must issue my timely health warning. I like the Irish as individuals and also collectively, when they are not involved in politics. I like the countryside; I like even the happy-go-lucky atmosphere which pervades everything. That is, of course, unless I have to be involved with that atmosphere in business. So, none of my remarks are meant to be insulting. On the contrary, they are intended to inform, on a relaxed basis, as to the views of a Unionist Ulster Scot. How do the activities of organs of the Irish state look today to Unionists, the very people that those in the Republic want to convert, if their national goal is to be achieved? Anyway, knowing what the other person actually thinks is a big help during a peace process.

I could write much about the ills of society in the United Kingdom and the changes that I would like to see take place. Anyone who is sad enough to follow my work in the House of Lords will get a feeling for my discontent. So, in the context of someone who has been offered a second-hand car (in this case, the imperialistic aspirations of some Irish) and wishes not to purchase, I outline my reasons for the decision, in order to help and support the salesman. This should mean that the next time the salesman contacts a potential purchaser, he may have upgraded the car and have a more convincing sales patter. (What about using the analogy of a beauty and the suitor?)

The slogan used by the Unionists during the Home Rule Crisis was: 'Home Rule is Rome Rule.' This became only too clear to be the case following 1921. The ethos of the founding fathers of that country, in particular of Fianna Fáil, a former IRA grouping under de Valera, envisaged a country dominated by the Roman Catholic Church, which values a kind of mystical living. The Roman Catholic Church had been in favour of the Union in 1801 and had only joined the nationalist bandwagon in the 1880s, as already pointed out. The understanding was that the Church would take control of education in a 'united Mother Ireland'. In this longed-for land, people could express themselves in song and poetry and the indefinable mystical things in life. There stood the image of the simple cottage, burning peat; the householder having a few acres to feed cattle and fowl and enough space to grow all that the kitchen could demand. Men would meet at the crossroads, suck their pipes and pass the day in the exchange of crack – of the banter type.

There is no smell that evokes a country of my forefathers more than the smell of burning peat. The idea of a simple, not too productive, living is also seductive. A quiet life away from worry and stress must seem ideal to all at some time. But right or wrong, their lifestyle is far removed from the industrial heartland that Ulster had become at that period. For a decade, Belfast was the fastest growing industrialized city in the United Kingdom. Being positioned near the major ports of Glasgow and Liverpool, it was well placed to play a role in ship-building.

At one time, the city had the largest independent shipbuilding yard in the world. The largest rope works, massive engineering factories and an all-important linen industry. Belfast was full of back streets where poverty, hunger, dirt and sickness patrolled every day, in search of further mischief. Men rose out of their shabby houses when the factory hooters blew and, robot-like, in light or dark, made their way to the factory. The concept of living in a Celtic mist was as far removed from their thoughts as the moon is from Artigarvan. The fullness of time will judge as to which lifestyle was the correct course but that is not the issue. Ulster men and women flocked into Belfast and other town centres, to partake in the Industrial Revolution that swept the country in the nineteenth century.

Many, including myself, believe that the Industrial Revolution in the nineteenth century was a product of the Enlightenment of the previous century. I have already examined the Enlightenment and the part played by the Ulster Scot, Francis Hutcheson. The Home Rule period starkly focussed the difference between New Light and Old Light and their effect on society. The openness of New Light, with its desire to inquire into all aspects of life, and the repetition of the words 'prove it', opens minds. What is today called 'thinking out of the box' became a way of life for generations of engineers, scientists, thinkers, businessmen and more. History informs us that Old Light forces, including the Roman Catholic Church and traditional, bible-based, Protestant groups, were against the advance of science and of freethinking. I have always felt that too much of religion is about control. 'I control you because I have the keys to heaven and you need them to get there.' Religion should not dull a person; it should inspire them to inquire and to 'think out of the box'. In fact, that should be the overreaching goal of all human activity. Supporting Manchester United or watching Coronation Street will fill a gap and might refresh the mind, but they should not be allowed to stunt human thinking.

The decision of my fellow countrymen at the turn of the nineteenth century was for freedom. But then, what is freedom? Having attempted to answer that question, one can see the battle lines drawn on the island from the 1880s, and see how they are still in place today. It is right to ask, did the Belfast shipyard workers of the period, living in squalor, have more or less freedom than the Irishman with his cottage, peat fire and access to a crossroads? The answer can only lie in what you think freedom to be.

Nature is the biggest force on the planet. Some consider God and nature to be the same thing. But nature, over its millions of years of hard work, has made the best of what it had; it innovated, experimented, got some things wrong, got some things right, but it always developed. It could not stand still in the face of problems; it found a way around them or scrapped the plan and started again.

I am taking the Belfast workers as an example. More than likely they did not know it, but they were the outworking of the New Light. Their plight was totally unacceptable and makes people like me ashamed of my forefathers, for allowing such conditions to occur. That was the thinking of the time. But nature has since made conditions improve, to keep up with its desire for advance and change.

New Light thinking was a driving force in Ulster nearly two hundred years ago. Freedom to me, and I suggest to the majority of Ulster Scots or Unionists, means freedom of the individual. I want to be able to think what I want to think, put forward any views that I consider correct and conduct my life with whatever cultural and ethnic values I wish. However, there is a vitally important point. My actions must be commensurate with values of the greater society. Maybe these rights are called human rights.

I use those words in the knowledge that in Northern Ireland the words 'human rights' have been devalued by a one-sided human rights industry. But I have dealt with that issue already.

So, the case that I make is that the people of Ulster, of whatever religion, background or colour, are different, with different values from those who live in our neighbouring country. That is no one's fault. Not better or worse, just different. Ulster people are different from the Welsh, all forms of English and the Scottish. By definition, we are all different and collectively so as well. But in the case of the Irish, the difference is very deep and fundamental. If a state is organised and run according to their ethos, then our (non-Irish) basic human rights would be infringed.

We can examine some structural problems with the Irish Republic. The central point is that the concept of freedom is different from that which is understood by those of us from the New Light tradition. In the Republic, the idea of freedom is collective while, for those like me, freedom is individual. This leads to the idea that, for the Irish nationalist, freedom is related to a piece of land, in this case the island of Ireland. Their cause is the cause of Ireland or Mother Ireland or Mother Catholic Ireland. People are required to die for the very ground, linked to some mystical idea of a time that never was, or could be. From my viewpoint, that idea is outrageous. I love areas of land but its freedom is nothing compared with my ability to think what I want to think and do what I want, inside a framework of standards of equality and human rights. But here again, human rights seem to mean something different in the Republic of Ireland.

Take another simple example. Several years ago, I tried to buy a property in Galway, as an experiment. Having checked out the suitable locations, I went into discussions with an estate agency. At a point in those discussions, it was made clear to me that, because I did not have a qualification in the Irish language, it was unlawful for the agent to sell me the property. In the twenty-first century, in Western Europe, what is, in effect, a certificate of ethnicity is required to purchase property. When I raised the issue with decision makers in Dublin, some said: 'Who wants to live in

Galway anyway?' That is not the answer. But it is the sort of glib response that Irish citizens cannot understand that Ulstermen so dislike.

Ask, in Dublin, why their national broadcasting network (RTE) plays the angelus several times a day. Ireland is the only modern country in Europe to do so. But it is infringing non-Roman Catholics' human rights, and when pointed out, you are told: 'It is only for a few minutes.' Again, that is not the answer. Why is the Irish Parliament able to, and it regularly does, pass sectarian legislation? Ask that question and you are likely to be told, as I was, that it has nothing to do with someone from the 'Black North'. And I agree. However, there are still people in Dublin who try and tell us about the need for greater human rights protection in Northern Ireland. If someone comes around to my garden and offers advice, I would like to see their garden before I take their words of wisdom. One gentleman who interests himself by providing such advice is the Irish Minister for Foreign Affairs, Michael Martin. I wrote to Mr Martin seeking his support in asking the authorities in Libya for compensation for all the victims of IRA violence. This is because that country had officially supplied boatloads of arms to the Republican terrorists. Despite his office confirming on several occasions that he had received the letter, I got no meaningful response. But then, I suppose Martin is an Irish Republican and so believes in 'fair play only for the Irish'. He is one of the same people who refused to meet me to discuss human rights for the twenty-five thousand Ulster Scots who are that country's national minority.

Ulster people of all backgrounds are straight talking people. Fancy footwork, patched up with mirrors and string, is not something that they consider clever. The period that brought the Celtic Tiger to the Republic was watched with support from the direction of Belfast. Everyone likes to see their neighbour getting on. But the aftermath is different. Ireland now looks more like a second rate banana republic, after the tide has gone out. I have studied Fintan O'Toole's recent publication, entitled *A Ship of Fools*. I gained no pleasure from its content. It describes a corrupt society whose politicians, bankers and developers are awash with money made through corruption. For the record, I repeat some of the information from O'Toole. It does not make good reading for genuine Republicans.

O'Toole clearly believes that the main author of the current political mess in Ireland is the unconvicted gunrunner and former Prime Minister, Charles Haughey. At the state funeral of Haughey, the serving Prime Minister, Bertie Ahern said: 'When the shadows have faded, the light of his achievements will remain.' Those shadows were cast, of course, by the towering skyscrapers of money the Boss (Haughey) had accumulated while holding high political office; the equivalent in 2006 of about €45 million, or 171 times his total salary payments as a full time politician. Corruption, Ahern was saying, even on such a heroic scale, was of little long-term consequence. This was a serving Taoiseach (Prime Minister) speaking at a formal state funeral.

> *The act of collective homage was solemnised by the party's young princeling, the future finance minister, Brian Lenihan; son, namesake and political heir of one of Haughey's closest allies. Haughey had stolen €250,000 from a fund set up to pay for a liver transplant for Lenihan's father, whom Haughey described as 'one of my closest personal friends and certainly my closest political friend'...* (page 27).

On page 31, O'Toole put the timetable of the whole downward process into context:

> *'From the mid-1990's onwards, it became ever more undeniable that corruption was deeply embedded, both at the top and the bottom of Irish public life. A deep but vague unease was gradually replaced with facts and figures. Three major figures – Haughey and Burke from Fianna Fáil and Michael Lowry, a minister for the major Opposition party Fine Gael – were caught bang to rights. A largely successful conspiracy to control the development of the capital city by systematically bribing large numbers of Fianna Fáil and Fine Gael councillors was*

uncovered. It became completely clear that the public interest was being literally sold out to an inner circle of businessmen.

Sleazy as these crimes were, they were not unique to Irish politics. What was peculiar to Ireland, however, was what happened next – virtually nothing.'

On page 94, referring to the Irish government, O'Toole said:

'The government failed so miserably to achieve its goals on poverty because it no longer actually believed in the Republican concept of equality.'

Fintan O'Toole is a columnist with the Irish Times. He is an acclaimed historian, biographer and critic. His book, *Ship of Fools*, is well worth reading for anyone who wonders why Unionists are Unionists.

The Roman Catholic Church, the state and the cover up of illegal sexual activity is something upon which I do not want to comment. Some of my good Roman Catholic friends are hurting badly on this issue and it is not for someone like me to add to the general misery.

For me, the issue of the Ulster Scots community in the Republic remains unresolved. And, I suspect, will remain so. There are two issues for me to deal with. There is my conscience and there is the question: 'How can I help these invisible people?' The feeling of guilt that I am left with dates from the time when twenty-six counties opted out of the United Kingdom. We are a people that believe in the importance of the individual's human rights. But we left supporters to their fate in an alien country. What else could we have done? Now, I feel I must help that invisible community – no one else seems to want to do so. It is not that they suffer violence, though some have; they are discriminated against in employment, provision of services and now in education. They feel under pressure. The major human rights issue that affects them is the need for a qualification in Irish language for government employment. That means that an Ulster Scot has to learn English in the local school and then go on to learn Irish, in order to obtain such employment. Two languages have been historically required and that is an infringement in human rights. Recently, the inventive Irish government has removed the Irish-language qualification requirement in certain cases, and replaced it with some fancy move that has the same effect. Now, if a person does an examination in history, or another topic, in the Irish language, they get up to ten per cent extra marks! So the 'Irish only' policy still operates. The Dublin authorities must think that we are stupid. They certainly do not deceive the Republic's Unionist population. Events from the ethnic cleansing of Protestants, in the 1920s and 1930s, to the treatment of the 'invisible people' today, are burnt deep into Unionists' thinking. They help to inform them in their determination to be Unionists, to this very day.

In recent years I have been invited to attend meetings in the Republic, to exchange views with others. This is a process that I value. But I have discovered two things. Firstly, the people there seem to hear only what they want to hear. Secondly, and more interestingly, I am taken aside by individuals who are from the Irish community, and, 'in confidence, you understand', provide me with information. For example, I was at a human rights seminar just across the border, in the summer of 2009. I gave my usual twenty minutes on the lack of human rights in the Republic to a stony faced audience and retired to wonder why there was no response. Nothing happened until the tea break. Then I was approached by several individuals who, one by one, would check that no one was listening before explaining their points. The main thrust of some was: 'Look, I need to get support from officialdom so I cannot be seen to be speaking to you. But I agree with all that you have said. Please keep up your work and do not tell anyone I was talking to you.' Some Republic!

Irish nationalism or its brother, Republicanism, is very strange. I have spent most of my life in a fringe activity to marketing. So let me just look at Irish nationalism in that light. The nationalists' wish is to create a so-called united Ireland, by consent. They have something to sell. So what do they do? Do they find out what the potential market wants? Do they set out to satisfy that need? Do they bring flowers to give to the target market? Of course not. What did Irish nationalists do to obtain consent? They treated us as if we did not exist; they created a state, the Republic, which is just about as bad as the worst predictions of our forefathers. Then they wonder why we are still Unionists. I am now in my sixties, and all that nationalism has done for me is insult me, ignore my requests, and allow its extremists to shoot or blow up my relations and friends. A new and original concept in marketing!

I have often wondered why the idea of making the Republic of Ireland open and welcoming to the non-Irish on this island never seems to have occurred to the Irish. As a people, they regard themselves as welcoming and friendly, when not roused in nationalist fever. Instead of attacking things that are British, why not try to include the non-Irish in cultural activities? In marketing terms, if you want to sell a product, you should find out what the target market requires and then so refine your product. Why not take the opportunity to explain the Protestant ethos and the importance of such iconic events as the Battle of the Boyne? In other words have a total revamp of the Irish system of teaching history.

In Northern Ireland we take it for granted that the Irish have a public holiday on Saint Patrick's Day. We can also enjoy the festivities. I hope that the days will return when, once again, my Irish fellow countrymen in Northern Ireland will join me in enjoying the celebrations on the Twelfth of July. But why not make that day one of equal rank to Saint Patrick's in the Republic? Would a bank holiday to celebrate the freedoms won at the Battle of the Boyne not be in keeping with some of the rhetoric of early Republicans?

I note with praise that the former Irish Justice Minister, Michael McDowell, has taken up the idea. It would be better sales tactics than trying to kill or drive out those with whom violent Republicans of today do not agree. Narrow-minded, inward looking Irish nationalism, when taken to extreme, has been a negative curse on these islands. The idea that an entire cultural group could be removed or subjugated just to appease 'Mother Ireland' is distasteful. Or perhaps Irish nationalism has not the self-confidence to allow other cultures to exist beside theirs.

In common with most folk brought up in Scottish culture, I have a high regard for our national poet, Rabbie Burns. When verse is used to describe something beautiful, I am left out, but when it is used to express an emotion, I can be much moved. My favourite is the bard's *A man's a man for a' that.* Nothing else expresses the Scottish desire for independence and equality. I will treat you.

Is there, for honest Poverty
That hings his head, an' a' that?
A coward slave, we pass him by,
We dare be poor for a' that!
For a' that, an' a' that.
Our toils obscure, an' a' that;
The rank is but the guinea's stamp,
The Man's the gowd for a' that.

What tho' on hamely fare we dine,
Wear hoddin grey, an' a' that;
Gie fools their silks, an' knaves their wine;
A Man's a Man for a' that:
For a' that, an' a' that,
Their tinsel show, an' a' that;
The honest man, tho' e'er sae poor,
Is king o' men for a' that.

Ye see yon birkie, ca'd a lord,
Wha struts, an' stares, an' a' that;
Tho' hundreds worship at his word,
He's but a coof for a' that.
For a' that, an' a' that,

His ribband, star, an' a' that;
The man o' independent mind
He looks an' laughs at a' that.

A Prince can mak a belted knight,
A marquis, duke, an' a' that,
But an honest man's abon his might,
Gude faith, he maunna fa' that!
For a' that, an' a' that,
Their dignities an' a' that;
The pith o' sense, an' pride o'worth,
Are higher rank than a' that.

Then let us pray, that come it may,
(As come it will for a' that,)
That Sense an' Worth, o'er a' the earth,
May bear the gree, an' a' that,
For a' that, an' a' that,
It's comin yet for a' that,
That Man to Man, the warld o'er,
Shall brothers be for a' that.

There are no other words that sum up Scottishness, for me, than those; independence, the sense of worth and the desire for something better in the future. Burn's words, of just over two hundred years ago, can be further qualified. In theory, I agree with the concept of equality. But what is equality? And how can it be created? Can someone born with only one leg be the equal of others with two? If he, or she, cannot, then why demand equality?

Is it equality of opportunity? But how does that affect the one-legged person?

Until future generations can sort out 'equality', if they can, let me take another section of Burn's poem for inspiration: 'That Sense an' Worth, o'er a' the earth.' Perhaps that is the point. Everyone should have a sense of worth in their community or circle of friends. Equality cannot be about the expectation that everyone can get to the same level. That is impossible. But if we consider 'sense of worth', then the calculation takes into account where a person started, what contribution they make to society and in what regard society holds them. The well-known Scottish Presbyterian, Gordon Brown, became the leader of his students at university. That must have given him a sense of worth. He felt that he could do more so he stood for Parliament, won a seat and gained a sense of worth from his new circle of associates. Thus he progressed to become Prime Minister.

I strongly believe that there are few occasions in which someone should be critical of another. In almost all circumstances, I think, it is possible to offer praise and support, (except in Belfast where male humour aims for the 'levelling' of others). In the army, if your job is to peel the potatoes, then you must believe that you are a vital part of the war machine. There will be no success unless you do your peeling correctly and in time. The paradox, for me, is that criticism can spur people on to show others that they are wrong. I could take my own example, at Inchmarlo. But that is too painful, and caused resentment and despair.

The same sense of worth can be applied to a community. The Romans and the Nazis believed that, before they could conquer a people, they had to destroy their culture. That is what was happening to the Ulster Scots community until recently. Now we are building a self-confident people, coming out from under a cloud of despair. Today the Unionist community is able 'to take its place at the table as equals'. Progress indeed! However, a small number of backward looking Irish, who are in influential positions, still think that they can destroy the Ulster Scots culture. To a few, insulting Ulster Scots people and culture is 'another blow for old Ireland'.

The vast majority of Irish folk who live in the Republic are decent, honest types without a political agenda. But they have been reared in an atmosphere in which they think that Irish is so good that everyone must want to be Irish. They cannot understand why anyone, like us, would not wish to be Irish. I have been exposed to Irish music and dancing in recent years and have a high regard for it. But it is not my culture!

The question is: 'Can we all live together?' I will tell anyone that Ulster Scots culture is as good as any other – not better. And this is where I come again into conflict with nationalism. The broad thrust of the Ulster Scots people is to see things on a wide screen. We are the people who want freedom for our minds, not for a lump of earth. If we cannot get freedom in one place we move on to another. Remember the quarter of a million who moved from Ulster to America, in search of a better place?

The Irish believe that the island of Ireland is a country. But there is no logic in that. That idea is what is now called the 'saltwater fallacy'; anywhere surrounded by sea must be a country. The concept will come as a considerable surprise to the English, Scottish and the Welsh, to mention but a few. Nationality is in your mind, not where your mother was on the day of your birth. As is the case with the rest of my family, I am not Irish. I am an Ulster Scot and if anyone insists that I am something different, they are infringing my human rights. Again there is a problem. Some Irish people cannot accept that position and so think that I, and people like me, have no place on the island. This is where nationalism is racist. In the 1880s, the Irish invented their own games and dancing, as well as revived the language. As a result, they underlined the split in the island. I never met my grandfather on the Laird side; he died before I was born. Examining his large collection of books, designed to self-educate, I note some references to Ireland. This was before the third Home Rule crisis. When he died in 1939, he considered himself not as Irish, but as an Ulsterman. I suspect that there were very many of that period who were born Irish but died Ulstermen; that should be food for thought for nationalists.

Coming from a Presbyterian background, I find the concept of Irish Republicanism to be totally revolting. Irish terrorists can call themselves nationalist, although I consider them to be like Fascists. The actual concept of Republicanism is very acceptable. It is a Presbyterian ideal, which embraces the equality of treatment of all men. Also, that every leader is elected to their position; one that it is changed regularly. Decisions are taken by a vote, after everyone has had a say. The idea of holding areas in the grip of terror is Fascist, not Republican. So is killing people in your own community because they do not agree with what you say.

There can be little doubt that there is a divide between those of the Irish community who live in Northern Ireland and those in the Republic. Almost one hundred years of the border has told a story. It seems to me that the majority of Northern Ireland Irish residents are happy to be part of a multicultural United Kingdom; especially with the recent disclosures of church and state in the Republic. All of us need to build a society where all nationalities and other groups are treated with fairness, and are recognised and valued. My experience of the Republic is of a deeply unhappy society that does not know how to get out of the financial and cultural mess in which it is now stuck. I wish it luck. I do not want to be a part of it. I prefer to exist in a bigger context, where there is a support for all people. If that is not available in one scenario, then we should just go elsewhere. For freedom of the individual, we will take on any odds. We would even take on the British government, if they presented a threat. If you need a few examples, just remember the American War of Independence, the Siege of Derry, the Rebellion of 1798, the gun-running of 1914 and the Workers' Council Strike of 1974.

As a community we must keep alert. Some of us can seem like Little Englanders, when we attempt to be more British than the English. 'For Queen and Empire' was all right at one time but things have changed. The Empire, I can argue anyway, is a thing of the past. For people like us, there is one worthwhile course and that lies within bigger political units. Distribution of wealth is more likely to happen when we become our brother's keeper. Little Englanders will not help the protection of our rights and culture. They will go with the tide. Remember the words of Kipling and of W. F. Marshall? Can we trust a Westminster government?

For example, the future could be in a new western state, currently known as the European Union. We must be able to go where there is a policy of looking after all regions. As we are a distinct region, that could suit us. Traditional Western values are our best chance. In this ever-changing world, we do not want to be Little Englanders if, for example, Scotland has left the Union. We must not be a part of the backward looking groups who would support nationalism by taking us out of Europe. These groups talk about British sovereignty. In our world of today, there is no such thing as sovereignty. We all live in a global village. What one country does affects others. British nationalism would be just as bad as the Irish version. All ethnic groups must be treated equally.

The fewer borders there are in the world, the sooner we will all arrive at the brotherhood of man, as envisaged by Rabbie Burns. Borders are only used for two things; to keep money in or to keep other people's culture out. They have nothing to do with equality. How can you be a nationalist and believe in the brotherhood of man?

What does the future hold in a fast moving world? We do not want to miss out if the eastern side of the United States moves to join the EU in the future. I would have liked Ulster to have been the fifty-first state of the United States. That is, of course, if we could not have joined up with Scotland, which is no more absurd than the concept of linking with the Irish Republic. Who knows? The only thing to remember is that we are an ethnic group and we must look to those who will recognise that. And, as I found out, that is not the Irish State!

If there is one thing that my life to date has shown me, it is that I am an Ulster Scot first and foremost, and anything else after that. I have taken a journey that was totally different to my father's. I have ended up as a dedicated Ulsterman supporting the current Union, as did my father. I am not a paper Unionist any more. I have been to the nationalist hell, looked in and decided that it was not for me. My freedom as an individual is the only thing of importance.

Today, I fight on for freedom in the knowledge that if we, as a minority, fail, then minorities all over the world will be in danger. People's rights must not be taken away by brute force. Our battle is their battle. I am also aware that, as a Unionist, we must succeed every day; we only have to fail once to be left to the mercy of our detractors.

My wife, and lifetime supporter, will soon retire from her hospital job. My daughter Alison is particularly interested in politics and I should not be surprised to find her, as the third generation of my family, fighting an election. My son, David, is a very successful online retailer. He also has an interest in things political, and, of course, in Chelsea. I am proud of them all.

So, there you have it. The reading is almost over. Sixty-five years of enjoyment and thrills. Learning all the way. In these pages are relived all of the major experiences which have helped to shape me.

'Ye see yon birkie, ca'd a lord …He's but a coof for all that.' More than likely!

'Big lad, you're getting above your self. Laird writing a book!' I agree!

APPENDIX

The Presidents' Trail

IT IS SIGNIFICANT that the Ulster Scots have to date contributed seventeen of America's forty-four presidents. Their ancestry is generally considered to embody defining characteristics that shaped the modern United States of America. To understand why this is, consider what drove the Ulster Scots from the northern part of the island of Ireland to a new life in the New World in the first place. Or, why did Scottish lowlanders move first to the English-inspired plantation and thence to New England? Some might see that as swapping one colony for another. Why, having maintained their essential Scottishness on the island of Ireland, did they choose to see themselves as 'American' in America?

The Ulster Scots, who were caught up in the plantations of Ulster, were not, for the most part, keen to be in the province. The natives were difficult. The land was wetter than that to which they were used. The Scottish desire for freedom and the right of self-determination was strong. After some decades, the idea of moving on to a better place had emerged. Events were to further unsettle some of the planters. The 1641 Rebellion, the Siege of Derry, the Battle of the Boyne, the attitude of a number of their landlords and increasingly oppressive laws, such as the Test Acts, bore down heavily on them. From the middle of the seventeenth century, an increasing number began to think of moving to the new land in the west, called America. Stories were filtering back about the prospects there, where a man could be free and be rewarded for his labour. In the region of a quarter of a million people sailed westward at that time and so a new series of pages were written, which would change the history of the world.

America, for all its resources and opportunities, was not always the gentle Eden of which early Ulster Scots pioneers dreamed. However, the struggle to forge a world based upon individual freedom as a result of hard work and uncommon daring was one for which Ulster Scots were very well suited. The patriotic ideals that evolved with the new nation worked upon the Ulster Scots identity, just as the Ulster Scots character worked upon the developing patriotism of Americans.

Jackson may rightly be considered one of the strongest of the early log-cabin presidents. His Ulster Scots successors did not all share the rawness of his background, but it is interesting to see how their various talents and personal values worked for progress, both social and political, in the developing nation.

Literally following in the footsteps of Andrew Jackson, Polk moved to Tennessee as a young man. Also a lawyer, he served as a state legislator and became Governor of Tennessee in 1839, having spent a term in the House of Representatives. (Altogether he served seven terms in Congress.) Polk is not remembered as a demagogue politician, but as a gritty statesman who oversaw a massive expansion of American state territory. This had been an ambition of Jackson's.

Polk's state acquisitions were not minor; Oregon in the north, Texas in the south and California in the west. Oregon he won by treaty with the British, as early as 1846. California, then under Mexican control, was more of a problem and involved both money and military action. His initial offer of twenty million dollars was not welcomed and Polk was forced to send troops to press his suit. This they did so effectively, that Polk was able to negotiate transfer of California to America for the reduced figure of fifteen million dollars. This hard-line prosecution of American interests took its toll on the president's health, however, and Polk died shortly after leaving office in 1849.

Eight years later, another Scots-Irish Democrat assumed the presidency. James Buchanan's family was from Pennsylvania, a state essential for the Democrats. You could say that Buchanan was a true log-cabin president, in that he was born in a log-cabin, in Franklin County, Pennsylvania. His parents came from Deroran near Omagh, in County Tyrone, arriving in America in 1783. Acutely aware of his Scots-Irish origins, Buchanan claimed that: 'My Ulster blood is my most priceless heritage'.

Buchanan's tenure coincided with the eve of the American Civil War. Slavery and the abolitionist cause were the key issues of the day and it is here that Buchanan is today remembered for dithering. As holder of presidential office, Buchanan was forced to uphold the Constitution. Private views along abolitionist lines could not be aired, but may have stayed Buchanan's hand when he should have acted. Jackson himself had been a slave-owner and his old nemesis Calhoun continued to speak for the necessity of the ownership of fellow human beings. Buchanan himself did not resolve the issue of abolition. This he left to his successor, the Republican Abraham Lincoln. Interestingly, Buchanan is the only president who never married. Instead, his niece, Harriet Lane, was appointed as First Lady.

Lincoln's own successor, Andrew Johnson, was an Scots-Irish Democrat (and another true log-cabin president), born in 1808 in Raleigh, North Carolina. His grandfather was a Presbyterian from Mountville, near Larne in County Antrim, who arrived in America in around 1750. Johnson's mother and wife were also of Ulster Scots families.

Johnson took office in 1865 after the assassination of Abraham Lincoln, for whom he had served as vice-president. Lincoln's death on Good Friday, April 14th, happened just a week after the Confederate surrender and did not make for a propitious political climate. In dedicating the military cemetery at Gettysburg, Lincoln had declared:

'That we here highly resolve that these dead shall not have died in vain – that this nation, under God, shall have a new birth of freedom – and that government of the people, by the people, for the people, shall not perish from the earth.'

This was a tough act to follow. It fell to Johnson, a southerner who was seen by the south as a traitor for his Union principles, to implement the civil rights laws that followed from the abolition of slavery. In this he was seen as having a mixed success. As well as benefiting freed slaves, Johnson was committed to reforms that saw justice for citizens at large, not just for the wealthy elites. Such a populist approach did not win Johnson admirers among the rich and powerful.

In addition to this, Johnson's attempts to reinvent the south conflicted with his policy of maintaining some of the pre-war leadership. Customs that went against the grain of the new egalitarianism upset both northerners, who felt that the abolitionist cause was not being properly upheld, and a group known as the Radical Republicans. This group refused to allow former Confederate leaders to hold power in the new administration. They also made legal provision for freed slaves, which Johnson opposed with his presidential veto. The Radicals then legislated successfully to overturn the veto, with the Civil Rights Act of 1866. This conferred citizenship upon former slaves.

The southern states of the former Confederacy particularly objected to the new Fourteenth Amendment to the Constitution, Section 1 of which states:

'All persons born or naturalized in the United States, and subject to the jurisdiction thereof, are citizens of the United States and of the state wherein they reside. No state shall make or enforce any law which shall abridge the privileges or immunities of citizens of the United States; nor shall any state deprive any person of life, liberty, or property, without due process of law; nor deny to any person within its jurisdiction the equal protection of the laws.'

All of the southern states save Tennessee, Johnson's own state, withheld ratification. Hostility towards Johnson grew and, when he contravened a restriction upon his office which guaranteed tenure to officials, he was impeached in 1868. He survived the impeachment, but with only one vote. The following year a Republican, Ulysses Simpson Grant, was elected to office.

General Grant was a very capable soldier, a characteristic that he shares with many others of Ulster Scots descent. He served under General Zachary Taylor during the Mexican War, the military leader sent by President Polk to facilitate the purchase of California. Grant was born in Ohio, at Point Pleasant, in 1822. The family of his mother, Hannah Simpson, originated from Dergenagh, between Ballygawley and Dungannon in County Tyrone. My county, Tyrone, comes out of this section well! Although himself a Methodist, his ancestors were Presbyterian. Grant's great-grandfather, John Simpson, left Ulster for America in 1760.

Grant's family background was neither wealthy nor influential and he came to prominence entirely through his own aptitudes. During the Civil War, he started his career in the volunteer force and rose rapidly through the ranks. As a military commander, Grant was both exacting and merciful. At Fort Donelson in the Mississippi Valley, he offered 'no terms except an unconditional and immediate surrender', which he duly received. He later accepted the surrender of General Robert E. Lee. Three years later, as a Radical Republican, General Grant was the nominated presidential candidate for the Republican Party.

It is generally conceded that President Grant lacked the verve of the general, and was not a very effective president. This may be partly due to political naïveté. Grant's straightforward and personally trusting character was not ideally suited to navigating a deeply corrupt environment. After leaving his second term of office in 1877, he went on a tour of the island of Ireland, where he visited the family farmstead at Ballygawley.

The supply line of Scots-Irish presidents did not stop at Grant, however, but continues to the present day. After four years, another candidate of Ulster Scots descent was elected, the first of five who formed a Scots-Irish chain that lasted, unbroken, until 1909. All but one was from the Republican Party.

Chester Alan Arthur, the twenty-first American President, was born in 1829. His father, who became the Reverend William Arthur, a Baptist, and his grandfather, came to Vermont in 1801, from Dreen near Cullybackey in County Antrim.

Like President Johnson, Arthur assumed presidential office from the vice-presidency, after the assassination of President Garfield in September 1881. Despite having a Baptist pastor as a father and numbering Baptists among his supporters, Chester Arthur was known for his prodigious whisky consumption. In contrast to his fellow whisky aficionado, President Grant, Chester Arthur's fortunes enjoyed a positive reversal once he entered office.

Arthur had come via the legal profession to be a high-ranking civil servant in New York. In 1871, he was appointed the Collector of the Port of New York, which put the Customs House under his control. He gained a reputation for nepotism as a means of preserving political factional power. After losing his job as a result of political reform in the Customs House, he became part of the Republican Party machine, finally achieving the position of vice-presidential candidate in 1880. Once installed as President the following year, however, Arthur demonstrated the sound principle of putting a thief in charge of the strong-box; he dedicated himself to reforming the civil service. Officeholders now had to pass examinations for some key positions and could no longer be removed for purely political reasons. President Arthur also oversaw the introduction of the first restrictions on immigration (limiting the entry of the insane, the poor, the criminal and the Chinese). Chester Arthur died in 1886 of kidney disease.

His Democrat successor was Grover Cleveland, who managed two four-year presidential terms, four years apart. Because American presidents are numbered by strict chronology, Cleveland was both the twenty-second and the twenty-fourth Presidents. He was born in Caldwell, New Jersey in 1837. Like Arthur, Cleveland's father, the Reverend Richard Falley Cleveland, was also a minister, but a Presbyterian one. Cleveland's mother's father came from County Antrim in the late eighteenth century.

Cleveland followed in the footsteps of Scots-Irish presidents before him; he was a lawyer. Practicing in Buffalo, he became Mayor in 1881, then Governor of New York. By 1885, he was the Democrat President of the United States. Although, by this time, the Democrat party was generally seen to stand for the common man, Cleveland's rapid rise to power owed a good deal to his willingness to promote the interests of big business. He also had the support of reformist Republicans. Cleveland was practical about money. He opposed handouts of government money on principle, upheld the US Treasury gold reserve and took a strong line against strikers. Such a hard line might have proved popular during an economic boom period, but was not so during the economic depression that took hold of the country during his second term of office.

Sandwiched in between the two bouts of Cleveland was Benjamin Harrison, the Republican president between 1889 and 1893. Yet another lawyer, and an excellent one at that, he was the son of a member of the House of Representatives. He was born in North Bend, Ohio, and was the Presbyterian grandson of the ninth President, William Henry Harrison. His mother was born in Mercersburg, Pennsylvania, and was descended from Ulster Scots immigrants. Like Grant, Harrison also fought during the Civil War. He worked to promote the rights of veteran soldiers, as well as those of Native Americans and, unlike Cleveland during his second term, did not fight shy of spending money where he felt it was needed. Nevertheless, Harrison left a country facing economic shortcomings, when Cleveland resumed power.

Harrison's fellow Republican, William McKinley, succeeded Cleveland. Also of Presbyterian stock, also from Ohio, and also a lawyer, McKinley's grandfather hailed from Conagher near Ballymoney, in County Antrim. His grandparents fought in the Revolutionary War. He was a member of the House of Representatives and Governor of Ohio. McKinley himself was not a revolutionary, but an imperialist and a supporter of the moneyed elites. In this he opposed the darling of the people, William Jennings Bryan, who campaigned tirelessly and, ultimately, fruitlessly across America, on populist lines. What was seen as the solid respectability of the Scots-Irish prevailed. Although he was elected for a second term, McKinley was unable to see it through. Not long after he resumed office, he was assassinated by an anarchist in September 1901 in Buffalo, New York.

The next Republican president of Scots-Irish extraction followed hot on McKinley's heels and was one of the major political figures of the early twentieth century. Theodore Roosevelt ensured a continuation of McKinley's strong line on foreign policy: McKinley had added Puerto Rico, Guam and the Philippines to US territory. Despite becoming the youngest ever president at the tender age of forty-three, Roosevelt was not remotely green. Roosevelt's idea of protecting his country's foreign interests was not rooted solely in conquest or defence, but was highly strategic. He oversaw the construction of the Panama Canal, which linked the Pacific and Atlantic oceans for the first time. He won the Nobel Peace Prize for his role in stopping war between Russia and Japan. He was, however, capable of being very firm in the national interest, preventing the expansion of foreign interests in the Caribbean. Roosevelt's connections to Ulster were not direct; he was from a wealthy, settled family in New York City. His mother's family was descended from emigrants from Larne, in County Antrim. Roosevelt himself wrote of the virtues of the Scots-Irish group, that 'stern, virile, bold and hardy people who formed the kernel of that American stock who were the pioneers of our people in the march westwards'.

Since the days of Jackson, there had been a progressive move away from the simple style of the 'log-cabin presidents'. Charisma and a ready way with a musket were no guarantee of a successful tilt at the top office of the land. Instead, respectability and the support of serious money were required. The traditional Ulster Scots emphasis on education, hard work and moral courage may explain the enduring strength of the Scots-Irish American presidential line. Woodrow Wilson, a Democrat, became president the year before the beginning of the First World War.

Wilson's grandfather had immigrated to North Carolina in the early nineteenth century. The family was from Dergalt, near Strabane in County Tyrone, yes Tyrone, and only a mile from where Polk's family hailed. His father was a Presbyterian minister; the Reverend Doctor Joseph Ruffles Wilson. Wilson, born in Staunton, Virginia, in 1856, took the Scots-Irish educational tradition one or two steps further, graduating in law before becoming a postgraduate professor in political science and, eventually, president of Princeton in 1902. During his time as professor, Wilson visited the island of Ireland. Of his Scots-Irish heritage, he said:

> 'My father's father was born in the north of Ireland. I myself am happy there runs in my veins a very considerable strain of Irish blood, and a Scottish conscience.'

After a stint as Governor of New Jersey, Wilson enjoyed two terms as President. The first focused a great deal upon business matters, lowering the trading tariff in order to foster international trade, and ensuring fair practice. Wilson also supervised the introduction of the Federal Reserve Act, which increased flexibility within the economy.

Although Wilson is known as the president who brought America into the First World War, he won his second term on precisely the opposite ticket. Americans did not want to fight in other people's battles. In order to persuade Congress to endorse America's entry into the global conflict, Wilson successfully waged one of the first full-scale political propaganda campaigns. The United States declared war on Germany in 1917, thereby ensuring Germany's defeat by the Allies the following year. Driven always by conscience and his belief in justice, Woodrow Wilson saw the job of America as being 'to make the world safe for democracy'. In so doing, he inadvertently strengthened greatly his own power base, but chose to focus on a worldwide future of peace and prosperity. After the war, he travelled to the Paris Peace Conference to promote his ideals, which were reflected in the proposed League of Nations. Although this forerunner to the United Nations was constituted as a result of the Treaty of Versailles in 1919, Wilson was unable to persuade his countrymen to sign up to it. Whether the ultimate failure lay in the inability of Europeans to create a credible world organisation in which Americans could place trust or whether it lay with an isolationist streak in American society is an interesting point. Wilson's dream was shattered. The treaty was rejected in the Senate by just seven votes.

The next president with Scots-Irish blood in his veins was not elected until the end of the Second World War; Harry Truman. A Democrat, Truman was born in Lamar, in Missouri, in 1884. He was descended from Ulster Scots settlers on his mother's father's side; Solomon Young had moved to Missouri from Kentucky in 1840.

Truman took over the mantle of power from Franklin D. Roosevelt (who did not share his distant cousin Theodore Roosevelt's Scots-Irish links) upon the latter's sudden death in April 1945. The Second World War did not end for another five months and Truman found himself centre stage at a critical time in both American and world history. Despite being ignorant of America's position with regards to the atomic bomb, he was faced with the decision of attacking Japan. The bombing of Hiroshima and Nagasaki led to Japan's surrender, and effectively ended the war. By June, the United Nations charter was signed. Much of Truman's work after the war was focused on reconstruction in Europe. NATO, the North Atlantic Treaty Organization, was created in 1949 to assure mutual defence, should any of its member states be attacked by a third party. It was put to the test by the Korean War, which also took place under President Truman's tenure. After an intense eight years in power, Truman chose to retire from politics, rather than stand again for office.

The Scots-Irish in America were not to be represented again at the top level for another sixteen years. Richard Millhouse Nixon, the Republican lawyer whose presidency ended in scandal, was elected in 1969. A Quaker, he was born in 1913 in Yorba Linda, in California. Both the Millhouse and the Nixon sides of his family had originated in County Antrim, the Millhouses coming from Carrickfergus and Ballymoney.

As vice-president, Nixon had originally hoped to take over from President Eisenhower, who took office after Truman. However, he lost the election to John F. Kennedy, and it took eight years for him to be reselected as the Republican party candidate. Nixon had himself served in the military during the Second World War, as a Lieutenant Commander in the Navy. It was towards the end of his presidential watch that an end to the interminable Vietnam War, which had begun back in 1959, began to come into sight. Tensions over the draft had dogged Nixon's time in office, however.

Although re-elected in 1972, the Watergate scandal erupted. During the run-up to the election, the offices of the Democrat National Committee were broken into; Nixon was later forced to admit that he had authorised a cover-up. Nixon was finally forced to resign in 1974, before impeachment proceedings could be brought against him. He was succeeded by his vice-president, Gerald Ford.

On the positive side, it was under Nixon in 1969 that the first American astronauts landed on the moon. Neil Armstrong, the first human being to walk upon the moon's surface, was of Scots-Irish descent. Armstrong's grandfather was a teacher in a school just outside Enniskillen in County Fermanagh. To this day, when visiting that beautiful town, I meet relations of the first man on the moon.

But back to presidents; Jimmy Carter was the thirty-ninth President of America. Around 150 years before his birth in 1924, his mother's ancestor, Andrew Cowan, was a Scots-Irish settler, from County Antrim. Carter himself is from Plains, in Georgia. Like his predecessor Nixon, he served as a naval officer. A farmer, Carter extended a growing preoccupation with the environment, taking a prescient but unpopular position on energy expenditure that cost him support. He held a statesman-like view on foreign policy, helping to broker peace between Egypt and Israel at the Camp David Agreement of 1978. It was therefore very unfortunate that the release of the fifty-two US Embassy hostages in Iran did not take place until the day that Carter left office. The ongoing crisis, and Carter's apparent inability to bring an end to it, destabilised him greatly, making it easier for Ronald Reagan, the Republican candidate, to defeat him in his bid for a second term.

After his two terms in office, Reagan was succeeded by another Republican candidate; his vice-president, George Bush. He was born in the same year as Carter, in Milton, Massachusetts. Although the ancestors of George Herbert Walker Bush are mainly English, he is descended from one William Gault on his mother's side; an Ulster Scot who emigrated with his wife to Blount County, Tennessee, in 1796. The Gaults became a prominent family in Tennessee.

George Bush became a pilot in the Navy during the Second World War, flying in fifty-eight missions. During one of these, he was shot down by Japanese gunfire and rescued from the water by a submarine. He was duly awarded the Distinguished Flying Cross. As a civilian, Bush distinguished himself in public service. Following his father into politics, he became a member of the House of Representatives, for Texas. His career included positions such as Director of the CIA, Ambassador to the United Nations and Chairman of the Republican National Committee. George Bush's four years as president, from 1988 to 1992, took in some critical points in recent world history; the fall of the Communist Soviet Union and the Berlin Wall, the defeat of General Noriega of Panama and, finally, the Iraqi invasion of Kuwait. Although these events represented triumphs over situations that originated outside American control, domestic economic woes overrode public support after the first Gulf War, and George Bush was replaced by a Democrat.

William Jefferson Clinton, the forty-second president, was born in Hope, Hempstead County, Arkansas, in 1946. A Baptist himself, he is descended from Ulster Scots Presbyterians; his ancestor, Lucas Cassidy, left County Fermanagh in around 1750. His presidential career was atypical only in its success, having managed to combine features of many other presidents' careers, except the experience of assassination. He acquired a law degree and then worked his way to the presidency through becoming Attorney General of Arkansas, rather than through the Congress route. He was the second president to be impeached by the House of Representatives (the first was Andrew Johnson), this time for the far more glamorous business of seducing (or being seduced by) a White House intern. And, unlike Nixon, who had faced likely impeachment, he survived the experience with his popularity and presidency intact.

Bill Clinton played an important role in the Northern Ireland Peace Process of the 1990s. A key function that he performed was to offer facilities and encouragement to all. I had the pleasure of working in Washington during one of the administration's economic conferences. I was deeply impressed to hear the most powerful man in the world speaking live on several occasions. Clinton never forgot his background. He was a class operator in his ability to engage a group of people, numbering from thousands to two or three, and hold them spellbound. When he talked, you thought that he was directing his remarks to you and that you were the only one in the world.

Although not the most recent president of Scots-Irish descent (he was succeeded by George W. Bush, who obviously shares his father's heritage), it fell to him to attempt to close the Ulster Scots circle. Bill Clinton is held in great affection in Northern Ireland. His wife, Hillary, is a different case.

George Walker Bush may consider himself to be lucky to have been president. His initial election against Al Gore was a first class cliff-hanger. In political terms, any one who was president during the attack on America on 11th September 2001 was always going to have a country rallied behind them. I think that it is unfair to judge George W's presidency yet. Historians will have much to consider in due course. However, I should record that he is not currently held as one of the 'greats'. But then, you cannot win them all.

Index

Abercorn Restaurant 66
Acheson, John 38
Adams, Gerry (MP) 233, 246
Agnes Street, Belfast 13, 14, 19
Agnew, Fraser 159
Ahern, Bertie (Taoiseach) 228, 252
Alamo, the battle of the 134, 135
Alexander, Harold (Field Marshal) 173, 175, 176
Allen, Jack 159, 162
Anderson, William (Willie) 141
Andrews, John M. 13
Ardoyne, Belfast 38, 232, 233
Arkansas, the State of 274, 275
Armstrong, Neil 273
Arthur, Chester Alan (President) 268
Arthur, William (Reverend) 268
Arthur Street, Belfast 35
Artigarvan 8, 10, 11, 21, 27, 30, 42–44, 64, 78, 134, 139, 140–143, 150, 152, 167–169, 178, 210, 248
Ashdown, Paddy (Rt Hon. Lord) 236
Attwood, Tim 161, 162
Auchinleck, Claude (Field Marshal Sir; 'the Auk') 174, 175
Auld, John McConnell (Reverend; 'Con') 70, 71, 73

Ballygawley, Co. Tyrone 267
Ballymena, Kells, Co. Antrim 14, 81, 133
Ballymoney, Co. Antrim 273
Ballynahinch, Co. Down 81
Ballynure, Co. Antrim 135

Ballyskeagh, Co. Tyrone
21, 42-44, 78, 137,
139–141, 143, 150
Beattie, Rev. Billy 63
Belfast Royal Academy 16, 70
Belfast St Anne's Division
20, 49–51, 58
Bell, Cecil Thomas (CTB)
34, 35, 71–73, 75, 118
124, 131
Bell, Eric (Captain; Victoria
Cross) 46
Berlin Wall 274
Berwick-upon-Tweed 14, 21
Bishop, Mervyn 38, 159
Black Pig's Dyke 244, 245
Blair, Tony (Prime Minister)
162, 165
the 'Blazers' 187, 188
Blood, May (Baroness) 192
Boal, Desmond (MP) 5
Bono, U2 162
The Boyne 79, 82, 151,
236, 237
Brooke, Alan (1st Viscount
Alanbrooke; 'Brookie')
175, 176
Brooke, Alan (Viscount
Brookeborough) 192
Brooke, Basil (Prime
Minister, Viscount
Brookeborough) 62
Brooke, Hon. John (Viscount
Brookeborough) 61
Brookvale 13, 27
Brown, Gordon (Prime
Minister) 258
Bruton, John (Taoiseach)
236
Bryan, William Jennings 270
Buchanan, James (President)
265
Buffalo, New York 269, 270
Burke, Ray (Fianna Fáil
minister) 252
Burns, Robert (Rabbie)
211, 256, 257, 261
Burnside, David (MP)
150, 159
Burnside, Ernest Everrard 150
Bush, George Herbert Walker
(President) 274
Bush, George Walker
(President) 275

Cahill, Kevin 236, 237
Calhoun, John Caldwell
(President) 154, 265
Caldwell, New Jersey 268
California, State of 264
Camp David 274
Campbell, David 162
Campbell, Don 38
Canada 223
Capitol Hill, Washington 223
Carrickfergus, Co. Antrim
76, 78, 273
Carson, Sir Edward 42, 45,
138, 209
Carson, Maurice 38
Carswell, Robert (Lord) 144
Carter, Jimmy (President)
273, 274
Cassidy, Lucas 274
Cather, Geoffrey (Lieutenant;
Victoria Cross) 46
Cave Hill, Belfast 9,10

Charles I (King) 76, 77, 178
Charles II (King) 77
China 216-218
Churchill, Winston (Prime Minister) 54, 116, 173-176
Cleveland, Grover (President) 268, 269
Cleveland, Richard Falley (Reverend) 268
Clinton, Hillary (Secretary of State) 275
Clinton, William Jefferson (President) 68, 274, 275
Clones, Co. Monaghan 31, 219
Coleman, Andrew 66
Conagher, Co. Antrim 269
Connelly, James 127
Convery, Pat (Councillor) 39
Cooke, Alec (Lord) 170
Cookstown, Co. Tyrone 31
Cornwallis (Lieutenant General Lord) 152
Coulter, Phil 186
Cowan, Andrew 273
Cowen, Brian (Taoiseach) 222
Cowpens, the battle of 153
Craig, Bill 68, 109
Craig, James (Lord Craigavon) 42, 149
Crockett, Davy 133, 134, 154, 155
Cromwell, Oliver 77
Curran, Edmund 159

Davidson, Samuel (Reverend) 15
Dennany, Martin 235
Dergalt, Co. Tyrone 271
Dergenagh, Co. Tyrone 267
Deroran, Co. Tyrone 265
De Valera, Eamon (President) 48, 54, 247
Devenney, Jim 208, 214, 216
Dickson, Anne 63
Dill, John (Field Marshal Sir) 174, 175
Dingley, James (Dr) 5
Donaghadee, Co. Down 244
Donaghey, Jim 143
Donaldson, Drew 72
Donegall Road, Belfast 16, 19, 52, 57, 67, 95, 111
Dreen, Co. Antrim 268
Drogheda 77, 79
Dromore, Derrygonnelly, Co. Fermanagh 60, 122
Drum, Co. Monaghan 219
Dublin 216–218, 221, 222, 224, 225–227, 234, 235, 241, 244–246, 250, 251, 254
Dublin Castle 76
Dungannon, Co. Tyrone 228, 267
Dunlap, John 152
Dunn family 21, 22, 25, 26, 42, 43, 82, 139, 143, 146
Dunn, Jack (John) 43, 137, 140–142
Dunn, James 140, 141
Dunn, John 43
Dunn Margaret (later Laird) 11, 17, 20, 21, 26, 39, 40, 51
Dunn, Rebecca 21
Dunn, Robert John 21
Dunseith, David 229
Durham 23

Edinburgh 23, 24
Egypt 274
Eisenhower, Dwight (President) 273
El Alamein 10, 173
Elizabeth I (Queen) 24
Elizabeth II (Queen) 187, 214, 219, 260
Elliott family 23
Empey, Reginald 159
Enniskillen, Co. Fermanagh 31, 76, 122, 133, 273
Erskine, John 207
European Economic Community (EEC) 109
European Union 27, 260

Falls Road, Belfast 15, 237
Faulkner, Brian 85
Ferguson, Fred 60
Ferguson, Mary Kathleen (Mary Kate, or Sadie) 60, 122–124, 169
Ferguson, Raymond 159
Ferguson, William John (Willie) 60, 169
Finner Camp, Co. Donegal 44
Fitt MP, Gerry (Lord Fitt) 50, 121, 125–132
Fitzpatrick, Rory 133
Flight of the Earls 25, 75
Forbes, Andy (Private; Military Medal) 44, 45
Fort Donelson, Mississippi 267
Francis Dinsmore Linen Mill 14
Franklin County, Pennsylvania 265
Franks, Lynn 208

Galway 250
Garfield, James (President) 268
Garland, Roy 159
George V, King 46
Germany 271
Gettisburg, Pennsylvania 265
Gladstone, William Ewart (Prime Minister) 73, 75
Glasgow 244, 248
Glenagoorland, nr Donemana 140
Glengall Street, Belfast 86, 93, 94, 162
Glenmaquin, Raphoe 139
Gore, Al (Vice President) 275
Gott, William (Lieutenant-General) 175
Gowdy, Colin 145
Grant, Ulysses Simpson (President) 267–269
Great Victoria Street Station 31, 34
Guam 270

Hadrian's Wall 23
Hancock, John 152
Harland and Wolff 9
Harrison, Benjamin (President) 269
Harrison, William Henry (President) 269
Haughey, Charles (Taoiseach) 252
Heath, Rt Hon. Edward (Prime Minister) 86, 96
Hermon, Jack (Sir; Chief Constable of RUC) 202
Hermon, Sylvia (Lady; MP) 202

Hooker, Joseph (Major General) 150
Hope, Arkansas 274
Hope Street, Sandy Row area 57
Horseshoe Bend, the battle of 154
House of Lords, Westminster 68, 131, 145, 160, 163, 164, 165, 167, 169, 170, 172, 176–179, 183, 184, 185, 191, 192, 229, 231, 233
Houston, Peter 5
Houston, Sam (President) 135, 154
Hull 181, 182
Hume, John 162
Hunter, Bob (Robert) 72
Hutcheson, Francis 80, 248

Inchmarlo School 27–30, 32, 36, 258
Inst (the Royal Belfast Academical Institution) 16, 19, 32, 33, 35, 36, 37, 70, 144–146
Irish Republican Army (IRA) 57, 64, 66, 73, 119, 120, 122, 129, 130, 180, 183, 184, 206
Iraq 274
Israel 274

Jackson, Andrew (President) 150–155, 264, 265
Jackson, Thomas 'Stonewall' (General) 151
James I, England; James VI, Scotland (King) 21, 24, 25, 171
James II (King) 77, 79
Japan 270, 272
Jay, Margaret (Baroness) 179
The Jewish Farm, Co. Down 12
John, King 163
Johnson, Andrew 265–268, 275
Johnston, Bryan 38, 39
Johnston, Helen 39

Kellswater, Co. Antrim 15
Kennedy, J.F. (President) 188, 273
Kennedy, Paddy (MP) 245
Kentucky, the State of 272
Kerr family 23
Kierkegaard, Søren 71
Kilfedder, James (MP) 125
Kilkeel, Co. Down 107
Killynaght, Co. Tyrone 42
King's Mountain, the battle of 134, 153
Kipling, Rudyard 62, 173, 260
Knox, Ian 143
Kuwait 274

Laggan Valley 138, 215
the Lagganeers 138
Laird family 14, 26, 82, 171, 259
Laird, Agnes 14
Laird, Alison Jane 112, 117, 118, 163, 168, 170, 262

Laird, Carol (née Caroline Ethel Ferguson) 39, 59, 111, 112, 117–119, 122, 123, 148, 163, 164, 168–170, 202, 228, 262
Laird, David (John David) 36, 118, 144, 163, 164, 166–168, 170, 262
Laird, James (Jimmy) 3, 10, 33, 36, 49, 50, 59, 81, 140
Laird, James Davidson 14, 15, 19, 259
Laird, Jesse William 14
Laird, Margaret (née Dunn) 11, 17, 20, 21, 26, 39, 40, 51, 61, 140
Laird, Norman Davidson 3, 4, 15, 17, 20, 21, 26, 34, 39, 40, 48, 49, 51
Laird, William 14
Lamar, Missouri 272
Lane, Harriet (First Lady) 265
Lansdowne Road, Dublin 185, 186, 188
Larne, Co. Antrim 270
Latimer, Kenneth 84, 159
Leckpatrick 44, 138
Lee, Robert E. (General) 267
Lenihan, Brian (Snr; Tánaiste) 252
Lenihan, Brian (Jnr; Finance Minister) 252
Libya 251
Lifford, Co. Donegal 218
Limavady, Co. Londonderry 148
Lincoln, Abraham (President) 150, 265
Lisnaskea, Co. Fermanagh 56, 62, 121
Lisnawhiggle 14
Liverpool 248
Lockett, Edgar 28
Londonderry 31, 44, 76, 138, 240, 241
Louis IV of France (King) 78
Lovatt, Andy 38
Lowry family 42, 43
Lowry, Isabel 43
Lowry, Michael (Fine Gael minister) 252
Lunney, Linde (Dr) 207
Lurgan, Co. Armagh 174

Magee College, Londonderry 223
Maginnis, Ken (Lord) 201
Maguire, Frank (MP) 120–122
Mansergh, Martin (Dr) 228
Marshall, W.F. (the Bard of Tyrone) 156, 260
Martin, John 234
Martin, Margaret 228
Martin, Michael (Irish Minister) 251
Massey, William Ferguson (Prime Minister) 148–150
the Maze Prison 119
McAdams, Gerard 38
McBride, Grace 141, 142
McCartney, Robert (QC; MP) 184, 202
McCorkall, Bertie 143
McDowell, Michael (Irish Justice Minister) 255
McElroy, Rev. Albert 73
McFadzean VC, Private William 45

McGlmpsey, Michael 207, 223
McGuinness, Martin (MP) 206
McIntyre, John 207
McKinley, William (President) 269, 270
McLucas, Herbert (Herbie) 141
McLucas, Maurice 141
McNamara, Kevin (MP) 181, 182
McNarry, David 159
Mercersburg, Pennsylvania 269
Methodist College Belfast 75
Mexico 264
Midgley, Harry 13
Missouri, the State of 272
Molyneaux, Jim (Lord) 109, 170
Montgomery, Bernard (Viscount; 'Monty') 172, 173, 176
Montgomery, Henry (Rt Rev. Bishop) 172
Mountville, Co. Antrim 265
Mowlam, Mo (Rt Hon.) 184
Murray, Len (General Secretary TUC) 105, 106

Nesbitt, Dermot 159
New Jersey, the State of 271
New Lodge, Belfast 232
New Orleans, the battle of 154
New York, USA 223, 268, 269
New Zealand 149
Newcastle, England 23
Newcastle, Northern Ireland 31
Newry, Co. Armagh 30, 244
Newton, Isaac (Sir) 171
Nicholson, Jim 160–165
Nixon, Richard Millhouse (President) 272, 273, 275
Noriega, Manuel (General) 274
North Bend, Ohio 269
North Carolina, the State of 271

O'Cuiv, Eamon (TD) 225–227
O'Donoghue, John (TD) 216, 217
O'Gara, Ronan 187
O'Hagan, Len 164
O'Hagan, Maureen 164
O'Toole, Fintan 251–253
Ohio, the State of 269
Oliver, Billy (MP) 126
the Orange Order 81, 126, 149
Oregon, the State of 264
Orr, Willie (MP) 109
Otterburn, Northumberland 22, 25

Paisley, Eileen (Baroness) 68
Paisley, Ian (Doctor; Lord) 68, 109
Paisley, Ian (Junior) 68
Panama Canal 270
Paris, France 272
Patterson, Paddy 186
Penn, William 151
Pennsylvania, State of 265
Philippines 270
Plains, Georgia 273

Point Pleasant, Ohio 267
Poland 211, 243
Polk, James Knox (President) 155, 264, 265, 267, 271
Pollock, Robert Bruce 155
Popplestone, Jack 33
Popplestone, Robin ('Pop') 33
Portadown, Co. Armagh 241
Portpatrick, Scotland 244
Portrush, Co. Antrim 31
Powell, Enoch (Rt Hon.) 108, 109, 121
Powell, Pam 110
Princeton University, New Jersey 271
Pryce, Irwin 72
Puerto Rico 270

Queen's University, Belfast 16, 71, 74, 176, 189, 201
Quigg, Robert (Private; Victoria Cross) 46

Raleigh, North Carolina 265
Raphoe, Co. Donegal 209, 219
Ravenhill, Belfast 185, 186
Reagan, Ronald (President) 274
Rees, Rt Hon. Merlin (Lord Merlin Rees) 93, 96, 105, 107, 112, 175
Reid, Ken 186
Richardson, John 72
Ridley, Michael 145, 146
Robards, Rachel (First Lady) 154
Robinson, Philip (Dr) 207, 212
Roden Street, Belfast 19
Rodgers, James 159
Rogan, Dennis (Lord) 159, 162, 166, 167, 170, 192
Rogan, Lorna (the Lady Rogan, née Colgan) 166
Rommel, Erwin 173
Rooker, Jeffrey (Lord) 231–234
Roosevelt, F.D. (President) 174, 272
Roosevelt, Theodore (President) 270, 272
The Royal Belfast Academical Institution (Inst) 16, 19, 32, 33, 35, 36, 37, 70, 144–146
Royal Ulster Constabulary Reserve (RUCR) 125

Saintfield, Co. Down 81
Sanderson, William (Billy) 93–95
Sands, Bobby (MP) 122, 123, 132
Sandy Row, Belfast 16, 19, 52, 57, 67, 111, 118
Santa Anna, Antonio López de (President) 134
Scullabogue, Co. Wexford 81, 83
Shankill Road, Belfast 13, 15, 16, 67, 82, 126–128, 192, 237
Sheldon, William (TD) 216
Simpson, Hannah 267
Sinclair, Thomas 74
Sloane, Hans 171, 172
Smith, Adam 80

Smyth, Clifford 159
Somerton Road, Belfast 11, 30, 61
Somme, the battle of the 45, 46, 209, 219
Speers, James 159
Staunton, Virginia 271
Stewart, James 159
Stewart, Robert (Lord Castlereagh) 83
Stormont 17, 48, 54, 68, 91, 129, 180, 222, 225, 240, 241, 245
Strabane 31, 44, 134, 138, 139, 140, 271
Stronge, James 63
Sunningdale 84–89, 96
Swan, Anthony 38

Tanney, Paul 217
Tarleton, Banastre (Colonel) 152
Taylor, John 159
Taylor, Zachary (General) 267
Templeton, Brian (BOT) 201, 202
Templeton, Elaine 202
Tennessee, the State of 264, 267
Texas, the State of 274
Thatcher, Rt Hon. Margaret (Baroness) 122, 231
Thompson, Hamilton ('Hammee') 139
Thomson, Charles 152
Tinman, John 81
Trimble, David (Lord) 160–165, 180, 192, 201, 205, 206
Truman, Harry (President) 272, 273
Turner, Fred (Sergeant) 35
Tyrone, Co. 21, 27, 30

Ulster Defence Association 58
Ulster Defence Regiment (UDR) 124, 125
36th Ulster Division 44–46, 138
Ulster Hospital 117–119, 185
Ulster Liberal Party 73
Ulster Scots Agency 206, 207
Ulster Solemn League 74
Ulster Volunteer Force (UVF) 42, 44–46, 138, 139
Ulster Workers' Council (UWC) 89, 90–92, 94, 105, 106
the Unionist Coalition 87
United States of America (USA) 150–157, 223, 230, 259, 263
the University of Ulster 146, 223
Union of Soviet Socialist Republics (USSR) 243, 270, 274

Van Buren, Martin (President) 155
Vermont, State of 268
Victoria College 36

Wall, Patrick 207
Wallace, William 22
Warnock, Edmund, QC 19
Washington, USA 223
Wells, Jane 161, 164, 202

West, Harry 68, 120, 123
Westminster 48, 49, 66, 87, 126
White family 42–44
White, Rebecca 42–44
Whitelaw, William (Rt Hon.) 67
William III, Prince of Orange (King) 78, 79, 151, 237
Wilson, Gordon 132
Wilson, Harold (Prime Minister) 50, 96, 107
Wilson, John (Professor) 223
Wilson, Joseph Ruffles (Reverend Doctor) 271
Wilson, Woodrow (President) 271, 272
Woking, UK 228

Yorba Linda, California 273
the York Fencibles 81, 84
York Loyal Orange Lodge 145 (Royal York) 82, 84
Young, Allister 38
Young, Solomon 272
Young Unionists 39, 56